Faith and Freedom / Essays in

Contemporary Theology

Faith and Freedom / Essays in Contemporary Theology

EDITED BY

Charles B. Ketcham and James F. Day

Allegheny College

WEYBRIGHT AND TALLEY
New York

DEDICATED TO THE MEMORY OF
CARL MICHALSON AND
H. RICHARD NIEBUHR

Preface

FREEDOM, LIKE THE WEATHER, is widely talked about and perhaps even more widely taken for granted in human discourse
and action. Yet when we take some time to examine either the
term itself or the sort of experience with which the term is
most frequently associated, we discover that it is, indeed, complex and elusive. This seems especially the case when we try,
as many have, to think about it in general or in abstraction
from some concrete setting. Even those efforts to reflect upon
the term's meaning within the context of ordinary language,
considering the variety of ordinary languages other than Oxford English in use, do not seem to provide any full or final
escape from the foregoing observation. It should not, therefore, be unusually surprising to discover that the essays in this
anthology reveal differences of perspective brought about by
the nature and character of each author's own specific involvement with the matter of freedom. We think it of more than
passing interest to note, in a time when so many are talking
about the ecumenical movement, that for a number of these
Christian thinkers the principal goal of that movement is a
fait accompli. What differences exist among them concerning
the matter of freedom, are, in other words, more obviously a

v

function of respective specialized concern, e.g. biblical rather than chiefly analytical, than of their national, sectarian, or denominational persuasion.

The editors' chief purpose in presenting this collection of essays is, however, to give the reader concerned with such matters an opportunity to participate in the serious and contemporary discussion of freedom in the Christian tradition. Each of these essays is a recent attempt to come to grips with some specific issues of freedom, and it is the view of the editors that each makes, in its own way, a positive contribution to this discussion of central importance for Christian theology, Christian ethics, and philosophy of religion. Thus merely occasional or chiefly polemical essays are not included in those here reprinted nor in the Selected Readings. Nor are essays of some difficulty or of unevenness of style omitted for such reasons alone. Our primary criterion in selecting these particular writings has been that each should itself be a significant contribution to the contemporary discussion of freedom in the Christian tradition. In accordance with this principle, each essay is reprinted as it was first published—with neither editorial alteration nor comment. The one exception to this is the Bonhoeffer selection which, due to the nature of the work in which these thoughts appear, has been "organized" by the editors from various pages of his *Ethics* as noted at the beginning of that selection. We think that the result of this rather unusual treatment is faithful to Bonhoeffer's views, insofar as those can themselves be determined, and we are especially grateful to the publisher for permitting us to reprint these words, phrases, and sentences from the English language text and to produce from them an essay which here achieves a literary existence for the first time.

One other selection requires a special comment, and that is the "Declaration on Religious Freedom" of the Second Vatican Council. While the large volume containing all the formal declarations of that remarkable Council has been widely circulated, and while the declaration here printed perhaps needs to be read in the context of the Council's other declarations for precise understanding of its whole meaning, we believe it a distinct addition to the discussion of the present volume to have it available in this anthology. Our readers may find it significant and revealing, for example, to examine this recent conciliar statement from the perspective of one or more of the other contemporary discussions. We have placed this document as an appendix not as a mark of derogation of its importance to our main theme, but rather to mark it off as a different sort of selection from the others. It is a "document," and, as such, represents a distillation of many discussions from varying points of view rather than merely a contribution to an ongoing discussion.

The editors' own primary vocations as teachers are undoubtedly revealed in the concluding essay which they have written especially for this collection. Our purpose there is to invite the careful reader of these essays to look at them again from a number of quite distinctive contemporary standpoints as these are represented by those intellectual movements widely known as phenomenology (including existentialism) and philosophical analysis. It seems clear that consideration of as complex a matter as that indicated by the term freedom requires every resource which the human mind and spirit may bring to it rather than any premature or over-simple sort of answer. The question whether the Christian claim about and stake in the issue of freedom can be fully arrived at apart from such considerations is certainly not a finally settled matter. Our concern is not so much to settle this issue as to raise again, perhaps in a fresh way, some of the questions which seem to us antecedent to any final such Christian stance.

There remains the pleasant task of acknowledging the various support we have received in the production of this volume. Publishers and other copyright owners receive formal acknowledgement at the beginning of each of the selections. We are, however, mindful that we are borrowing other people's property, and the cheerful and friendly responses we have had from editors and their assistants has redeemed from tediousness much of the business of securing permission to reprint. Miss Virginia Moulthrop, our student assistant, has performed a multiplicity of chores with such intelligence, humor, and

attention to detail as to place us in her debt. Mr. Victor Weybright, our editor and publisher, encouraged us to bring this
project to fruition both by his initial response to our proposal
and also by his friendly, competent, and immediate attention
to problems and questions directed to him. Allegheny College
provided us with a Summer Study Grant which provided assistance of an essential kind at a time when we most needed
it; and we wish to express our thanks to the College and to its
President, Lawrence Lee Pelletier. Our wives, Janet and Joyce,
have given us the support which comes only from that mutual
concern and understanding which are themselves perhaps life's
most concrete expression of the freedom that is bondage and
of the bondage that sets men free.

Allegheny College
March, 1969

Contents

PREFACE   *v*

Introduction / The Context of Freedom:
  A Theological Investigation   *1*

PART I / INITIAL PERSPECTIVES

Gustave Weigel / Theology and Freedom   25

Waldo Beach / Freedom and Authority in Protestant
  Ethics   40

PART II / PERSPECTIVES OF BIBLICAL
  THEOLOGY

John L. McKenzie / The Freedom of the Christian   59

Karl Barth / The Gift of Freedom: Foundation of
  Evangelical Ethics   69

ix

PART III / PERSPECTIVES OF EXISTENTIAL THOUGHT

Carl Michalson / Christian Faith and Existential Freedom   97

Sister Mary Aloysius / Freedom and the "I": An Existential Inquiry   115

PART IV / PERSPECTIVES OF NEO-TRADITIONAL THOUGHT

Dietrich Bonhoeffer / Responsibility and Freedom   151

Mark John Farrelly / God's Sovereignty and Man's Freedom   165

PART V / PERSPECTIVES OF RATIONAL THEOLOGY

Karl Rahner / On the Theology of Freedom   197

Austin Farrer / Liberty and Theology   214

Charles B. Ketcham and James F. Day / Freedom as Experienced and as Thought: The Question of Freedom   234

Appendix / Declaration on Religious Freedom of the Second Vatican Council   251

SELECTED READINGS   277

INDEX   283

Faith and Freedom / Essays in

Contemporary Theology

Introduction / The Context of Freedom:
A Theological Investigation

CONCERN FOR FREEDOM is widespread in the contemporary world. It has personal, political, racial, economic, and social aspects as anyone who participates in or even reads about current affairs certainly knows. It should occasion no surprise, then, to discover that the question of freedom has become a focal point for contemporary theologians who seek to explicate and to wrestle with the issues of Christian Faith. Perhaps, one will say, that of course every Christian generation since St. Paul wrote his letter to the Galatians has been concerned about freedom; and the general truth of such an observation can be cheerfully acknowledged. However, in all too many of those past centuries it has been thought about and written about as one among a number of other issues. Rarely in Christian history—and perhaps only in the second and third decades of the sixteenth century—has this issue provoked such fundamental concern in so profound a theological sense as in the contemporary epoch. Something of the response to this provocation and of the nature of this concern is evident in each of the essays we have collected for this anthology, and none of these writers needs an editor to speak for him. But just because thought about and experience of freedom does not take place in a vacuum, we propose to sketch in the following few pages some of the principal aspects of contemporary Christian thought which provide the context for these discussions of freedom.

The essays which follow have been written by contemporary western theologians. Along with millions of other western men and women these thinkers have lived through and have been influenced by many of the tragedies and triumphs of western civilization in the decades since World War I. That such events constitute a significant aspect of the context within which these theological reflections concerning freedom have been carried on is indubitable. That such events constitute either the primary focus of Christian Faith or the substance of theological reflection is, even though quite widely maintained, open to serious question. For even where some cultural movement or some apparently decisive historical event is taken with theological seriousness, such an interpretation involves seeing the movement or event as an instance of, or an occasion for, the will, the hand, the mind, the judgment, or the revelation of God. So, at any rate, the Editors understand the matter; and thus if we say nothing here about bombs or United Nations, about guerillas or new nations, it is not because we think such things are either irrelevant or insignificant. Rather, it is because we have a different purpose in mind for this Introduction.

That purpose is to provide some background for understanding and interpreting the essays in this volume by describing briefly each of the theological perspectives which seem to us to characterize the work of these particular theologians. An inspection of the Table of Contents will reveal the four organizational themes or perspectives under which we have grouped, in pairs, the main essays of this volume. We do not, of course, maintain either that these themes together exhaustively characterize the scene in contemporary Christian thought, or that any one of them adequately defines the total perspective of any one of these thinkers. As to the former, it is perhaps enough to mention the pervasiveness of the "urge to reform" of the institutional churches as well as a correlative impulse toward grappling with those affirmations which most fundamentally characterize Christian Faith—both are embraced by the term "ecumenical." As to the latter, we note, just for example, that Karl Barth's major theological work is called *Church Dogmatics*, and that Karl Rahner has had a deep concern for biblical theology as well as for many of the insights and expressions of the existentialist thinker, Martin Heidegger.

Nevertheless, when such acknowledgements have been made, it still seems to us both intelligible and helpful to group the particular essays we have selected according to the categories or "perspectives" we here employ, so long as none of them is used either reductively or simplistically. At any rate, our intention in this Introduction is to say something about each of the perspectives as they have, in turn, emerged in contemporary Christian thought.

The Perspective of Biblical Theology

Every serious Christian thinker from the Church Fathers to the present day has had to reckon with the Bible, but not everyone who has so reckoned with this varied set of the documents of faith has done so as a biblical theologian. Thus, for example, in the nineteenth and early twentieth centuries there were at least four kinds of concern about, or ways of regarding, the Bible; but no one of these was, in the present meaning of the phrase, *biblical* theology. So we proceed to define the phrase initially by saying what it is not; then we shall examine briefly its primary concerns.

First of all there is the view, which certainly did not originate in the nineteenth century, that the Bible contains either words that God Himself spoke or that His Holy Spirit caused or inspired certain writers, such as Moses or St. Paul, to write down. So understood, the Bible is a self-authenticating, transhistorical set of writings in Hebrew and in Greek, and each word is the bearer of a literal, decisive, definitive, and exclusive description, instruction, or counsel from God to everyman. That no one finite human can fully comprehend or finally reconcile all that is here recorded is to be expected, but here is gathered all the wisdom that any man needs for life, whether on earth or in heaven. If he would know about the beginnings of all things, let him turn to the Book of Genesis; if he would inquire concerning approved human conduct, let him turn to Exodus 20 and to Matthew, chapters five, six, and seven; if he is concerned about the future, let him study the prophets, Daniel, the apocalyptic sections of Mark and Matthew, and the Revelation of St. John. Faith is defined as assent to the proposition that the Bible—most often, for English-speaking Protestants, the King James Version—is all-knowing, all-wise, all-saving. The method of interpretation, roughly indicated above, is to gather together all of the texts bearing on a certain issue, then to codify them, next to memorize them, and finally to practice them.

In the second place, and at the opposite extreme, culminating in the nineteenth and early twentieth centuries, there is the view that regards the Bible as a composite work of many hands, times, and cultures, as a *pastiche* of memory, wisdom, and hope assembled through the centuries by many groups of unknown editors and thus quite properly the object of study by the scientific historian, the philologist, and the student of comparative cultures. Such dispassionate study vitiates, or at least blurs, traditional claims to the Bible's *verbal* authority in its disclosure of disparate strands of competing or even of contradictory accounts of creation, the birthplace of Jesus, or the number of trips that St. Paul made to Jerusalem. Old Testament accounts of creation and of floods have earlier and parallel accounts in Babylonian literature; Gospel narratives of the crucifixion and resurrection have earlier and contemporary parallels in the mystery cults' celebrations of their dying and rising "lords"; Pauline and Johannine attempts to universalize by spiritualizing the Gospel reveal the influences of an older and widely attractive Gnosticism. In the light of these and literally dozens of other historical and humanistic sources of the actual biblical documents, eminent scholars came seriously to debate such questions as the historicity of

Moses and of Jesus. As a consequence of such inquiries, discoveries, and debates, not only was doubt raised concerning the dependability of the biblical records at every crucial point but also the Christian claim to the uniqueness of its faith was called into question at its very foundation.

A third way of regarding the Bible which contemporary biblical theology has had to transmute may be summarized as the idealist influence. This came to fruition in two principal forms, one metaphysical, the other, moral. The former saw in the Bible a variety of primitive, rudimentary "testimonies" to the emergence of universal "Spirit" as particular men, or groups of men, awakened gradually from their primitive struggles amidst the primeval slime to the presence in and around them of the Absolute. Its emergence into a higher, more universal, and thus more creditable expression of self-consciousness in the faithfulness of a Ruth, the exalted visions of peace in Isaiah, the hymn of praise to love (*agape*) in I Corinthians 13, and most notably the identification of the "essence" of Jesus with the "Logos" in the First Chapter of John's Gospel are especially praiseworthy. But of course the Philosophy of Idealism transcends the incipient particularism and the manifest emphases upon incarnation of both Testaments, paradox is removed, and the darkest corners lighted by the philosopher's vision of Truth made concrete and universal.

The idealist perspective in its moral form, as one may rightly infer from its expressed concern, is to seek out the moral nuggets of the Scriptures and then to separate them from their grosser contexts such as the wars, the slayings of false prophets, the sacrifices of sons to propitiate a tribal Jahweh, the incipient religion, faith, and theology about the Christ which obscures the goodness of Jesus. In this case the Bible is made to subserve man's moral concerns by the use of such extra-biblical principles of selectivity as man's fundamental goodness, the allegedly self-evident principle of pacifism which selects and praises Jesus' teachings about the peacemakers and ignores such a passage as the one which proclaims, "I come not to bring peace, but a sword." The Gospel is interpreted in terms of what will inspire or produce moral uplift, and whatever authority is ascribed to Jesus, to Jahweh, or to God, is to be made in terms of their moral insight and ethical relevance.

The fourth and final interpretation of the Bible with which the biblical theologians have had to contend is to be found in a development variously described as "comparative religion," or the "history of religions." By whatever name it may be known, this movement is significant for our present purpose for at least three related phenomena. One is its approach to the Bible as only one among the great scriptures or "bibles" of the world's religions, with the clear implication that, as one among many of the same *genre*, its universal significance is most truly visible when it is seen as supplementing and as supplemented by other great masterpieces of inspiring or religious literature. As such, it finds its place in a "Bible of the World," its truth in what it shares with the others, and its significance in its power to bring some men to an awareness of the need for a world religion. This concern for a world religion, made possible in part on the basis of a foundation to be constructed from the stones and bricks of the "great passages" from various scriptures, is the second phenomenon of this movement. And the third of these phenomena, closely associated with the other two, was the "discovery" that the real key to understanding the Bible, in both its grossest and most sublime passages, is to regard it as a record of the evolution of man's religious awareness. So seen, one can follow, for example, the development of man's understanding of God. Beginning with a primitive tribal chieftain through such stages as those of a God of jealousy, of wrath, of judgment, of law, we are finally brought to the universally compelling and admirable portrayal of a God of mercy, forgiveness, and love. Similar evolutionary developments may be traced through the Bible with respect to its ideas of man, of right and wrong, of immortality, etc. In any case, the suggestion is clear that it is to be read and understood in terms of this particular set of criteria selected from and imposed from outside upon what would otherwise remain a strange or even alien world.

This image of the Bible as, in some fundamental sense, a

strange world is deliberately introduced at this point to indicate two things. First, it suggests that each of the four emphases we have just briefly outlined represents an attempt to
come to terms with the Bible by interpreting it in a way that
is already familiar, an effort to eliminate or at least to mitigate
its foreignness. As such, these interpretations, profound and
scholarly as they may be, fail to bring their readers into the
world of the Bible, with its emphatic God-centeredness, its
focus upon the concrete events of history as the primary arena
of man's confrontation in judgment and renewal with God,
and its "realism" about the ambiguity of human existence
within the context of man's freedom and destiny. Second, the
emphasis upon the strangeness of the biblical world is a
characteristic which is fundamental to biblical theology. This
means that, as with any document we propose to consider
seriously, we must be willing to listen, to allow ourselves to be
brought into its world, and to participate in its strangeness.

It is not that the biblical theologian proposes to ignore
either the questions or the methods or the reports of those
other investigators whose work we have briefly discussed.
Many, if not all, of these earlier methodologies and conclusions have become part of the warp and the woof of the
biblical theologians' own investigations. What is so different is
the point of fundamental departure, of orientation, of perspective. What must be recognized as a matter of first importance
is that the documents of the Bible are the products of two
communities of faith, that what we have here is a set or some
sets of claims about what some men have come to believe God
has done, is doing, and promises to do in relation to human
existence. In it are no philosophical arguments, no answers to
specific geological or biological questions, and certainly no
economic advice. Its context is faith and its purpose is proclamation of the faithfulness of God. It makes a claim upon the
trust and the loyalty of those who will or who can hear and
asks for decision: Answer "Yes" or "No"; don't wait for the
translation! Yet it bespeaks a God of infinite patience who
exercises lordship in His Kingdom not by over-ruling the un-
ruly wills of men but at great cost by forgiveness unending

and mercy unfathomable. Not *in* the particular words or accents of the Scriptures but *through* them is the Word of God to be heard, in faith and in freedom.

The Perspective of Existential Thought

The mode of thinking called "existential" which has come into prominence in recent decades is both old and new. The excitement about its "newness," with its concern for human freedom, "authentic" existence, and "truth-for-me" in a world overwhelmed and wearied by inevitability, inauthenticity, and abstract truth, has largely operated to conceal its intellectual connection with classical voluntarism. This voluntarism, whose source seems more largely biblical than Greek and whose earliest and most articulate spokesman was St. Augustine, may be briefly characterized as a view which asserts the primacy of will over intellect. It has, therefore, in contrast to those modes of thought which stress the priority of reason, traditionally placed greater stress upon freedom than upon Truth, upon a dynamic rather than a static view of reality, and upon the provisional or problematic character of human existence than do those *a prioristic* views which assert that the answers are, in principle, already given. Although carried out in a far different historical setting and expressed in much sharper accents, the central concerns of contemporary existential thinking are not, in principle, as novel as some of its most ardent practitioners would have us believe.

At the same time it is, however, new. This newness is chiefly a function, as it seems, of the novel historical situation of the twentieth century in relation to which the existential mode of perceiving and thinking reveals a "world" sharply different both from that envisioned by the bland doctrine of progress and from that sharp, brittle, bright, and "external" vision of the technological manipulators. In a revolutionary age, where change—rapid, breathless change—is the order of the day, the categories of inevitable human progress seem increasingly irrelevant. In a time of passionate struggles for freedom and self-expression, the procedures of the technicians and the social engineers seem not only stultifying but also terrifying. What we can attempt here, without in any way presuming to state as certified a set of doctrines to which all existential philosophers would agree, is simply to characterize the "stance" or "perspective" of existential thinking. So seen such a mode of perceiving and thinking is, at a minimum, concerned about the following themes: truth as "subjective"; authentic existence; radical freedom; historical seriousness; and personal involvement. And its concern in all these matters is both primarily and fundamentally within the context of *human* existence, with life as "lived" by concrete and particular rather than "average" and depersonalized human agents.

This emphasis upon the character of life as "lived," in depth and in passion, becomes immediately evident in the existentialist concern for truth. Truth is neither some high and abstract or remote state of affairs in an objective, impersonal, "closed," realm, nor is it a least-common-denominator consensus expressed in mores and codified in the "laws" of science, state, or church. Rather, the truth that counts *for me* is that which gives meaning to my existence as a total person— not some abstract and irrelevant "two plus two equals four" to which I give only the assent of my mind. Every armchair or laboratory quest for truth is both too impersonal and too abstract to provide me with significant answers in my quest for the meaning of *my* existence. To "know" in this deeply inward existential sense requires venture, commitment, involvement. Other kinds of truth and knowledge are not here regarded as "wrong" but as misleading both as to the nature of the way to personal truth as well as to the criteria for it. Furthermore, to a person in agony over a difficult decision which he confronts, it is not merely misleading but an affront to pat him on the back and point out that others have faced similarly difficult situations; for the existential fact is that no one can make my existential decisions for me, and the anguish is compounded by the realization that even my failure to choose is a choice in which I commit myself to the inauthentic, the merely common, the inhuman.

This brings us, with a sort of existential "inevitability," to the concern for authenticity. If the sole method of truth-finding for the existentialist involves commitment, action, then its sole criterion is authenticity. For the non-religiously oriented existentialist there seem to be no criteria for authenticity; for such, an authentic decision or act is self-certifying. Its credentials do not lie in its satisfaction of any biological or psychological desires, and they are certainly not to be found in terms of any set of rational categories. The observer may be left to suspect that this self-certification lies in something not dissimilar from a feeling of the "rightness," the relevance, of such an act or decision; but then he is reminded that, in any case, no other existing being is ever in quite the position to judge the authenticity or inauthenticity of another person's decision or action. Made only in the "moment" amidst the profound anxiety which marks their all-or-nothing character, the truly momentous commitments of human existence are enacted as decisive, ultimate, with the awareness that they constitute the "to be or not to be" of one's unique, concrete, and personal "being." Every truly real and creative act thrusts one against the edge of his being to a confrontation with the "sea" of non-being, with the abyss of meaninglessness whose permanent horizon is at least symbolized by death. There is no help, no Helper, no dependable guide, no Pole Star, no compass, no chart, no model, no rule, no law. Human existence, so conceived and so specified, is a series of specific and unique ventures into an unknown where no one else, as a matter of existential and historical fact, could ever set foot. Only one thing seems sure, and that is that authenticity is not served by those who only stand and wait!

The almost nihilistic implications of the foregoing are redirected by those of religious, and specifically Christian, persuasion as they find a criterion for authenticity in an encounter with the holiness and mercy of the Being of God. He it is whose presence looms beyond the horizons of being and non-being, toward whom, by the mercy of whom, and in relation to whom the isolation, the anxiety, and the meaninglessness of human existence may be understood and transformed. As the One, the Wholly Other, the Stranger, even the Enemy with whom we have ultimately to do, He manifests Himself in Jesus Christ as the Friend, the Authentic One who in mercy which ever over-reaches our most servile self-abnegation searches out the Prodigal and the lost. He, as the patient, loving "Thou" for every detached or wandering or questing "I," offers hope, courage, restoration, and meaning without negating His "otherness" or annihilating human freedom. This encounter becomes the ground for meaningful identity. So, at any rate, have the insights and language of existential thought become powerful instruments in the hands of some contemporary theologians as they seek to confront their alienated and biblically illiterate contemporaries with the *evangelion*, the Good News, of the Christian Gospel.

As it was difficult to discuss the existentialist view of truth without coming to grips with the problems of authenticity, so it is with freedom: the existentialist quest for truth and for authenticity brings us to, or better reveals, how absolutely fundamental to human existence is freedom. Renouncing as it does any idea of a "fixed" human nature, freedom nevertheless serves existential thought almost as though it were the "essence" of human existence; it is, for man, the occasion if not the ground for both the misery *and* the grandeur of his life. As existentialists treat it, freedom does reveal human existence in its problematic character. It is not to be equated with the situation we confront in the restaurant or cafeteria in being able to select only one among a number of entrées; nor is its dimension revealed in crossroads situations while driving from one place to another. Neither is the existentialist really a party to the age-old debates among and between various kinds of determinists and supporters of free will. His concern is at once more temporal, more profound, and as he sees the matter, more decisive. For freedom is each person's participation in non-being, his venture into creativity, and his involvement with the anxiety of having to act in situations in which he can never be certain of the consequences of his acts, yet with the certitude that he becomes those acts "for better or for worse." So envisioned, freedom is not only not the "holy light" of our forefathers; it is not even the "inner light" of human reason;

it is a darkness which fascinates and repels, which is awesome and terrifying; and it is inescapable. Temporal beings that we are, each with a determinate past for some parts of which we are existentially responsible, we stand always in the present moment with the not-yet of an unknown and unknowable future beckoning as an inescapable dimension of every significant decision we shall ever as humans make. One writer, Marjorie Grene, has thus been led to characterize the entire existentialist movement as "dreadful freedom." If there were only some definite object in the future, then we could begin by fearing it and perhaps learning how to deal with it, but anxiety, dread (*angst, l'angoisse*), is a condition in which there is no specifiable object—only the nothingness of the future with as yet no determinate character. The future is a *tabula rasa* upon which each person is called to write—not with chalk, brush, or pen, but with and for his own existence. For our encounter with this most profound dimension of our existence, no person, young or old, is ever equipped with the truth or the measure of authenticity; yet, inexorably, freedom (as Spengler wrote of fate) "leads the willing and drags the unwilling."

And our consideration of freedom brings us, really without transition, to note the historical character of human existence. Bound to a time as to a place, it seems the case that not only are we in time but also that, even more profoundly if also more elusively, time is in us. Our existence as lived is always a present in the light of an open and indeterminate future out of a past. But the latter is significant only as it relates to defining the "me" of the present, never as a trustworthy existential key to the future. It is now that I must decide, never knowing the one thing I most need to know if I am to move with genuine but non-existential confidence to implement my decision; for in my capacity for self-transcendence I can know both a time-when-I-was-not and a time-when-I-will-not-be, and the strange thing is how the former gives rise at most to nostalgia, but the latter to nausea, terror, dread. And so I am squeezed into a temporality not of my own making with a beginning and an ending neither of which is really under my control. Beyond this, my very thought of myself, or of anything, is somehow "infected" with temporality—not so much in the sense of now at noon I see it and then at six I don't, as with the character which all things I know exhibit, that they come to be and they pass away. Existentially speaking, there is no opportunity for trial and error as I seek to be the truth, to live authentically and in freedom. And for the theologian who comes to reflect upon the Christian Faith, there is the profound enigma of the Eternal as the one who is not alone creator of time but beyond this involves Himself with the temporal in the event to which Christians point with the term "incarnation." Here, too great an emphasis upon the "otherness" and transcendence of God at the expense of the significant reality of time and its events risks the loss of the human, temporal dimension; whereas, too great a stress upon the events of time merely as lived and experienced can lead to the loss of the transcendent dimension for which we have the name "humanism." Whether there are resources in existential thinking adequate to holding these poles together in a significant way yet remains to be seen; and the issue may well lie with a test of the adequacy of the existentialist view of the incarnation.

Finally, as a theme really secondary to none of the foregoing, is the existentialist concern for involvement. Without it none of the others can be complete. As already implied at each of the points of our investigation so far, what is most evidently at issue here is a rejection of any view of human existence which holds that either "objectivity" or "neutrality" is the way to truth, authenticity, or freedom. Although physical action does not seem always required, what is demanded is the total self with nothing held back, a willingness to put one's money where one's mouth is. Without such a total commitment, one is condemned to be an observer in the safety and anonymity of the bleachers, to live a life as irrelevant as the Monday morning quarterback. Without involvement existential truth does not "become," authenticity is not achieved, fredom is not "real," and history becomes a story about someone else. Manifestly, given the nature of our contemporary age—with living from crisis to crisis in a time of quite revolutionary change—this existential perspective is very much attuned to the character and demands of such a world. One cannot but think that, if it had not had its precursors in Kierkegaard, the early Marx, and Nietzsche, it would have had to have been invented! Certainly its preoccupation with the problematic nature of human existence and with the urgent demands of freedom cannot safely be ignored by any thinker who would participate sensitively and creatively in the contemporary world.

The Perspective of Neo-Traditional Thought

Every thinker and worker in the field of ideas carries on his work within a community of scholars and on the basis of achievements already attained, conclusions already established. The training of the scholar-in-the-making involves him, always to some degree at least, in the effort to appropriate the ideas and perspectives of those who have gone before. This process also requires the adoption of some standpoint, some tradition, on the basis of which to begin to make sense of his own studies. Thus Einstein was once a Newtonian in physics, Bertrand Russell an Idealist in philosophy, and Karl Barth a liberal in theology. However, as he gains a certain mastery within his chosen field, the thinker is confronted with the possibility either of consciously making a sharp break with his own tradition or of consciously choosing to identify himself with one or another of the established traditions. Although we acknowledge that this is greatly oversimplified, the point is that not every significant and creative scholar has, as a mark of his genius, to make a sharp break with tradition. He may, rather, devote himself to the task of relating the fundamental and viable elements of some tradition to a present cultural scene. It is the continuation—or persistence—of such past, established patterns of theological thinking in the twentieth century that we have in mind when we speak of the perspective of neo-traditional thought.

Involvement in one or another of such traditions by a majority of contemporary men and women of Christian persuasion, and by many Christian theologians, seems clearly to be the case; but our interest in this perspective is not prompted primarily by such gross quantitative considerations. For one thing, it certainly must be acknowledged that many who think of themselves as Neo-Lutherans, Neo-Thomists, Neo-Calvinists, etc. do so on the basis not of careful or hard thinking but as a family inheritance, as something familiar and comfortable as an old shoe, or simply due to sloth. Such passive followers of traditional ways of believing and thinking honor their tradition in religion no more than those activistic but mindless devotees of radical change serve the cause of creativity. It is neither of nor for such that we speak here. Our interest in this perspective, and its significance in contemporary Christian thought, lies in a quite different direction. We consider, briefly, its three principal strengths and, even more briefly, three of its potential limitations.

One strength of the neo-traditional perspective is it service as an active and living reminder that Christianity is an historical faith. This means two things. It means, first, that the events of history are understood and witnessed to as a primary arena of man's encounter with God's self-disclosure. And, secondly, it serves as a reminder of those significant events in the Church's own continuing effort to witness to and to explicate the meaning of Christian Faith in specific historical situations. To become a Christian, or even to come to an understanding of what this Faith is, requires not only an awareness of this year's foliage and fruit but also some sense of involvement with the roots through which every living present receives some of its essential nourishment.

A second and related strength of this traditionalist view is its function with respect to new insights and situations. Christianity is not interested in novelty for its own sake; and neither churches nor its theologians are commissioned to dart hither and yon seeking out the most titillating or *avant garde* ideas as its primary media of expression or self-understanding. It is difficult to see how a sense of responsibility can be successfully maintained apart from a sense of history, and it is this latter sense, exercised in service of the former, that the traditionalist brings to bear upon the lords of the passing hour.

In the third place, the traditionalist posture is a factor of strength because it guards the particularity and the variety of Christian witness and understanding. No one traditional or historical way of understanding or expressing Christian Faith is the absolute or final truth; but when we have a number of viable traditions, then each may teach and learn from the others. Such has clearly been the experience of those denominations within Protestantism in the past two decades and more as they have sought a closer sense of unity and a clearer understanding of the mind of Christ in ecumenical efforts. Before one denomination can seriously come to talk with another about some sort of organic union, each has first been driven to seek anew an understanding of its own characteristic emphases before it can begin to understand what and how it is that the other may bring to such a merger. This seems to be almost a first law of ecumenism, if not of life—that before one can come to understand who and what another is he must first come to know in some genuine depth who and what he himself is.

There is, however, another side to this whole traditionalist matter, and it is this of which the neo-traditionalist seeks to become aware—namely, that there is a companion weakness for each of the above strengths. It is apparent—and this is certainly not limited to theological or religious existence—that in coming to grips with the events of the past one may go beyond seeking to conserve what is viable and end up as a backward-looking reactionary. Such a peril point has become all too evidently a clear and present reality in recent decades as the churches have all too often found themselves confronting a worldwide, revolutionary, urban age with a parochial, pre-revolutionary, and rural set of conceptions and expectations. From such an abject surrender of freedom and responsibility the neo-traditionalist would seek to preserve both himself and his tradition. For him the tradition is never an end in itself, to be preserved inviolate at all costs; it is rather the definition of the ground upon which he initially stands and that through which he has come both to self-understanding and to confrontation with God in Christ; and he seeks only new expression of that in it which is clearly vital, creative, and responsible.

A second weakness of traditionalism of which the neo-traditionalist soon becomes aware is the temptation to confuse its justifiable reluctance to pursue novelty for its own sake with an unjustifiable refusal to confront the present age. Thus in order to preserve a sense of history its guardian ends up in a most ahistorical stance. Such a view is ahistorical in two ways; for, on the one hand, it refuses to look at the present except through the eyes of some ancient saint—be it Augustine, Thomas, Luther, Calvin, or Wesley—and in the process, on the other hand, it demonstrates that it has not learned the fundamental facts involved in the creative vision of these great men themselves. The Christian's authentic obligation to the past is not to learn some formula from the lips of either Thomas or Luther, but to try to see what he saw and how characteristically he went about acting upon that vision. And what is significant from the past for the newness of every present must never be understood as a consolation against, as a fall-out shelter from, the urgent issues of the hour.

Finally, traditionalism without critical control and careful appropriation may serve to stifle the contemporary and living Word of God, to deafen us to the meaning which the free and responsible exercise of Christian Faith has in the time and place where we live. It is such control and such appropriation which the neo-traditionalist seeks. He does not glory in secularism nor in the secular age for the sake of the secular, but rather because he understands and comes to see creation as the work of God Himself. And for the same reason, he cannot indulge, either lightly or even seriously, in a so-called "death of God" theology. Rather, the point of his dispute with the more unthinking traditionalists is over the latter's apparent efforts to keep everything "just the way it was" in the name of the creative Lord of history. Such an attitude verges on paranoia when it persists in seeing only the redness of the fire in the worldwide revolution of our time; it challenges the creative wisdom of God when it seeks to cling to racist doctrines; and it claims prerogatives which are not its own when it acts to veto responsible participation in the ecumenical movements of the day. These strengths and these weaknesses of traditionalism the neo-traditionalist seeks to understand in at least some of the ways suggested above. As such, he, and the perspective through which he envisions his theological task, is both a responsible and an essential participant in the theological work of every contemporary age.

The Perspective of Rational Theology

Religious claims and theological utterances are addressed not only to men's hearts but also to their minds. The rational theologian, no less ardent in the strength of his beliefs than others, conceives his task as the careful working out and analysis of the implications and problems involved in such claims and utterances. This is a critical task in at least two senses. In the first place, it is critical because it is difficult to carry it out seriously without seeming to be presumptuous with respect to the revealed elements of religious faith. It has sometimes seemed to critics of such an activity—and these critics have not always been wrong—as though the rational theologian were trying to usurp the role of God Himself. But such a clear and ever-present danger to such an activity must not be understood as relieving the Christian theologian from the responsibility of confronting the issues and problems with which the rational theologian is concerned. As is the case in much of life, real problems do not go away if we just pretend they do not exist; nor will they evaporate, in this case, under the bright sunshine of faith. For the task is a critical one in a second sense, namely, that if theology is to be done at all some continuing and serious attention must be paid to its rational components. The only alternative, then, to careful and systematic rational theology is to let such issues go by default; and the consequences of such a move, in ways both silly and serious, no devotee of Christian Faith ought either to want or accept.

Among the many issues which might be discussed here, some subtle and hidden and others more self-evident, we select four which seem to us of unusual significance on the present scene: the problem of language; man and society; nature and history; and the matter of dogmas themselves. What we propose in each case is neither a definitive statement of the problem nor anything like a theological solution to it, but rather an indication of the way in which the perspective of rational theology itself may be delineated.

The religious person, if he is to take with any seriousness his capacity to speak about the varieties of his experiences with any precision, must come to grips with the issue involved in his language about God and faith. A moment's reflection will establish that we mean something different when we say, "I believe in God," than when we say "The sun is shining." The latter statement is open to immediate, sensory validation and is ordinarily intended and understood as a literal assertion of a factual state of affairs. But what does the former utterance mean, and how is it to be validated? We would certainly not understand the religious speaker to be making a claim of the same literal sort as is involved in the assertion about the sun. Is the religious statement to be understood as a parable, as symbolic, as poetic? Is it in every ordinary sense of word usage entirely meaningless, as some thinkers have claimed in recent years? It is no final settlement of such questions to observe that Jesus spoke often in parables or in even more ambiguous ways, although the theologian may well profit from a careful study of the modes of religious discourse in the Scriptures. In the end, however, if religious faith is to be received, witnessed to, and articulated, some attention must be paid to the very nature of the language used in such fundamental religious activities. The only significant alternative would seem to require that Christian Faith be seen as fundamentally an unutterable mysticism, but such an admission would undercut the principal thrust of Christian Faith itself—*toward* the world, *for* man, and not *away* from him.

The person to whom religious faith comes finds himself already a human being in the setting of a social environment. What sort of creature is it who finds himself addressed by the Lord of redemption? What implications, for and against, this gift of faith which has come to him are there in the achievements and failures for which he and his fellow men hold themselves responsible? What suggestive possibilities are there for

him in his natural communities which might help shed some
light upon the meaning of what Scripture calls the "Kingdom
of God"? Dare any single person ever think that he, a social
being, could hope to confront God in solitariness? How is he,
in the midst of his "worldly" calling, to be or to become a
good neighbor as he works and votes and plays? Is it ever
enough, especially in our complex modern world, to say that
love of neighbor is a genuine possibility for anyone without
careful consideration of the nature of human selfhood and of
human community? These and other associated questions, for
which there are no specific answers in the revealed data of
religious faith, press in upon anyone who would seek to discover the responsible meaning of faith for him. It is with
fundamental aspects of such questions that the rational theologian must be concerned in the area of man and society. He
seeks neither to displace nor to confute the work of such
specialists as psychologists and sociologists and political scientists; but he must be deeply involved in trying to work out the
implications of Christian Faith in relation to such issues and
also to represent the interests of that faith when confronted
with theories which assert psychological determinism or societal environmentalism as the whole truth and nothing but the
truth.

So it is also with respect to the extremely knotty problem
concerning the relationship of nature and history. We have
already seen the importance of history as somehow the primary arena wherein man confronts God, but what then is to
be done about the natural environment? In its earliest con-
troversies and creeds, the Church has always refused to
separate the work of redemption, or the person of the Redeemer, from that of the "creator of heaven and earth." That
the temptation to make such a separation is not merely an
ancient or dead temptation is witnessed to today by the continuing flirtation between some theologians and existential
philosophy. The existentialists, seeking more humane or "personal" categories than those offered by philosophical perspectives informed more largely by logic and science, seem to
provide theology a way of coming to grips with the imperson-

alism, the anxiety, and the alienation which grip the modern industrialized world. But the rational theologian feels moved, not by some alien or more perverse philosophy but by the demands of the first article of the Creed, to raise his voice in warning against those of his fellow believers who would seek to explicate Christian Faith through categories for which creation is alien and nature little more than a distant background.

Finally, the rational theologian is concerned to understand Christian dogmas themselves not simply as blind assertions nor merely as liturgical or evocative celebrations, but as efforts at various times and places to explicate the Christian Faith. Thus the Nicene Creed, admitting the limitations of much of its rhetoric for our contemporary world, is to be seen as an effort to make explicit what is involved in saying "Jesus Christ is Lord." It is possible that this ancient formula may be improved upon, but the rational theologian is concerned to point out to those who would abandon that Creed entirely on the grounds of its archaic language or of its alleged involvement with the static categories of Greek metaphysics must face up to the problems of polytheism which such abandonment so often entails. On the one hand there is the oneness of God, and on the other the richness and variety of the ways of His dealing with the created order; and to focus one's thought upon either at the expense of the other inevitably leads to theological confusion and runs the risk of religious idolatry. In such matters the rational theologian claims neither the first and certainly not the last word, but he does claim the responsibility of bringing to bear some intermediate words that others may come to serve the Lord with their minds as well as heart and soul and strength.

These are the perspectives, then, which in varied combinations exercise their influence upon the labors of the contemporary Christian theologian. Each in its own way supplies both a way into the question of the freedom of faith and also at least a hint concerning the responsible exercise of that freedom in service to the Living Word in the Church for the world.

PART I / INITIAL
PERSPECTIVES

Gustave Weigel / Theology and Freedom

THIRTY YEARS ago when a young collegian manifested his intention to dedicate his life to theology, eyebrows rose. In the second and third decades of this century, the thinking world of the West put theology on a par with phrenology and astrology. No serious man would have anything to do with such occult arts. They were supposed to be based on false assumptions and, practically, they had nothing to give to man.

All that has changed. Theology has once more achieved respectability, while astrology has only acquired popularity and phrenology has withered away. The reason for this change is manifold, but one reason is certainly the collapse of the optimistic naturalism which flourished at the end of the nineteenth century and through the first two decades of the twentieth. It was not the naturalism which annoyed the men of the late twenties and middle thirties. It was the optimism.

GUSTAVE A. WEIGEL, S. J. *(1906–1964) taught at the Catholic University of Chile and then at Woodstock College. He was a lecturer and the author of a number of essays and books, including* CATHOLIC THEOLOGY IN DIALOGUE *(1960); the present essay was originally delivered as a lecture at Fordham University and is reprinted here from* THOUGHT, *vol. 35 (Summer, 1960) by permission of the Editor.*

By strictly empirical tests there was no ground for optimism. Things were getting different but not better nor was there any visible hope for improvement. Insecurity and threat faced men all over the world. The United States had its economic depression. Europe had the turmoil of naziism, fascism and stalinism. Imperialism agitated the East not so much because of Western action, which was bad enough, but because of the ambition of Japan. Technology indeed was advancing in gigantic strides. Aviation, radio and electronics shrunk distances and there were machines for every human effort. But all this evident progress did not make the lot of the earth-dweller any more tranquil. In some respects the machines were a cause of the trouble. The leisurely production of the ancient craftsman who adjusted his instruments to his own needs and temper was gone. The new machines worked at a fixed tempo to which man had to adjust and when he used his new tools as perforce he had to, he was under tension. It was not now the eagle eye of the foreman which had caused him nervousness in the past, but rather his mechanical tool which was next to him and in accelerated operation every minute of his working day. Technology was seen as absolutely necessary but it alone was not going to solve the problems of the human situation.

Things were certainly not getting better of themselves. You had to put your collective mind to it. When the collective mind did go to work in the League of Nations and in the Rooseveltian Braintrust, it was suddenly discovered that "the best laid schemes o' mice and men gang aft a-gley an' lea'e us nought but grief and pain for promis'd joy." The reason why they often "gang a-gley" is because there is an uncontrollable factor in human action which for ages had been called man's freedom. In other words, the heart of the human situation was the problem of human liberty. No matter how you treated man, this stubborn indeterminism showed its ugly head. Force and coercion were applied to men; persuasion most skillfully employed was directed toward him; knowledge was deluged over him; but there was no known medium which could infallibly control that freedom. The existentialist philosophers who were coming to the fore in that time invented the phrase, "Man is condemned to freedom."

Freedom was not a new word in the twenties and thirties. It had come down to us from the past and there was a glorious ring to it. In fact we had the Liberty Bell as one of its most revered symbols. It was the mark of the United States that culturally it was a champion of freedom, while other Western communities had lost their faith in it: Italy, Germany and Russia, for example.

Yet freedom was on trial. It was universally recognized that it was not true that its only possible fruit was good. It was evident that it could also bring forth much evil. In man freedom produced the problem of evil. Evil had not been the object of man's contemplation for many decades, and the men who spoke of evil did not explain it. They only explained it away. Their usual solution was that evil was only a manifestation of bad organization, which through education would automatically evolve into good organization. Evil in this view was only the birth pain of the better. This was consoling doctrine but it was not satisfactory to a world which experienced evil and saw no great good burgeoning out of it.

[I]

It was here that theology suddenly took on a new significance. This discipline had for millennia dealt with the problem of freedom and evil. It was the only discipline around with something profound to say about the matter. In consequence, Cinderella suddenly became a princess. Karl Barth, Emil Brunner, Reinhold Niebuhr and Paul Tillich, theologians all, talked to our time about the concerns of the age. And they were heard. The dignity of theology was recognized again and this dignity has survived to our day. It is not the majestic eminence once enjoyed by theology in the distant past but at least the theologian no longer has to apologize for his presence among the molders of ideas.

What has the theologian to say about freedom? Very much, and he has been doing it for many centuries. As Mortimer Adler in his *The Idea of Freedom* (New York: Doubleday, 1958) has pointed out, most theologians have seen that freedom is a complex notion having as many as four or five levels of meaning. Political freedom is hardly the heart of the matter and even the psychic capacity for choice is a superficial aspect of liberty.

Theologians of the Catholic tradition have without exception taken the human capacity of choosing for granted. They never went into great investigations of this obvious phenomenon, which even determinists freely admit. As a phenomenon, the choice of alternatives is evident in all conceivable agents when they are thrust into situations which permit a variety of reactions. Even the dog must choose which of two chewable bones he will chew on. But the Catholic theologians felt that the problem of choice of future lines of activity took on a peculiar freedom when the different possibilities of reaction were previously contemplated. In such an event, and only a contemplating agent is capable of it, we have deliberate choice, and this is free in a sense higher than mere contingency. Granted indeed that the resulting action was contingent, its contingency was in function of the deliberation, decision and responsibility of the agent. Catholic theologians never bothered to prove that man acted in this way. They simply considered it to be an existential datum and as a datum it presented man with problems. They wisely refused to solve the problems by denying that the ground of the problematic was real.

This is the first contribution of theology, the serene and unbefuddled admission of man's freedom as an experienced datum. In this admission theology did not confuse contingency and liberty. Liberty is a quality peculiar to rational action. It says more than the truism that all things are possible; it affirms that man can comprehend possibility and control its actualization. Liberty is, therefore, a dignity and a sign of human worth. What is more, liberty does not make man worthy but man is free because he is antecedently worthy.

This first theological affirmation concerning liberty is of immense consequence. To suppress a man's liberty by coercion, duress or meddling with his being is to treat man in disaccord with his worth. He is being unworthily treated and if the man himself succumbs to such interference, he is conducting himself unworthily. There is in this position the firm basis for an effective humanism. Man becomes an agent of peculiar value for no other reason than that he is a man. Christianity's approach to slavery ended slavery not by banning the institution but by removing the postulate which justified the system. If any man is by his very being free, then he cannot because of his essence be a slave, and accidental slavery is only an economic arrangement agreed upon by those concerned with economic ends. The pagan's contempt for the slave always rested on the supposition of the unworthiness of the slave, a notion patent in the writings of such men as Plato and Aristotle, though attacked by Stoics like Epictetus, Seneca and Marcus Aurelius. But even the Stoics considered the slave's worth as something he could achieve by asceticism and not as something antecedent to his own behavior. The Christian theologians went beyond both the Academy and the Stoa by insisting that man was worthy before he acted. In this situation master and slave were really equals, and in consequence the system lost any advantages it may have had. When it lost its advantages, it lost its reason to exist, and in Christianity the system could only wither away and finally disappear. We have here an eloquent instance of the way theology works. It does not necessarily attack objectives by direct assault; it simply floods them with light under which the objectives melt away.

[II]

The mere recognition of the fact of human liberty is not of itself a superlative achievement. As it is a datum, it really is not denied by anyone, if we limit liberty to its phenomenological level, namely, deliberate, responsible decision. Every man knows that he posits such acts and there is no use telling him that he does not do so. The problems of liberty arise when we go beyond the mere experimental fact and relate it to the whole framework of universal meaning. What are the metaphysical implications of freedom? What does it tell us about the world and its structure? What does it tell us about the ground of being? What does it suggest as a decent pattern for human coexistence? These are the real questions which are brought to man's attention because he is involved in deliberate, responsible decisions. In answering these questions only theology is competent to give ultimate answers, and every ultimate answer will be theological, even though it may be a very bad theology.

From the very phenomenon of choice we know that freedom is self-affirmation. The question immediately arises whether it is only self-affirmation, or to put it in its ultimate form, what is the self who affirms? Is the self an isolated, unrelated consciousness, floating without orientation or direction on the mysterious sea of existence, itself selfless? There are those in the past and present who have answered affirmatively. Of course, this answer supposes that history is a seething mass of maggots in an opaque puddle, unlovely, without pattern and beyond judgment. This answer is reckless and has only the glory of wildly manifesting freedom, which as we have seen is a noble thing. When man is confronted with the real, he inevitably looks for its meaning, so that the meaningless and nothing are synonymous. The fury of chaos is unthinkable. The self is somehow definable; it is not a mere splutter in an ooze.

From this basic insight Catholic theology has had much to say about freedom and self-affirmation. It begins with the supposition that the self is structured and its affirmations must be related to that structure. Any affirmation inconsistent with such structure is not a self-affirmation, but a self-denial, and by that very fact treason to the self. Such a preposterous affirmation is indeed a manifestation of freedom but it is not its proper fruit; not its use but its abuse. This was basic to the Christian theologian's conception of freedom. Liberty does not mean absolute indifference to either of two alternatives, though it did in finite agents suppose that physically either alternative could be chosen. But only one *should* be chosen, that which accorded better with the structure of the human self. Freedom was conceived as an instrumentality for perfection, not as an expression of unconditioned autonomy. In this conception freedom is a responsibility rather than an absence of law. Freedom is not man's possession in order to enable him to do what is good or evil; it is an enablement to do the good in a rational way.

It is at this point that Catholic theology takes a stand on freedom which opposes it to almost all other forms of visions of liberty. Theology sees three dimensions in the self. First of all, it is an agent rooted in the ground of being which transcends the particular human agent but without which the agent is nothing. Man's being derives from a source distinct from himself and man's activity shows up not only the finite self but an infinite self, the last and first spring of being and action. Second, any reference to an inbuilt design in the human self is unrealistic if only constructed in the light of an atemporal idea of man achieved by abstracting from history. To understand man's true design we must study man in his historical context. Third, man's history will not be adequately achieved by consulting man alone. It will be necessary to contemplate the vision of man as possessed by the author of history. The purview of this vision is granted only by divine graciousness in a personal self-revelation inviting man to faith.

These three principles have weighty consequences. According to Catholic theology, historical man has a flaw in his structure. This flaw is labeled by the term "Original Sin." The term affirms that the active human self is a disturbed personality and nothing which man can do can eliminate the disturbance. At most he can reduce the disturbance but he cannot get rid of it. As a consequence man will freely express his own split self by split action, which will be simultaneously self-realizing and self-defeating. He cannot by himself reach the goal of liberty which is perfect self-affirmation, for when he affirms self, he is affirming a self torn between being and nonbeing. Here we find theology's criticism of all optimistic naturalism which supposes that man can by education, training, guidance or asceticism achieve a totally satisfactory self-expression. There is a death or destruction impulse vitiating all human effort. This view of man and his freedom has exasperated all naturalists because it flatly denies the basis of their own philosophy. It has been a constant temptation of Catholic theology to compromise its own basic insight in its dialogue with the thinkers from beyond its own circle, but the compromise has always been resisted by the major voices of the Catholic tradition. Augustine rose to attack Pelagianism and Semipelagianism and his views have prevailed. The Augustinian conception of man has often been caricatured by its own friends as a doctrine of total depravity shows. But Augustine never thought that man was a monster; he only denied he was a balanced agent.

What makes Augustinian anthropology most distasteful to naturalists is the doctrine held by all Catholic theologians that man's self-affirmation, to be adequate, must ultimately be an affirmation of God in the self. This demands a consciousness of God derived from the self's returning to the ground of its being. Such a state is not natural because in it man leaves the order of nature and only beyond nature can he truly realize himself. To make such a goal the dynamism of man, irritates the secularist because he wants man to occupy himself only with secular goods. But Catholic theology has always denied that such an orientation can have ultimate meaning for mankind. All being is divine in its ground and the elimination of the ground of being from the consideration of man directs him not to what absolutely is but to what is absolutely not, and this is a frustrating activity. From the point of view of the Catholic theologian, secularism and naturalism are self-defeating and therefore are lamentable programs of human action rather than liberating saviors. In the bitter dialogue between the theologian and the secularist, the secularist has one defense: he does not believe that God has made any revelation concerning the destiny of man. Here he stands impregnable and that is why he glories in his unbelief and exalts the fact of freedom. It never dawns on him that he is not defending freedom but only using it, for to believe is as free as unbelief. To say that there is a revelation is just as much a manifestation of freedom as to say that there is not. The only difference is that, if there is a revelation, to reject it freely is an abuse of liberty and not its proper function. Freedom gives man no grounds for rejecting the real, though it does make it possible.

[III]

For the Catholic theologian, then, absolute freedom, the freedom of the unconditioned creator, is not and cannot be the
freedom of man. To treat human freedom as if it were divine
is nonsense in any hypothesis, but it is tragic nonsense if we
consider man as he historically exists, since this man is prone
to abuse freedom in every instance. Yet Catholic theology is
not a despairing pessimism. It has an optimism of its own
which stands up better than the naive optimism of the natural-
ist and secularist.

Man indeed is a split personality; he will always abuse his
own freedom, and this abuse will bring suffering to individual
man and to the human community. However, man operates in
function of an original divine will and God is good, kind, wise
and all-powerful. His beneficent design cannot be thwarted by
human willfulness for He uses even the wrath of man to praise
Him. What is more, He can overcome the schizophrenia of men
by interiorly inspiring and gently moving them to proper
choices in their freedom. This action is called grace, the
gracious sanating intervention of God in a bent world, whereby the kind designs of the Creator become real. The weakness
of man and the limits of human freedom need not depress the
human agent. In his weakness the power and majesty of God
are at work, and human history, produced by human agents,
will bring glory to God and peace to men of good will.

On hearing this gospel, one might think of Leibniz who
considered ours the best of all possible worlds, a theory which
was savagely ridiculed by Voltaire in *Candide*. Others may see
in it the Stoic principle of detached resignation. Actually the
doctrine neither rests on delusion nor leads to passivity. Suffering and disappointment are not denied nor is it pretended
that they can be transmogrified into pleasures. It is not suggested that we have no part in the formation of the destiny
of the self or history. Above all it is affirmed that history is a
divine comedy and not a Greek tragedy.

What is demanded by the Catholic theology of freedom is
intense activity and, as far as is possible, the elimination of

all obstacles to free choice deriving from human duress or neurotic compulsions. The capacity for free choice must be heightened to the degree compatible with the limiting situation of Original Sin. Action is called for in the framework of my little world with its stimuli and challenge. The man envisaged by Catholic theology does not retire from the external world into the cave of his isolated self, not even when he becomes a hermit. He is always open to the world and its impinging action. In the light of his faith, and of reason enriched by faith, he tries to solve the problems, individual and social, which come his way. He makes the most of his being, which is active and creative, nor is he afraid to trust his understanding of things, extremely fallible as it is. However, he is under no illusions. He knows that whatever is ultimately valuable in his contribution comes not from him, but from the good God working in him in a way he does not understand. The evil which results even from his best-intentioned efforts will not dismay him, because he knows that he is a faulty organism, and the very evils will set the stage for something extremely good when seen from the viewpoint of eternity, which he now can only grasp by faith, not by vision. Wisely he will not expect Paradise in the secular order nor is his eye fixed on such a goal for his actions. Yet nonetheless he will with wisdom fight injustice and unrighteousness, strive to acquire more knowledge wherever it may lie, always remembering that his wisdom is shot through with folly and his projects of amelioration fraught with strains of old and new injustice. He can do this because in the long run, in the moment beyond time, it will work out unto definitive good. In defective freedom he creates his world because the great free Creator is using him as he is for the awesome glory of total creation. In part he understands, and this partial understanding is buttressed by faith, but much he does not understand and he accepts on trust the meaningfulness of it all. He may be weak, perverse and purblind, but God writes straight with crooked lines.

I submit that this man is free in the fullest sense of human freedom. It is not here a question of the physical possibility of choosing this or that, but the capacity for action, creativity and insight for the fullest liberation of human potential. We are not dealing with mere freedom *from* something as if that were all of the question, but we are proposing freedom *for* something, rendering freedom dynamic, liberating and creative.

[IV]

As a vision, the theological conception of freedom certainly commands respect. The main objection to it, when not derived from metaphysical assumptions, comes from the patent fact that Christian history does not show this conception at work. Rather the Christians, and even the theologians, have shown themselves foes of freedom not once or again but constantly. For many thinkers Christianity is rejected because it is repressive, employing duress and coercion whenever it can.

It would be childish simply to dismiss this objection by blithely denying that it is true. The Christian fact is an historical fact with a hidden transhistorical dimension. In its purely historical dimensions it will be homogeneous with all other historical facts, and these, as we have seen, are shot through with Original Sin. The Church is waiting for the Kingdom of Heaven; it does not think that it is the Kingdom of Heaven except in an imperfect, relative sense. The Church more than anything else is the perfect example of the theologian's vision of human freedom. Even human efforts at justice and righteousness are not without their vicious elements, and an overall good intention does not purge the action of its perverse factors. The theologian constructs his schemes by stepping back from the existing thing he wishes to describe and he foreshortens the object. The impurities of existence are thus invisible to his view. In so doing he does not falsify but he does give us a representation which is less than a photograph but definitely more than a fantasy.

Unlike a pure philosophy which is only in the mind, Christianity is an earthly society in its own right and compenetrates another society which is the secular commonwealth. Now it is precisely in society and the contact of society with society that Original Sin shows up most clearly, and society must guard itself against Original Sin lest it perish. It is in free choice that Original Sin manifests itself most and society will always try to curb free choice as effectively as it can in those areas where a threat can arise to its own well-being or survival. The consequence is that all societies exercise a repressive force on their members. The Catholic Church will be no exception to this rule but since membership in that society is on a voluntary basis, those who join the society are merely actualizing their freedom, and others in principle have no complaint. The complaint does arise because the presence of the Church in the secular commonwealth is conceived as a threat to the freedom of those outside of the society which is the Church.

Although political liberty is only one facet of human freedom, yet political liberties have always loomed large in the questions raised by freedom. That man needs society and without it is not fully human is granted by all thinkers. That society will increase the area of choice for the human agent is just as obvious. That a bad choice on the part of the individual in a social context can threaten the existence of society is admitted by all who are not anarchists, the most romantic of all deniers of Original Sin. The question to what extent society can prevent such bad choices has one answer all men are agreed on: organized society should use duress and persuasion to cut off possibilities of choice only insofar as the survival and well-being of society demand, neither more nor less. Man's own urge to self-expression must enjoy the widest range of possibilities permitted by his limited condition. In consequence it is not the function of the community, religious or secular, to curtail these possibilities unless it must in order to preserve itself. Nor does the social nature of man imply a conflict between individual and social drives. It is one and the same man who is an individual and a member of the republic. A balance of interest is required but there is no conflict in the abstract. The situation is polar and dialectic, but hardly antithetical.

According to Catholic theology the Church is God's medium for divinizing man, and to that extent she is divine herself.

The Church consequently feels that she speaks not in her own name but in the name of God, and His will is her law. To be sure, the divine will is implemented by human church law, but even this human product is considered only as a concrete application of the will of God. The application obviously supposes an historical situation to which it applies. Hence church law is subject to change because situations change or are better understood with time.

In rigor of logic the Church should outlaw all sin in its own community and in consequence the repressive action of the Church on its own members should be extreme. Actually this logical conclusion was never accepted by the Church which has always rejected the counsels of puritans from the days of Christ to our own. Let the wheat and the cockle grow together. There will be a division and separation in the last judgment. Before that moment, to pull up all the cockle would entail pulling up or weakening the wheat plants which grow with the cockle side by side. There is here a stand for liberty, even though it is recognized that liberty can be abused. Liberty is so great a good that it is proper to allow it even though it is capable of evil. God does not force man to virtue even though He calls him to it, and so the Church feels that her exhortation to the godly life can be no more narrow-minded than is He in whose name she speaks.

Yet in the community of the Church there will be restrictions on liberty which are not recognized as necessary to those beyond the Church's family. Can the Church in God's name subject them to its laws? Many a non-Catholic thinks that this is the position of Catholic theology. Many a Catholic thinks that it is the doctrine of the Church, though it must be modified by the Church's capacity to enforce it. Yet the serene tradition of the Church favors neither of these two views. From the days of the Roman empire to the day of Russian dominion, it was the Church alone who withstood the tyrant in the name of freedom. The despot can kill off all Catholics in his domains, but if he allows only one to survive, he will have to face one champion of freedom.

The concerned non-Catholic sees this well enough, but he

asks whether this concern for freedom is merely a love for the Church's freedom rather than for the freedom of man. The Catholic theologian will answer the question by pointing out that the Church loves her own freedom because she is human and sees her freedom as a facet of all human liberty. She cannot defend her own without defending the freedom of all. In her predilection for freedom, the Church sets strict limitations on the authority of society.

The Church believes that there is a law of God freely revealed by Him to men. The Church also believes that she is the sole custodian and interpreter of this law, nor will she permit any other entity to apply or execute that law. The Church also believes that there is a natural law embodied in the very nature of things and man by his rational nature is capable of knowing it, even if only imperfectly. It is not for the Church to execute that law, less is it the function of the secular commonwealth. The Church will deal with the natural law only insofar as it is made manifest in God's revelation and the secular community should respect it by making it possible for man to live up to it. The law of nature which is the same as the law of reason is not what is to be enforced by the political society. The law of nature enforces itself. Political society by the leave of natural law makes its own laws which have only one end: the balanced liberty and prosperity of the citizens. These laws must tolerate much that is condemned by the law of reason, because the human being is not only rational but unreasonable as well, and for him as he is society exists. If the Church cannot make a heaven on earth, the political society is hardly more capable. The ambiguities of the human situation are essential to it and any attempt to remove them will destroy the human situation. Hence in the light of theology the non-Catholic need not fear the presence of the Church in his secular society. She has no intention to take over the functions of political government nor even use these functions as implements of her own concern.

But the non-Catholic insists that he has seen in history the efforts of the Church to do precisely what theology says it does not do. Instead of denying such facts, the theologian can only point again to his basic insight. All things in history, the Church therefore as well, will show evidences of the heavy influence of Original Sin. The Church is not a sinner but she is made up of sinners. The non-Catholic's complaint is not with the Church living up to herself but with the human situation. To complain about that is not wise. To recognize it as a datum which is both a challenge and a humbling truth is the wiser course. To judge benignantly the faults of others is one of the lessons which Original Sin teaches. My neighbors are sinners and so am I. We can only turn to God and say sincerely, "forgive us our trespasses as we forgive those who trespass against us."

In brief outline we have tried to distill the bimillennial doctrine of Catholic theology in its meditations on freedom. The work of so many thinkers, some of whom were singularly gifted, must be enlightening for our time. The readiness of the moment to hear the theologian makes it imperative for the theologians to speak to the world concerning something which concerns all men always, especially today. Any given moment is wall-eyed. It sees things exclusively in terms of its own anxiety. A wall-eyed vision distorts the truth and truth so achieved will not make us free. The long ponderings of so many ages of theologians on so complex a question as human freedom are of immense help for the student of liberty in a particular age. He will see other dimensions of the problem than the one suggested by his contemporary crisis and he will be able to see his own problem in the light of a holistic approach to his question.

Theology deals with what concerns man ultimately. There can be no discussion which is not based on ultimate concern. In consequence I have given a theology of freedom, because only this will ultimately illuminate our quest.

Waldo Beach / Freedom and Authority
in Protestant Ethics

"THE QUESTION OF authority, . . . in its religious form, is the first and last issue of life. It is indeed the question of Lordship. As soon as the problem of authority really lifts its head, all others fall to the rear." So wrote P. T. Forsyth some forty years ago in a classic work, little studied now, on *The Principle of Authority*.[1] Any careful student of Protestant thought in the last three or four decades, watching it as it attempts to find its footing below the swirling waters of modern culture, would acknowledge that this claim of Forsyth's is not extravagant. Yet, oddly enough, relatively little attention has been given in modern Protestant writing to a frontal attack on the problem of authority.[2] Possibly the Protestant mind has been too preoccupied with the problem of moral freedom to pay sufficient

WALDO BEACH *(1916–   ) is Professor of Christian Ethics at the Duke Divinity School and the Duke University Graduate School of Arts and Sciences. He is the author of a number of essays and monographs and, with H. Richard Niebuhr, was editor of* CHRISTIAN ETHICS: SOURCES OF THE LIVING TRADITION *(1955). The paper here printed was originally read at a meeting of the Society for Theological Discussion and is reprinted from* THE JOURNAL OF RELIGION, *vol. 32 (April, 1952) by permission of the University of Chicago Press.*

attention to the other pole of the dialectic, authority, which has been the preoccupation of the Romanists. Yet certainly the question of authority is as urgent for Protestantism as for Catholicism. All the persistent quandries of ethics, theology, and ecclesiology point beyond themselves to the issue: What is the final authority for the believer, the rule for the private conscience and for the public community of the church, the arbiter of oppositions and the Supreme Court of moral litigations?

[I]

The distinctive Christian view of the freedom of the will may be the most fruitful lead into the problem. Along with "secular" philosophical ethics, Christian ethics must affirm a genuine and primal freedom of choice, the ability of man to say a real "Yes" or "No" to the options of life within which he moves. Over against all absolute determinisms and fatalisms, environmentally or psychologically conceived, the Christian view of man's nature has maintained the irreducible power of free choice. This is entailed in the concept of man as a responsible creature, raised above the level of the beast by the power of rational choice. Without this, ethics would be meaningless.

Yet contemporary philosophical ethics, taking this moral freedom as an absolute, has constructed ethical theories on its foundation which are sharply different from Christian ethical theory. The major number of non-Christian moralists, since Kant, have resumed the Greek tradition of formulating the pattern of the good life in terms of the rational individual, completely autonomous, who chooses wisely the right "values" by mental discernment, thereby finding "self-realization." [3] Among many of these writers, "religious values" are acknowledged important, but devotion to them is encouraged as simply supplementary assistance in achieving the good life. Ethical theory is never theologically grounded; at best it is theologically buttressed. The beginning and end of ethical endeavor is the sovereign, rational self.

Christian ethics in general, and Protestant ethics in particular, follows a very different road. While acknowledging with secular ethics the power of responsible and rational choice in man, its view of human nature leads it to a radically different ethic. For one thing, it is much more voluntaristic. It stresses the will more than the mind as the core of man's being. The will is the crucial agent of ultimate choice. The final attachment of the heart, rather than the discernment of the mind, determines the moral worth of a man. Moreover, as Christianity understands human nature, man as creature is made with a will which must be directed toward some center of value. The will is not autonomous in the sense of being unattached to an object outside itself. The will must be dynamically related to some god, either true or false, either God or some *Abgott*, in devotion to whom it attempts to find the meaning of its life, and the trust in whose sovereignty redeems its endeavor from despair.[4] Man's freedom of will, then, is always freedom-in-responsibility to someone or something.

Within and by the sovereignty of God, man is free to attach his will to one or another god. The will is not free to choose whether it will have a master, but it is free to choose among masters. Yet the divine determinism operates even here, since the self is ineluctably bound by the consequences of this primal choice. Where it chooses an *Abgott*, it falls into the hands of a tyrant who does not liberate but enslaves the will. This enslavement itself does honor to the sovereignty of God, whose Kingdom reaches over the man who chooses to make his bed in hell. Where it chooses the true God as its final object of love, it is only then liberated. But here "freedom" is meant in a sense far different from that of *liberum arbitrium indifferentiae*.

Paul Tillich's distinctions among autonomy, heteronomy, and theonomy serve to clarify the Christian position. Christian freedom is not the freedom of the autonomous will, obliged to nothing beyond itself. Nor is the Christian view heteronomous, in the sense that the will is enslaved by the dictates of a despot alien to the self's will, so that its authority cripples the self's spontaneity. Rather, the Christian view is theonomous: under God's authority the self is bound by its own consent to that which liberates rather than enslaves. The "freedom" of the will bound to God is the freedom of spontaneity, the freedom of power, freedom *for*, primarily, rather than freedom *from*. Here is the "true" freedom of Christian thought, the freedom intended in the familiar Gospel references,[5] in the Fathers, in Luther's *On Christian Liberty*, in Calvin,[6] and in the whole of the classical Protestant tradition. *Deo servire libertas.*

This "perfect freedom" is the power not of the autonomous self but of the theonomous self. "The maximum of dependence on God is the maximum of man's freedom; any attempt to get out of the dependence on God leads to slavery." [7]

[II]

There are certain corollaries of this view of freedom which illumine the distinction between Christian and secular theories of ethics.

1. This familiar freedom-in-bondage of Christian thought does not preclude the real area of moral maneuver, where the self makes its choice of one action versus another on the basis of rational analysis. Within the determinism set by the commands of the God to which the will is attached, there is a great range of alternatives, where man is free to choose this action rather than that, just as there is a wide variety of ways in which man is free to serve the devil. There is a multiplicity of routes whereby one may head north instead of south. The matter of ultimate aim is "set" by the final affection of the will. The matter of the choice of roads is relatively indifferent; one changes *en route* by free decision according to one's present insights.

Here Christian thought makes contact with the kind of freedom dear to the children of the Enlightenment and secular liberalism. But, whereas for the secularist the occasionalist freedom of choice is the all-important thing, for Christianity this freedom of moral maneuver is secondary to the primary issue of the ultimate direction of the will. The one-directional quality of the Christian life, bound to serve God, is not then inimical to specific freedoms-of-choice wherein I decide to do this thing one day and that thing another. "Love God and do what you want." This aphorism of Augustine is the affirmation of freedom-in-bondage, not the rationale for the autonomy of the free-lancer.

2. Christian freedom, as bondage to God, is the ground for all the freedoms *from* those constraints of the "world" which run counter to the Christian's transcendent loyalty. Freedom from the law, from the state, even from the church (as an external institution) are rights integral to the Christian faith, which the Christian seeks and defends for others as well as for himself, but only as they are derivative from religious obligation. They are in no sense autonomous rights, given to man as an unobliged and independent being. Christian liberty of conscience is first an obligated conscience. The very language of conscientious objection ("I can do no other"; "I cannot go against my conscience") is a semantic symbol of this freedom-in-bondage. A Christian bill of political rights must be a corollary of a Christian constitution of religious duties. For the Christian it is never man against the state but man-for-God against the state.

Here again is where the Christian concept of the freedom of the individual goes deeper than that of secular liberalism. Though the Christian might well subscribe to such a document as "The Declaration of Human Rights," approved by the General Assembly of the United Nations, he would differ in his belief as to the ultimate ground and sanction of its affirmations. Whereas the United Nations document seems to ground its bill of rights in the sanctity of persons, the Christian would find his sanction in a theological affirmation of the higher obligation of the self to an Infinite Being which calls for his emancipation from the exploitation of any finite economic or political institution. It is precisely at this point that a Christian view of man and his true freedom is needed both to undergird and to correct the modern secular democratic philosophy of "rights," which veers toward anarchy, since it has no centripetal force of obligation to counteract the centrifugal force of rights which permits the individual to do what he wants to do without responsibility to community.

3. Christian ethics, then, is quite unashamedly authoritarian. The will of God in Christ is the objective norm which constrains the subjective conscience. Erich Fromm is correct in classifying traditional Christian ethics as "authoritarian," over against the "humanistic" ethics which he espouses.[8] But he is quite incorrect in his attack against authoritarian ethics on the ground that it cripples moral responsibility and zeal. For Fromm, the obedience of the Christian to the wilful despotism of God paralyzes creative energy partly because it represents an authority alien to the real self. So the real self has to knuckle under to an authority it resents in the deep heart's core. All this is premised on Fromm's view of the ideal nature of man as the autonomous self, whose conscience should have no objective authority outside itself, and whose highest good is self-fulfilment.

Here Fromm has failed to discern the more subtle relation of the external authority of the believer and its internal appropriation in the conscience. He makes too facile a distinction between "autonomy" and "heteronomy" and fails to do justice to Christian "theonomy." He acknowledges that in "authoritarian" ethics the authority is internalized in the conscience.[9] But he fails to make much of this acknowledgment. Christian ethics makes a great deal of it. For when the self really acknowledges the sovereignty of God over him, that acknowledgment is an inward appropriation so intense that the self no longer feels the authority to be something "over against" him, something hostile to his true self, but rather the expression of his true self. The authority now compels him from within, not from without.

Since the Christian accepts the authority of God for himself, his voluntary consent makes his authority the King of his inner castle rather than a foreign power. In the consciousness of the regnant power *within*, the Christian feels the more deeply his *freedom for*, since he is convinced his will is in accord with the true nature of things. The tussle of his moral decisions is not as between his essential self and an alien outward compulsion (*à la* Fromm) but between his higher true self and his lower false self which may still be inclined to obey contrary authorities. Thus, while Christian ethics is authoritarian, it is not tyrannical, since its authority, the will of God, involves both objective Will and subjective consent.[10]

[III]

The rub comes for Protestant moral theory, not as to the locus of final authority ("God alone is Lord of the conscience"), but as to the mediate or proximate authority which stands between the will of God as revealed in Christ and subjective decision. God's will in itself is notoriously elusive. The character and content of his revelation in person, principle, and institution have been the perennial bafflement of Christian history. For the Roman church, of course, the final norm, given in Christ, is channeled into the authority of the one church, which provides the sole continual mediate authority for the spiritual sanctification and moral guidance of the "faithful." The problem of authority is *a priori* resolved in the presumption of the finite institution of the church. The Reformation arose in part as a protest against the idolatry implicit in such a presumption. But, since Luther, Protestantism has agonized over the problem of the new mediate authority it might settle on to supplant the claim of the Roman church. What shall be the "rule" of conscience, which can surely if not infallibly guide the will in its attempt rightly to serve the will of God?

There is no normative answer in Protestant theology. Indeed, there cannot be. For it is precisely of the Protestant genius (or "the Protestant principle," to use Tillich's concept) to criticize, under the Judgment of God, the finality of any *finite* authority as representing exhaustively the authority of the Infinite. At certain points in its history, to be sure, this Protestant principle has been submerged or lost in one or another type of Protestant practice, where the authority of the Bible as such, or of the sect, or of the individual's intuition has assumed an unquestioned finality. But certainly in its most dynamic eras it has kept itself under judgment, in unease, receptive to the new truth which may yet break forth out of God's holy Word or elsewhere. Yet, at the same time, Protestantism has had to avoid its perennial peril of anarchy and to affirm its consensus as to the proximate and available guide for the perplexed.

Though the issue of mediate authority has been crucial for Protestants from Luther down to the present, it was in seventeenth-century English Protestantism that the most honest and thoroughgoing attempt was made to arrive at the Protestant persuasion on the matter. Though of course no unanimity resulted, the issues were squarely joined and the various answers normatively given, as far as doctrinal formulation was concerned. All parties to the ecclesiastical and civil conflicts of that turbulent century agreed to the sole Lordship of God over the conscience. And there was a general unanimity in accepting the authority of the Bible as the full and sufficient guide for faith and practice. But within this biblicism there were wide differences which expressed the full range of Protestantism's difficulty with authority and which in effect qualified considerably the biblicism itself. There were three main positions: Anglican, Presbyterian Puritan, and sectarian.

The Anglican position represents a *via media* on the question of authority, as on most other matters. In steering between "popery" and Presbyterianism, the Church of England historically came to follow neither the former's reliance on the infallible church as the final authority nor the latter's reliance on the infallible Bible but looked upon both church tradition and Scripture as authoritative. In the execution of this task, Anglicanism relied much on "Reason," to the extent that "Reason" itself might be called its ultimate proximate authority. "Reason" is here understood, not as a subjective criterion, but objective, since it is the expression of the structure of objective Natural Law. In matters of salvation the authority for Hooker, for Chillingworth, and for those who followed them lay with Scripture.[11] The Anglican found no fault with the Calvinistic Puritan when he bespoke the authority of the Bible in this area. But he criticized the bibliocracy ideal of the Puritan: the extension of the sufficiency of Scripture to cover all the minutiae of ecclesiastical, moral, and political decisions. Seventeenth-century Anglicanism found the Law of Reason the guiding norm in the moral concerns of this temporal life, where the Scripture is silent. Here it followed the Thomistic tradition of Natural Law, perceptible by the reason of man and conceived as perfectly congruous with Scripture. Natural Law is embodied in the historic tradition of the church. Here was the bulwark against the anarchy which would follow inevitably from the sectarian's claim to "special illuminations" and the authority of private judgment. Here was the guide to distinguish the true norm of conscience from "Humor, Fancy, or Passion." In the main, this position has remained normative for Anglicans down to the present.

The seat of authority for Anglicanism, then, is more a bench than a chair. It is broad enough to include Reason, Natural Law, "church tradition," as well as Scripture, in somewhat ambiguous and overlapping fashion. Its inclusiveness is its strength and also its weakness. Who shall cast the deciding vote if the occupants of this Supreme Court bench should disagree? Moreover, Anglicanism has the same trouble as Roman Catholicism when it comes to specifying the *content* of the law of nature, where the problem of relativism enters in. The dictates of a Universal Reason become not so unanimous as the Thomistic tradition expects when the specific measures of Natural Law are under debate.

Presbyterian Puritanism, inspired by Calvin, located authority unambiguously in the Scriptures. Here the will of God was totally and definitively and specifically set forth. Viewing the authority of Natural Law as vague and ambiguous, and the sectarian's claim to immediate inspiration as anarchic and fictitious, the Puritan found the Scriptures certain and infallible, the sure Rock for all true believers. The Westminster Confession crystallizes the Puritan conviction:

> The authority of the Holy Scripture . . . dependeth not on the testimony of any man or Church; but wholly upon God (who is truth itself) the author thereof. . . . Our full persuasion and assurance of the infallible truth and divine authority thereof is from the inward work of the Holy Spirit, bearing witness,

by and with the Word, in our hearts. . . . Nothing is at any
time to be added—whether by new revelations of the Spirit or
traditions of men. . . . The infallible rule of interpretation of
Scripture is the Scripture itself.[12]

Note that Puritanism follows Calvin in acknowledging the
substantiating authority of the Holy Spirit, whose testimony
in the heart of the believer acknowledges and confirms the
objective authority of the Scriptures.[13] But note also that the
authority of the Spirit is not something set *over* the Bible as
a superior court of authority. It is set *under* the Bible, con-
firming subjectively its self-authentication. There is no higher
authority over the Word save Him who is its Author. It is thus
its own rule of interpretation, its own court of appeal.

Puritans conceded to the Anglicans that there is a "law of
nature," which guides the heathen and unregenerate to a
measure of civil decency; but Scripture supersedes this authority for the Christian, "since it made explicit all the promises which the light of nature could discover, and in addition
gave the precepts of redemption." [14] It was granted, too, that
Reason has an authoritative role. But it was a secondary role,
to illumine the witness of the Word when the words were
dark or obscure. Within the framework of data given in the
objective Word, the reason had a necessary selective function,
but it was obligated by the data which it interpreted and so
was under its authority.

Sectarianism—a term here used to include a wide range of
groups: Congregationalists, Baptists, Quakers, and those even
further to the left—is very elusive on the question of authority.
While strongly biblical, in true seventeenth-century fashion,
extolling the authority of the Scripture along with Puritans,
the sectarians came to shift the locus of authority from the
"outer" to the "inner" Word, or from the Word to the Spirit
which interprets the Word aright. They sensed the inherent
difficulty of the Presbyterian Puritan logic: that its objective
authority proved a fallible and self-contradictory court of appeal in polemics. "The argument will not hold from Israel to
England," one wry anti-Puritan sectarian remarked. In greater

or less degree, sectarianism came to exalt the "Holy Spirit" or the "Inner Word" as an authority over, though never contradictory to, the external Word itself.[15] Most moderate sectarians settled on a double authority, the outer Word and the inner Spirit, without working out clearly the relation of the two. Those of more radical bent were ready to assert the priority of the Spirit over the Word. Two quotations must suffice as examples of the left-wing view, one from John Smyth, a Baptist, the other from Robert Barclay, a Quaker:

> Although it be lawful to pray, preach, and sing out of a booke . . . yet a man regenerate is above all bookes and scriptures whatsoever, seeing he hath the Spirit of God within him, which teacheth him the true meaning of the scriptures, without the which Spirit the Scriptures are but a dead letter, which is perverted and misconstrued, as we see at this day, to contrary ends and senses.[16]

> The scriptures' authority and certainty depend upon the Spirit by which they were dictated: and the reason why they were received as truth is, because they proceeded from the Spirit. . . . If by the Spirit we are to be led into all truth, and so be taught of all things, then the Spirit, and not the Scriptures, is the fountain and ground of all truth and knowledge, and the primary rule of faith and manners.[17]

In Quakerism, as representative of sectarianism, we find, then, the "spiritual" type of religion, the belief that there is a direct and continuing revelation of God to man, which cannot be formalized into any rigid pattern of Law, whether contained in Scripture or in the dictates of a church. The absolute authority is the Holy Spirit of God itself, in the heart of every believer, self-evident and self-authenticating.

The sectarian view of authority was horrifying, of course, to any decent and law-abiding Puritan or Anglican. It immediately allowed any sort of whim or "enthusiasm," sprung from a "heated imagination," to be authoritative for Christian conduct. It was anarchic and subjective. To trust sheerly the Inner Spirit would be to trust the wind for constancy. All the polemical literature against the sectarians brought the obvious charge of antinomianism. In reply the Quakers affirmed, against opponents to the Puritan right and the Ranter left, (1) that the Inner Light was an objective authority, coming from "without" to illumine the natural conscience, which in itself is fallible; (2) that it is a *group* authority ("the sense *of the meeting*"), which can check the vagaries of an individual's conviction; (3) that it is marked by moral results, "the fruits of the Spirit," by which its presence is known; and (4) that, while its testimony does not contradict Scripture, the Scriptures are a secondary rule of faith, since themselves inspired of the Spirit. Thus the Quakers disallowed "any old" subjective conviction of right and wrong to pass for authoritative. Nonetheless, the Quaker could not on his own ground subsume the Holy Spirit under any more ultimate authority; the final recourse of the Quaker case is to the self-evidence of the Spirit's own authority. It is sure to those who possess it, who can "by a living experience easily refute their ignorance who ask, How dost thou know that thou art actuated by the Spirit of God? Which will appear to thee a question no less ridiculous, than to ask one whose eyes are open, how he knows the sun shines at noonday?" [18]

One cannot argue with intuitionism. It is free from the questions that other ways to truth must abide. Yet the charge of antinomianism against the Quaker view of authority is a persistent one. It never quite escapes the temptation to subjectivism, as the subsequent history of Quakerism attests. In latter-day practice of the Friends the theological context of the seventeenth century in which Quakerism arose, which identified the Holy Spirit in severely christological and biblical terms, has well-nigh disappeared. The modern Quaker is likely to identify any generalized humanitarian sentiment as a dictate of the Holy Spirit or the Inner Light. Theologically, it is sometimes difficult to distinguish modern Quakerism from Unitarianism or from the kind of liberal humanitarianism which does not claim any Christian or theistic foundations.

The point of this brief perusal of seventeenth-century English Protestantism is twofold: (1) to show the full range of standards of authority around which various traditions within

Protestantism gather and (2) to recall that the general pattern was then set for subsequent Protestantism in the various declarations and confessions of faith.[19] So that, as far as doctrinal formulation is concerned, the matter of the mediate authority between God and man was largely closed: for Anglicanism, Reason, Natural Law, church tradition, and the Bible in somewhat uncertain combination; for Calvinism, the Bible; for sectarianism, the inner promptings of the Spirit.

[IV]

Where do matters now stand? Though doctrinal formulations remain set on the surface, it is obvious that powerful undertows have swept in from secular as well as sacred sources, currents which have radically changed the Protestant mind over these three centuries and made these doctrinal formulations a matter of difficulty if not embarrassment. It is clear that the issue of authority for Protestant faith, and particularly for moral action, is in a stage of the greatest confusion. We can only mention briefly the main factors that appear to have been influential in creating this state of affairs and that put the problem of authority high on the agenda for Protestant deliberation.

For one thing, patently the impact of biblical criticism has required a sharp re-examination of the authority of the Bible for Protestants. The Scriptures as such, that is, the external words, can no longer stand in the sacrosanct position they held for the Westminster divines, surrounded by an aura of infallibility, the guidebook to be searched and used in all the minutiae of daily moral decision. The inner dynamic of Calvinism somehow kept the authority of the Bible for the Puritans from a stultifying legalism. But now the absolute authority and inerrancy of Scripture has become the household God of an arthritic fundamentalism, hardly the inspiration for a dynamic and creative Protestant influence.

The return-to-the-Bible theme of modern Protestantism, in this postliberal era, has been by a new route, through rather than around or away from biblical criticism. This way has led

"Neo-Protestantism" to affirm again the authority of the Word, but it is the authority of the Word within the fallible words, the final and definitive Word given to man once and for all in the Christ of faith, whose authority is not one whit affected by what biblical criticism may discover about the Jesus of history.[20] This is an impressive solution, which appears to resolve nicely the fundamental issue raised by biblical criticism, but it has its perils, both for Christian theory and for Christian practice. In theory its peril is that of splitting faith from science completely. In Christian ethical practice its peril is that of providing a formal principle of "the mind of Christ" or the divine agape in Christ, which bears only tenuous relation to the content of the ethical teaching of the Sermon on the Mount. In short, one is left quite in the dark about the moral authority of the "Word" in relation to the moral authority of the detailed "words" of the Gospel record. Does the impact of biblical criticism upon the "words" affect in any way the authority of the "Word"?

The authority of the Bible for the contemporary Protestant is altered by a second factor: the changed context of ethical decision. Since the latter part of the nineteenth century the concern of Protestant moral theory has shifted from the pietistic preoccupation with "private" morality, household virtues and vices, to "public" morality, or what is loosely called "social ethics." The crucial moral decisions for the Christian appear to lie in the area of racial, economic, and political behavior. He is confronted with the problem of finding the "Christian way" in dealing with the complexities of institutional power, systems of economic production and consumption, racial segregation, nationalism and war, and the like. The Bible, particularly prophetic morality, can readily be shown to provide indirect guidance for confronting these issues. But New Testament thought, especially in Paul, with its eschatological world view, its consequent nonchalance about the "structures" of society, its individualistic and "unilateral" treatment of moral problems, does not enable it to provide direct authoritative guidance for these questions of "multilateral" social ethics. A Christian social ethics can be based on the Bible only in a derivative sense. The Protestant in the twentieth century is acutely aware of what John Bennett calls "the distance between Christian Ethics and Social Policy." [21] Biblical morality throws light only obliquely on such pressing moral questions as the relation of justice and love, the criterion for choice among competing neighbor-claims, the issue of compromise and strategy within a social order which constricts all feasible choices down to evil options, the dialectic of freedom and order, etc. These are the central working problems of the Christian in the social arena. The New Testament "law of love" can and must preside over the Christian debate on these matters, but in itself it is a remote judge. Mutually self-contradictory policies can often claim its sanction.

There has certainly been a return to a biblical base in current Protestant ethical theory, in contrast to the liberal era, and a rash of books on biblical ethics.[22] At the same time, it is significant that, when Emil Brunner comes to the discussion of the social order, he must have recourse to extra-biblical as well as to biblical authority for normative principles. In *Justice and the Social Order* he really reverts to a disguised Aristotelian-Thomistic "Natural Law" tradition as the basis of his proposed solutions to the problems of social ethics. The "Amsterdam Assembly Series" can hardly be called simply an application of the Bible to the problems of techniques, power, and the international disorder. Perhaps it is no accident that in the last few decades Anglicans, such as Temple, Hudson, Reckitt, and Demant, have been taking the lead in creative contributions to Christian social ethics. Their appeal to Reason, Natural Law, and church tradition may provide resources supplementary to the Bible for guidance in determining Christian social policy. This clear trend toward the acceptance of other-than-biblical authority is an indication that Protestantism is finding the Word of the Bible in itself insufficient in speaking the things needful to contemporary culture. Can the contemporary Protestant subscribe without misgiving to the Article of Religion: "The Holy Scriptures contain all things necessary to salvation," if he construes salvation in societal terms?

[V]

Despite the qualification of the authority of the Bible, or Reason, or church tradition, or the Holy Spirit—indeed, emergent above them—the reaffirmation of the authority of Christ is a clear and positive trend in contemporary Protestant ethics. The law of love, incarnate in his life and teaching, reincarnated again and again in the history of the Christian community, confirmed in the testimony of the conscience of the believer, and applied freshly to new moral situations, is the definitive "fixed point," the inspiration, the guide, and the critic of moral decision. As noted above, there is considerable ambiguity on the matter of the content of the law of love, particularly in its relation to social justice. But the sovereignty of the norm itself is unambiguous.

Adherence to this authority enables Protestantism to steer between legalism and lawlessness.[23] It avoids legalism in that the law of love transcends any specific legislation into which it may be translated. It avoids lawlessness, since the individual conscience is not on its own but is bound by this objective norm in Christ.[24]

It is difficult always to maintain a sure course between these opposite perils. Legalism lures from one side, with its temptation to exalt some relative and transient measure, required by love at one time and place, to the status of the absolute and eternal. From the other side the temptation is to adopt so inclusive an understanding of the law of love as to baptize all actions indiscriminately as Christian. This is simply a disguised antinomianism. Perhaps it is the task of Protestantism, its misery as well as its genius, to keep forever in this precarious "middle" between the tyranny of too much authority and the anarchy of too little.

NOTES
1. P. T. Forsyth, *The Principle of Authority, in Relation to Certainty, Sanctity and Society* (London, 1912).

2. One recent Anglican book reopens the question of authority from the side of biblical criticism and church history, R. R. Williams'

Authority in the Apostolic Age, with Two Essays on the Modern Problem of Authority (London, 1950).

3. The reference here is to such moralists as Nicolai von Hartmann, John Stuart Mill, W. M. Urban, Philip Wheelwright, E. Jordan, R. A. Tsanoff, and innumerable others, who amid wide divergencies share a common affirmation of the autonomous and rational self as the crucial factor in ethical theory.

4. Augustine's *Confessions* and Emil Brunner's *Man in Revolt*, trans. Olive Wyon (Philadelphia, 1947), are classic expressions of this voluntarism normative in Christian thought.

5. II Cor. 3:7; John 8:36.

6. *Institutes*, Book III, chap. xix.

7. Emil Brunner, *Christianity and Civilization* (New York, 1948), Part I, "Foundations," p. 132. Cf. *Man in Revolt*, pp. 262–263.

8. Erich Fromm, *Man for Himself* (New York, 1947), pp. 8–14.

9. *Ibid.*, pp. 141–158, 143–146.

10. R. R. Williams points out convincingly that this double aspect is characteristic of New Testament thought (*op. cit.*, pp. 128–129).

11. Richard Hooker, *Laws of Ecclesiastical Polity*, Book I, chaps. xi and xiv; Book II, chap. viii.

12. *Westminster Confession of Faith*, chap. i.

13. John Calvin, *Institutes*, Book I, chap. viii.

14. Perry Miller, *The New England Mind* (New York, 1939), p. 193.

15. To date, the most important study of this trend is Geoffrey Nuttall, *The Holy Spirit in Puritan Faith and Experience* (Oxford, 1946).

16. John Smyth, *Works* (Cambridge, 1915 ed.), II, 755.

17. Robert Barclay, *Apology for the True Christian Divinity*, "Defense of Proposition III," Par. II.

18. *Ibid.*, "Defense of Proposition II," Par. XVI.

19. Cf. Philip Schaff, *Creeds of Christendom* (New York, 1877), Vol. III.

20. Emil Brunner, *The Mediator*, trans. Olive Wyon (Philadelphia, 1937), chap. vi.

21. John Bennett, *Christian Ethics and Social Policy* (New York, 1946), chap. ii.

22. To cite but a few Paul Ramsey, *Basic Christian Ethics* (1950); L. H. Marshall, *The Challenge of New Testament Ethics* (1947); Lindsay Dewar, *An Outline of New Testament Ethics* (1949); Sidney Cave, *The Christian Way* (1949).

23. Reinhold Niebuhr, *Faith and History* (New York, 1949), chap. xi.

24. *Ibid.*, p. 179.

PART II / PERSPECTIVES

OF BIBLICAL THEOLOGY

John L. McKenzie / The Freedom of the Christian

I AM ONE of those who is old enough to remember when a declaration of religious liberty seemed as unlikely from the Roman Catholic Church as the canonization of Martin Luther. But the declaration has been made, and more than that, it has been made with no great disturbance and by the vote of an overwhelming majority of the bishops. The Church did not depart as much from an established pattern as we thought, for the pattern really never was established. What we heard was a noisy and persistent minority who knew what they believed. The great majority remained silent, either from fear or from the lack of a clear understanding of their own belief. The Church discovered no new principles in arriving at the Declaration on Religious Liberty, nor did she abandon any old principles. The Church simply reconsidered her identity and mission, and once having recognized herself, she could have

JOHN L. MCKENZIE S.J. *(1910–   ) is Professor of Theology at the University of Notre Dame, is a noted New Testament scholar, and is the author of a number of works, including* AUTHORITY IN THE CHURCH *(1966). Reprinted with permission of the Macmillan Company from* RELIGIOUS LIBERTY: AN END AND A BEGINNING *by John C. Murray. Copyright © The Macmillan Company 1960.*

arrived at no other conclusion. That the Church ever failed to state the principle of religious liberty firmly—and she did fail—was due to a loss of identity. Deeply engaged in politics, the Church could not recognize herself, and her decision became partly or even entirely political.

My task is to discuss the decree against its Biblical background. If I were to limit myself to the explicit discussion of the New Testament and to the texts quoted, particularly in article 11, my treatment might be thought not altogether sympathetic with the decree. A fuller and better selection of texts could have been made and I could produce a very dull paper by listing the texts I think should have been used, adding a brief comment to each. This part of the decree is disappointing because it can leave many with the impression that this handful of texts is the Biblical background of the decree. It seems that it will be more profitable and, I hope, more interesting to the reader to attempt to state some of the Biblical themes on which the decree reposes.

The central idea of the decree is the dignity of the human person. Personal dignity demands that the person be permitted to realize his personal fulfillment. He can do this only by exercising his power of responsible decision. The notion of personal dignity can be viewed philosophically, and, if it is so explained, a very convincing statement can be produced. Once the nature of the person is understood, it becomes obvious that only the person can make himself fully what he has the potential to become. He must do this in society, of course, but society exists in order that persons may reach their full development within it. I do no more than notice the philosophical presentation, because it is not my task to expound it or to criticize it. I do no more than notice that historic man has rarely been aware of the dignity of the human person. Historic man has almost always considered that some human beings are more persons than others, or that some human beings are ends and other human beings are means. Historically, human societies have rarely been principles of freedom. This does not imply that the philosophical presentation is invalid; it suggests that a consideration of the nature of man does not always coincide with a consideration of the history of man.

We approach the dignity of the human person via the New Testament, not because the Old Testament has nothing to say, but because the full dignity of the person as a religious subject does not emerge in the Old Testament. In the New Testament all Christians become one in Christ, so that differences of race, social status, and sex cease to be meaningful. Baptism gives all men freedom in Christ. This is not specifically religious freedom in the modern sense of the word. Rather it is freedom from sin and concupiscence, it is freedom from slavery to the world. There is a sense in which the Christian freedom of Paul is very close to the Stoic freedom of the wise man. The difference, however, is seen when the basis of the two freedoms are viewed more profoundly. For the Stoic, the wise man liberates himself. The Christian has been liberated by God through Christ, and the freedom of the Christian is the freedom to act as a religious subject. No member of the Church has more or less of this freedom than another member, for this would mean that some members are more baptized than others. And since it is God who bestows this freedom, it is not for man to take it away.

It is worth stressing the fact that Christian freedom and Christian equality go together. Any conception of the inequality of persons destroys freedom—if not at once, then in the course of a very short time. Unless we are speaking of equality, we are not speaking of persons; we are speaking of persons with something added—of persons as Jews, Greeks, Scythians, or women, to draw an example from a Christian writer so remote in time that no contemporary allusion can be suspected. We can fill in the more contemporary names and titles for ourselves. These are the factors that Paul says make no distinction between Christians; these would destroy the unity of Christ. What he says fits quite well with the saying of Jesus that those who are officers of his community should become the slaves and lackeys of others. Where inequality might creep in, we have a specific recommendation that it should be compensated. For the Christian can achieve a distinction from other persons only by taking something away from them and what he takes away might turn out to be their power of responsible decision, the only means they have of achieving fulfillment as persons. The dignity of the person is invested with a new sacredness, for the person is a member of Christ and a son of God. Thus it is God's freedom that is attacked when human freedom is attacked. For God has a fulfillment in each person that cannot be achieved through other persons.

This freedom, I said, is freedom to act as a religious subject. This ought to have been explained in more detail and in New Testament terms. The decree speaks of *faith* as the religious commitment, and emphasizes that faith is a personal commitment. But the decree makes the point that no one believes except by his personal decision, and it accepts the principle that compulsion is alien to the genius of the New Testament. When we say, as we so often do, that faith is a gift, we must not forget that the gift carries no compulsion to receive it. I think that the decree would have been stronger, and the notion of compulsion as being alien more plausible, if more consideration had been given to the Christian fulfillment, which is not faith but love. When James said that faith without works is dead, he meant, as we can see clearly in the context, the works of love. Now love, by its nature—here we can appeal to the philosophical consideration—is the height of personal freedom and personal decision, personal commitment and engagement. That love can be compelled is an absurdity; if it were compelled it would not be love. Of course, this is true of love on the merely human level, but what is given to the Christian is love on the divine level. The Christian loves his neighbor not because of his lovable qualities but simply because the neighbor is there. The Christian is to exhibit the sovereign love of God, which is free from all compulsion and free of any particular attraction; therefore, it can be given to all equally, and no one can be excluded from its scope. This is the supreme religious act of the Christian, and he cannot perform it unless he does it with supreme freedom. He must engage himself; no one else can do it on his behalf.

The concrete ideal of Christian love is Jesus himself, who did not employ coercion. The decree refers to those passages of the Gospels in which coercion is explicitly rejected. Jesus employs persuasion and demonstration, but he does not employ physical or moral force. In the crisis of his life he met coercion with nonresistance, and thus he achieved the saving act. Why should Christians ever have thought that the character of the saving act had changed? If the Church is the enduring presence of Christ in the world, should not her share in the saving act manifest the same qualities as the saving act of him whose name the Church bears? It is shocking to think of the Church as continuing the role of the Sanhedrin and Pilate in the passion rather than the role of Jesus. I said that the Church has not always clearly recognized her identity, and this is what I meant. At times her leaders have appealed to means of fulfilling her mission that Jesus refused. No one doubts that this was a demonstration of his sovereign freedom, a freedom that is communicated to his members.

Love is fulfilled in the works of love, and the New Testament in more than one context states what some of the works of love are. I find it piquant that the New Testament is most explicit about the works of love just where more recent Christian moralists have insisted that these works are optional. (I mean such things as nonresistance and the total donation of one's goods to the poor.) More recent moralists may place greater emphasis on these acts than the Gospel does, but their position clearly makes these works of love a matter of personal decision. The principle of love must be worked out in detail by each Christian in a manner suitable to his own situation and his own resources, for ultimately no one except the person who loves knows whether his love is genuine and full. It is not for another to impose a ceiling upon his love. Nor is it for another to teach how to love, since love is an action that cannot be taught as history and geometry are taught. It is communicated by love received, by love shown in example, by immersion in an atmosphere of love, which ought to be the atmosphere of the Christian community.

This thought leads into another consideration that I have treated elsewhere, and I must beg pardon for being repetitious. I am aware that the consideration is controversial even among interpreters of the Bible, but the proposition is important enough to be set forth once more, especially since it is still open to discussion. The proposition, based on the Gospels and the Epistles of Paul, is that Christianity confers freedom from law. I interpret this proposition to mean that Christianity does not impose obligation on its members. It is clear in St. Paul, and scarcely less clear in the Gospels, that the law of Judaism is annulled for Christians. No distinction is made between various laws or types of law in this annulment. We do not keep a few and throw away the others. Of the 613 precepts that the rabbis counted in the five books of Moses, Jesus retained only two—the love of God above all things and the love of the neighbor as oneself. Paul wrote that he who loves his neighbor has fulfilled the law. And Christian interpreters have never contended that the law of Judaism remained valid, even when they have been uncertain about some of its contents.

That the annulment of obligation is a consequence of the annulment of the law I deduce from the fact that no other law is substituted for the law of Judaism. The Christian will do the acts of love from the motivation of love or they are not Christian acts. We may put it this way: the Christian who does not commit adultery from a motive of obligation has done nothing wrong, but he has done nothing good in the Christian sense. He has not risen above the morality of the law, and he has not made his righteousness more abundant than the righteousness of the scribes and Pharisees. If one thinks of morality as comprised in love instead of law, it is extremely difficult to define a point at which one has done all that one ought. Love is not considered in terms of what one ought to do.

It is a real question whether we have ever shown full confidence in the freedom and responsibility implied in the morality of love, and therefore whether we have allowed Christian personal dignity to reach that fullness that lies within its power. It seems undeniable that Jesus released the power of love as an adequate principle of an entirely new set of human relations. Christians who are endowed with the Spirit have the capacity to execute the commandment of love by their personal decisions. Some will never reach it, others will fail to reach its fullness, and all will fail at times to reach even its minimum level. Jesus seems to have preferred these risks to other risks, risks involved in the principle of obligation. Certainly these other risks include the preservation of the principle of pharisaism, and the risk of creating a class of Christian scribes. They include the risk of reducing the ideal of love to a controllable minimal level of obligation that can be imposed. These risks we have run, and I will not go into the consequences.

The New Testament speaks of freedom of the Christian; the decree on freedom speaks of the religious freedom of all men. How is the Biblical base of freedom extended to those who are not members of the Christian community? Here it might seem both wiser and safer to rest the principle on philosophical reasoning. I am not sure that the philosophical basis of freedom is more meaningful here than elsewhere. For Christian freedom does touch the freedom of others very deeply, and for the Christian this is ultimately the factor that will mean most to him. In its simplest terms, Christian freedom means that other men must have the freedom to become Christians. If they do not become Christians by a free personal decision, they do not become Christians at all. They cannot be compelled into the way of freedom, for it would cease to be the way of freedom if they were.

However, historically, Christianity has often shown little confidence in the power of the Gospel, preferring to strengthen the Gospel by various types of pressure. Christians have shunned the encounter with the world, the free encounter of the market place. Had they deep faith in that which they profess, they would fear an encounter with no one, confident that the power and truth of the Gospel is greater than all human arguments and all human force. Yet it is precisely these means, arguments and force, that have sometimes been employed to propagate Christianity or to maintain it. Although the unbeliever is quite safe from an authentic Christian, it is not difficult to understand why he is apprehensive when he is confronted with any other kind. It is the other kind that makes this decree necessary and valuable. The declaration does not create any more authentic Christians, but it at least keeps any other kind from being the spokesmen of the Church.

Ultimately the assurance of freedom of religion for all men rests on the conviction of the Christian community. I am aware that this may appear to some to be a foundation less stout than they could wish, but what is to substitute for this Christian conviction? The conciliar decree is a beginning and not an end. It should help Christians, and in particular Roman Catholic Christians for whom it speaks, to understand that religious freedom for all men is not a matter of tolerance or concession or compromise with a lesser evil. It is an act of virtue, an act of Christian love, and an act of apostolic zeal. It guarantees the Gospel against corruption. And I spare you the obvious comments on how it might make Christianity a little more attractive. I do not think it is in our power to make Christianity attractive, but it is unfortunately within our power to make it repulsive.

There is a final aspect of the decree that does not really fall within the scope of the decree. The topic pertains to and is opened in the constitution of the Church. That it is opened will permit further discussion, for the topic has been discussed extensively in recent years. This aspect is religious freedom within the Church as well as outside it. I hesitate to add this consideration, because it may appear irrelevant, and may even be thought a hobby-horse that I brought along because I have a chance for another ride. But I think it is pertinent, and I shall try to explain why. Perhaps a simple, if incomplete, way to say it is that freedom is of one piece; either you believe in it or you do not. It has been my effort here to set forth the Biblical basis of religious freedom. Examination shows that it is Christian freedom within the Church that best guarantees, at least for Christians, freedom of other religions. The Church can be no more convinced of the right of freedom of those who are not her members than she is convinced of the right of freedom of those who are her members. The history of the failure of the Church to speak clearly on religious freedom is accompanied by a history of her failure to accord her members that personal dignity and power of decision that is theirs as Christians. This history is so long and so complex that we now find ourselves in the position of reaching for something we are not sure we want and defending something we are not sure we like. Let no one be apprehensive about demands for excessive freedom. For what it is worth, my experience is that most Catholics are afraid of freedom and do not even want as much as they have. And because they are afraid of it for themselves, they are afraid of it for others. No doubt this attitude is changing in what is called "the new breed," and it would be interesting to be around long enough to see how "new" the new breed is in 1986. But at present it is still true, as it has been for a long time, that practically no important decisions in the Church are made by any one under forty, and very few by any one under fifty. The change in attitude may be coming, but it is not just around the corner.

In evading freedom, Catholics evade responsibility. They permit the character of their Christian fulfillment to be determined by another. Where they ought to look for leadership they look for control, and it must be said that they have little trouble in finding it. By doing so they renounce the freedom to act as a religious subject. This can be ultimately the renunciation of Christian love. I am optimistic enough to think that discontent with this type of managed Christianity will grow, and that more and more people will see that they will be as free as they insist on being. To some of us older and more timorous churchmen, it will look as if the whole structure is tottering; but that is because our perspective is from the past.

We are, I think, on the eve of some important structural changes. These changes can put Christian fulfillment within a nearer reach of Catholics than is now possible. These changes can be conducted in an orderly fashion, for the Church has the resources to grow without the mess of a revolution. But she will grow, and those who attempt to stop history will have the difficulties usually experienced by those who attempt it. Recently I have been going over the Epistles to the Corinthians. It is simply impossible to imagine a church of this type today. But if the Christians of Corinth were really able to move where Paul led them, we have little reason to think we are better than they because we are more organized. The Church can survive the disorder of development better than she can stand the living death of organized immobility. We have not yet seen that the Declaration on Religious Freedom has profound implications within the life of the Church as well as in her posture toward the world. With the declaration the Church has disclosed her true identity, and it will be impossible to conceal it in the future.

Karl Barth / The Gift of Freedom:
Foundation of
Evangelical Ethics

It is my task to discuss the gift of freedom, and to do so with the foundation of evangelical ethics in view. Let me anticipate the solution to the problem inherent in this theme in three summary propositions. The first describes the freedom which *God* Himself possesses; the second delineates it as the gift bestowed by God upon *man*; the third relates the consequences of these two to the problem of the foundation of evangelical *ethics*.

First: *God's freedom is His very own*. It is the sovereign grace wherein God chooses to commit Himself to man. Thereby God is Lord as *man's* God.

KARL BARTH *(1886–1968) in his last years lived in retirement at Basle, Switzerland, after an almost unbelievable career as preacher, teacher, lecturer, and writer. His most substantial work, the multi-volume and uncompleted* DIE KIRCHLICHE DOGMATIK *(1932–   ), is one of over four hundred published works. This essay was originally given as an address at a meeting of the* "GESELLSCHAFT FÜR EVANGELISCHE THEOLOGIE" *at Bielefeld in 1953, was originally published under the title* DAS GESCHENK DER FREIHEIT *as a separate monograph in the* THEOLOGISCHE STUDIEN *series by Evangelischer Verlag A.G., Zollikon-Zürich. The English translation by Thomas Wieser is a part of Karl Barth's* THE HUMANITY OF GOD, *published by John Knox Press. © C. D. Deans 1960. Used by permission.*

Secondly: *Man's freedom is his as the gift of God.* It is the joy wherein man appropriates God's election. Thereby man is God's creature, His partner, and His child as *God's* man.

Thirdly: Evangelical ethics is the reflection upon the *divine call to human action* which is implied by the gift of freedom.

[I]

We begin by examining what man may know about *God's own freedom.* Must I justify my starting with God's own freedom rather than with anything else? Must I justify my not beginning with man's innate or given freedom? I, too, have heard the news that we can speak about *God* only by speaking about *man.* I do not contest this claim. Rightly interpreted, it may be an expression of the true insight that God is not without man. This means in our particular context that God's own freedom must be recognised as freedom to be a partisan for man.

We may not speak of God's own freedom apart from the history of God's dealings with man. Man's God-given freedom, then, must be acknowledged from the very beginning. But this claim, correctly understood, calls for a counterclaim. We can speak about man only by speaking about God. This general statement is hardly disputed among Christian theologians. There is, however, sharp disagreement as to the priority of the two claims. It is my firm conviction that what I have just called the counterclaim is the true claim and must come first. Why deny priority to God in the realm of knowing when it is uncontested in the realm of being? If God is the first reality, how can man be the first truth?

Those holding the opposite view go so far as to say that the God-given freedom of man is, first of all, freedom of man from himself. But how does this bold statement prompt man to begin as a thinker with himself as a starting point? Why, of all concepts in Christian theology, should the concept of God merely have the function of a boundary term? Why should it connote only a vacuum to be filled at best with subsequent and nonessential assertions about the ideal or historical conditions of human existence? Is it so self-evident that man is intimately known to us, whereas God remains the great and doubtful Unknown? Is it, then, a law of the Medes and the Persians that our quest for God must proceed on the basis of our supposed knowledge of man? Does not this freedom, bestowed by God upon man and, as we shall discuss later, specifically upon the Christian theologian, prompt man to overcome this mental block and to think in a new perspective, to think even exclusively in a new perspective? Is not this new perspective mapped out for man in God's revelation, showing forth first and foremost God Himself, and in this way and only then revealing man to himself? Where else can we learn that freedom exists and what it is, except in confrontation with God's own freedom offered to us as the source and measure of all freedom? We do not speculate beyond man nor do we abandon him and his freedom by first inquiring about the One who is man's *God* and about His own freedom. On the contrary, we then may seek and find true man and his true freedom.

God's freedom is not merely unlimited possibility or formal majesty and omnipotence, that is to say empty, naked sovereignty. Nor is this true of the God-given freedom of man. If we so misinterpret human freedom, it irreconcilably clashes with divine freedom and becomes the false freedom of sin, reducing man to a prisoner. God Himself, if conceived of as unconditioned power, would be a demon and as such His own prisoner. In the light of His revelation, God is free in word and deed; He is the source and measure of all freedom, insofar as He is the Lord, choosing and determining Himself first of all. In His own freedom, as the source of human freedom, God above all willed and determined Himself to be the Father and the Son in the unity of the Spirit. This is not abstract freedom. Nor is it the freedom of aloof isolation. Likewise, man's God-given freedom is not to be sought and found in any solitary detachment from God. In God's own freedom there is encounter and communion; there is order and, consequently, dominion and subordination; there is majesty and humility, absolute authority and absolute obedience; there is offer and response.

God's freedom is the freedom of the Father and the Son in

the unity of the Spirit. Again, man's freedom is a far cry from the self-assertion of one or many solitary individuals. It has nothing to do with division and disorder. God's own freedom is trinitarian, embracing grace, thankfulness, and peace. It is the freedom of the living God. Only in this relational freedom is God sovereign, almighty, the Lord of all.

In this freedom God is, again according to His revelation, *man's* God. To put it more concretely: He is the God of Abraham, Isaac, and Jacob. He is man's God not because man projected, patterned, and exalted Him, not because Israel chose Him, but because He chose, decided, and determined Himself for His Israel and with Israel for mankind. The well-known definitions of the essence of God and in particular of His freedom, containing such terms as "wholly other," "transcendence," or "non-worldly," stand in need of thorough clarification if fatal misconceptions of human freedom as well are to be avoided. The above definitions might just as well fit a dead idol. Negative as they are, they most certainly miss the very centre of the Christian concept of God, the radiant affirmation of free grace, whereby God bound and committed Himself to man, making Himself in His Son a man of Israel and the brother of all men, appropriating human nature into the unity of His own being. If this is true, if this is not an accidental historical fact but in its historical uniqueness is the revelation of the divine will, valid and powerful before, above, after, and in all history, then God's freedom is essentially not freedom *from*, but freedom *to* and *for*. (We shall have to remember this point in our discussion of human freedom.) God is free for *man*, free to coexist with man and, as the Lord of the covenant, to participate in his *history*. The concept of God without man is indeed as anomalous as wooden iron.

In His free grace, God is for man in every respect; He surrounds man from all sides. He is man's Lord who is before him, above him, after him, and thence also with him in history, the locus of man's existence. Despite man's insignificance, God is with him as his Creator who intended and made mankind to be very good. Despite man's sin, God is with him, the One who was in Jesus Christ reconciling the world, drawing man unto Himself in merciful judgment. Man's evil past is not merely crossed out because of its irrelevancy. Rather, it is in the good care of God. Despite man's life in the flesh, corrupt and ephemeral, God is with him. The victor in Christ is here and now present through His Spirit, man's strength, companion, and comfort. Despite man's death God is with him, meeting him as redeemer and perfecter at the threshold of the future to show him the totality of existence in the true light in which the eyes of God beheld it from the beginning and will behold it evermore. In what He is for man and does for man, God ushers in the history leading to the ultimate salvation of man.

Though in a different way, God is beyond doubt also before, above, after, and with all of His other creatures. However, we may at best venture some ideas of this difference in the meaning of God's freedom for these creatures, of the gift of freedom to them. In reality we have no precise knowledge about this. Through His revelation God is known in His lovingkindness to us as the God of *man*. However, God was not and is not bound to choose and to decide Himself for man alone and to show His loving-kindness to him alone. The thought of any insignificant being outside the human cosmos being far more worthy of divine attention than man is deeply edifying and should not be lightly dismissed. But it remains true that God who gave His Son to become and to remain our brother assures us that He willed to love *man*, that He loved us and still loves us and shall love us because He chose and determined Himself to be our God.

This freedom of God as it is expressed in His being, word, and deed is the content of the *Gospel*. Receiving this good news from those who witness to it, the Christian *community* in the world is called to acknowledge it in faith, to respond to it in love, to set on it its hope and trust, and to proclaim it to the world which belongs to this free God. It is the privilege and the mission of the Christian community to acknowledge and to confess the Gospel. By acknowledging and confessing Jesus Christ as the creation and revelation of God's freedom, this community is incorporated into the body of Christ and becomes the earthly and historical form of His existence. He is in its midst.

We do well to keep remembering that the existence of the Christian community, through its preaching and its works, is already an expression of man's God-given freedom. Let us therefore respect the difference in perspective! The existence of the Christian community in its faith, love, and hope, and in its proclamation, is unmistakably part of the divinely inaugurated *Heilsgeschichte*. It is part of it insofar as to acknowledge and confess God's freedom is an act of the freedom bestowed upon man in the course of this history. But it is and remains an act of human freedom. The divine freedom was not initiated in and by this act of human freedom. Nor is it accomplished and somehow encompassed in it. Rather, God's freedom is and remains above and beyond human freedom. Measured against the act of divine freedom, the act of human freedom has its own beginning, its own course, and its own preliminary and relative ends. None of these coincide or are to be confounded with those of the *Heilsgeschichte*. It remains the prerogative of the divine freedom to set the end of this history, the beginning of which it set also.

God's own freedom and its realisations is the source and object of every Christian act of recognition and confession. It is sufficient that this human act takes place in the context of the freedom of God to which it bears witness. Yahweh lives and will live in solidarity, but not in identity, with Israel. The same holds true for Jesus Christ, the word and deed of God, with regard to his community, to the task it has to perform in response to the gift of freedom, and to its *kerygma*. The head does not become the body and the body does not become the head. The king does not become his own messenger, and the messenger does not become king. It is sufficient that the community be called into being, be created, protected, and sustained by Jesus Christ, and that it may confess Him who came into the world, is present now, and shall come in glory. It may confess Him who was, is, and shall be the word and deed of God's freedom and of His all-embracing loving-kindness.

[II]

God in His own freedom bestows human freedom. Here we must point to so-called *natural* freedom which constitutes and characterises human existence in its creatureliness, and to the freedom of eternal life *promised* to man. Here, for once, we must daringly include both in what is to be said about *Christian* freedom. Christian freedom is divinely bestowed upon man despite his sin, despite his existence in the flesh, and despite his being threatened by death. "Natural freedom" and "freedom promised" must, in any event, be understood on the basis of "Christian freedom." This is because freedom is made known to us by God as the "freedom of the Christian man."

Human freedom is the *gift* of God in the free outpouring of His grace. To call a man free is to recognise that God has *given* him freedom. Human freedom is enacted within history, that history which leads to the ultimate salvation of man. Human freedom never ceases to be the event wherein the free God gives and man receives this gift. God freely makes Himself available to man by granting him the freedom he is meant to have. Whatever the subsequent events of this history may be, they take place within the context and under the judgment of this divine act of mercy. Seen from the vantage point of the free gift of the free God, the concept of unfree man is a contradiction in itself. Unfree man is a creature of chaos, a monster begotten by his own pride, his own laziness, his own lies.

The concept of freedom as man's rightful claim and due is equally contradictory and impossible. So is the thought of man's acquiring freedom by earning it or buying it at any price. The idea that man can conquer freedom as God's antagonist and defiantly wrench it from Him is untenable. Man has no real will power. Nor does he get it by himself. His power lies in receiving and in appropriating God's gift. The event of man's freedom is the event of his thankfulness for the gift, of his sense of responsibility as a receiver, of his loving care for what is given him. It is his reverence before the free God who accepts him as His partner without relinquishing His sovereignty. This event alone is the event of freedom.

The gift of freedom, however, involves more than being offered one option among several. It involves more than being asked a question, being presented with an opportunity, and having a possibility opened up. The gift is total, unequivocal, and irrevocable. It remains the gift of freedom even though it may be turned into man's judgment if misunderstood or misused. We are dealing with the gift of the free God. God does not put man into the situation of Hercules at the crossroads. The opposite is true. God frees man from this false situation. He lifts him from appearance to reality. It is true that man's God-given freedom is choice, decision, act. But it is genuine choice; it is genuine decision and act in the right direction.

It would be a strange freedom that would leave man neutral, able equally to choose, decide, and act rightly or wrongly! What kind of power would that be! Man becomes free and is free by choosing, deciding, and determining himself in accordance with the freedom of God. The source of man's freedom is also its yardstick. Trying to escape from being in accord with God's own freedom is not human freedom. Rather, it is a compulsion wrought by powers of darkness or by man's own helplessness. Sin as an alternative is not anticipated or included in the freedom given to man by God. Nor can sin be explained and theoretically justified by this freedom. No excuse can be provided for sin. In human freedom there is no room for sin by fiat. Sinful man is not free, he is a captive, a slave. When genuine human freedom is realised, inevitably the door to the "right" opens and the door to the "left" is shut. This inevitability is what makes God's gift of freedom so marvellous, and yet at the same time so terrifying.

As a gift of God, human freedom cannot contradict divine freedom. This leads to certain limitations regarding human freedom which are similar to those mentioned in our earlier attempts to define the freedom of God. We now make bold to say:

(1) Human freedom as a gift of God does not allow for any vague choices between various possibilities. The reign of chance and ambiguity is excluded. For the free God Himself, the giver of man's freedom, is no blind accident, no tyrant. He is the

Lord, choosing and determining Himself unmistakably once and for all. He is His own law.

(2) Human freedom is not realised in the solitary detachment of an individual in isolation from his fellow men. God is *a se* (for Himself), but He is *pro nobis* (for us). For us! It is true that He who gave man freedom because He is man's friend, is also *pro me* (for me). But I am not Man, I am only *a man*, and I am a man only in relation to my fellow men. Only in encounter and in communion with them may I receive the gift of freedom. God is *pro me* because He is *pro nobis*.

(3) Human freedom is only secondarily freedom *from* limitations and threats. Primarily it is freedom *for*.

(4) Human freedom is not to be understood as freedom to assert, to preserve, to justify and save oneself. God is primarily free *for*; the Father is free for the Son, the Son for the Father in the unity of the Spirit. The one God is free for man as his Creator, as the Lord of the covenant, as the beginner and perfecter of his history, his *Heilsgeschichte*. God says "Yes." Only once this "Yes" is said, He also says "No." Thereby He reveals Himself to be *free from* all that is alien and hostile to His nature. Only once this "Yes" is said, is He free for Himself and for His own glory. Human freedom is freedom only within the limitations of God's own freedom.

And thus we can see that freedom is *being* joyful. Freedom is the great gift, totally unmerited and wondrous beyond understanding. It awakens the receiver to true selfhood and new life. It is a gift from *God*, from the source of all goodness, an ever-new token of His faithfulness and mercy. The gift is unambiguous and cannot fail. Through this gift man who was irretrievably separated and alienated from God is called into discipleship. This is why freedom is joy! Certainly, man does not live up to this freedom. Even worse, he fails in every respect. It is true enough that he does not know any longer the natural freedom which was bestowed upon him in creation; he does not know as yet the ultimate freedom in store for him at the completion of his journey, in the ultimate fulfilment of his existence. It is true enough that man may presently know and enjoy this freedom through the abiding Spirit of the

Father and the Son only in spite of sin, flesh, and death; in spite of the world, his earthly anxiety and his wordly nature; and in spite of himself in his persistent temptation. This however, does not prevent man from being enabled to know and to live out this freedom in incomparable and inexhaustible joy, limited as his own awareness may be. Some may not want any part of it, and at times we all feel this way. But this does not change anything. God's gift is there for all. It is poured out at the beginning of our journey, at its destination, and most certainly also in our present plight. Freedom is waiting here and now to be received and lived out in joy, albeit a joy that is not without travail.

Human freedom is the joy whereby man appropriates for himself God's election. God has elected Himself in His Son to be the God, Lord, Shepherd, Saviour, and Redeemer of mankind. Through His own election, He willed man to be His creature, His partner, and His son, He, the God of the community of men, and we, the community of men, His people! Freedom is the joy whereby man acknowledges and confesses this divine election by willing, deciding, and determining himself to be the echo and mirror of the divine act. Each individual is called to this commitment in the midst of the community of men, not as the first disciple but as a follower in the visible and invisible footsteps of many; not as the only one but together with many known and unknown fellow Christians. He may be accompanied by the comforting help of several or by at least a few. He may be a rather sad member of the rear guard or he may be way ahead of the crowd where he is temporarily alone. He lives for himself, but not only for himself. He is constantly in living relationship to others, as a member of the people of God who appropriates for himself God's election and is responsible for the brothers. Each individual is called by his own name as a member of the people of God. Each one is responsible for his relationship with God and his fellow men. He is free because he chooses, decides, and determines himself to be this person. His freedom is the joy of that obedience which is given to him. This is a daring venture whenever it is undertaken. A venture at one's own risk and peril? Never! It is the venture of responsibility in the presence of the Giver and the fellow receivers of the gift—past, present, and future. It is the venture of obedience whereby man reflects in his own life God's offer and his own response. This is the life of obedience, allowed for by man's freedom: to will himself to be that member of God's household which God willed him to be.

Free man wills himself to be God's *creature* according to that distinctive structure and limitation of his human nature which sets man apart from all other beings. God wants man free together with his fellow men in the greatness and the misery, in the promise and the anxiety, in the richness and the poverty of his humanity. True enough, man no longer knows what it means to be truly human. Alienated from God, he is alienated from himself and from his true nature. But God does not cease to call and to claim this estranged creature for His own. Likewise, man does not cease to be called and claimed by God as this estranged creature. The gift of freedom makes man free to be not more and not less than human. Whatever God's other intentions for man may be, they will always be a confirmation of his nature as a creature of God. And whatever man may choose to do with his God-given freedom, it always will have to be carried out within the framework of human possibilities. If he cannot boast of his human condition and achievement because they are a gift of God, he need not be ashamed of them either. God does not expect extraordinary accomplishments nor does he expect a jaded or lazy response. He does, however, expect man to realise in his life the divine intention of true humanity inherent in the gift. Glorifying God and loving his neighbour are sure signs of man's commitment.

God wants man to be His creature. Furthermore, He wants him to be His *partner*. There is a *causa Dei* in the world. God wants light, not darkness. He wants cosmos, not chaos. He wants peace, not disorder. He wants man to administer and to receive justice rather than to inflict and to suffer injustice. He wants man to live according to the Spirit rather than according to the flesh. He wants man bound and pledged to Him rather than to any other authority. He wants man to live and not to die. Because He wills these things God is Lord, Shepherd, and Redeemer of man, who in His holiness and mercy meets His creature; who judges and forgives, rejects and receives, condemns and saves. This is not the place to describe the divine act of reconciliation even in its main outline. It is enough to say that God's "Yes" and "No," spoken in His act of reconciliation, is not proclaimed apart from man. Even in this central act God declines to be alone, without man. God insists on man's participation in His reconciling work. He wants man, not as a secondary God, to be sure, but as a truly free follower and co-worker, to repeat His divine "Yes" and "No." This is the meaning of God's covenant with man. This is the task man is called to fulfil when God enters into the covenant relationship with him. This is the freedom of discipleship bestowed upon him.

The sovereign God alone saved man from the alienation and depravity of which he was and still is guilty. He delivered him from the imprisonment and slavery which was and still is his human lot. In the death of Jesus Christ, perfect reconciliation, beyond any need for improvement or repetition, took place once and for all. In His resurrection, and nowhere else, as long as time lasts, God's act of reconciliation is unmistakably revealed. There is no need whatsoever for this divine act to be re-enacted by man in order to be efficacious. This is not to say, however, that man is confined to the role of an approving spectator. The gift of freedom becomes operative at this critical point. Man's freedom always remains human freedom and is not to be confused with the divine freedom whereby God in Jesus Christ took man's part.

Human freedom is the God-given freedom to obey. *Faith* is the obedience of the *pilgrim* who has his vision and his trust set upon God's free act of reconciliation. This obedience confirms and evinces the transition from sin to righteousness, from the flesh to the spirit, from the law to the sovereignty of the living God, from death to life in the small and preliminary, yet determined, steps of the daily journey. *Love* is the obedience of the *witness* who is summoned to announce this transition. The witness announces God's victorious deed, offered to all his brothers and sisters far and nigh so that they might greet it as their light. This obedience in love and faith is the human response to the divine offer of justification, sanctification, and calling in Jesus Christ.

Thus human freedom is freedom to respond with thanksgiving. It is the *freedom of the Christian man* whom God chooses to be His partner and whom He does not abandon. God does not expect from man more than this gratitude, this faith, and this love. Nor does He expect less, and He certainly expects nothing else! For this service of thankful obedience, for this participation in the *causa Dei,* God has set man free.

God wants man to be His creature and His partner. Even more, He wants him to be His *child.* God is not content with man living as a reverent creature *before* Him, or as a grateful partner *alongside* Him. He wants him to be a man *with* Him, and to enjoy the glorious assurance of belonging to God. This assurance points to man's future, his eternal life. But man as he is here and now, cannot see himself enjoying this eternal relationship. He cannot understand himself in this dimension, not even in faith and love. Man bestowed with eternal life is future man; he is the object of God's promise and of our hope. And yet he is not devoid of reality. In God's free deed, in Jesus Christ, man *is* God's child. But as long as man lives he remains a pilgrim and a witness. He can only call on God from afar and out of the depth, *"Our Father who art in heaven!"* He does not yet understand himself as the child who enjoys the glorious assurance of belonging to the Father. For as yet he is an enigma to himself, and his brothers and sisters in the Christian community are enigmas to him as well. As yet his eternal destination is hidden and not revealed.

Even though man as he is here and now does not see or understand himself as a child of God, the God-given freedom breaks through in a new dimension, in a decisive and definitive way. Man is free to call God "Our Father," here and now. Man is free to see things from the standpoint of the beginning, the revealed act of the free God in the here and now. He can see his end in the ultimate revelation of God's act, his belonging to Him in glory. Frustrated, yet comforted in the midst of frustration, he will steadfastly look to the end. Human freedom is to live, to suffer, and finally to die in this expectation. But before he dies, as long as the day lasts, man is free to work, to rise after each fall, to labour and not to grow weary. Whether or not we rise or tire depends on the use we make of our freedom to look to the end. "Jesus, give me eyes, and touch my eyes that they may serve" ["Jesus, gib gesunde Augen, die was taugen, rühre meine Augen an."] says a well-known hymn. Man is free to bring his plea before God. In so doing he is free to hope for the great light, the great vision that will illumine the world, the Church, his fellow man, and himself. A Christian is one who makes use of this freedom to pray and to live in the hope of the end which will be the revelation of the beginning.

[III]

We now turn to the question of what these assumptions may teach us about the foundation of *evangelical ethics*. Although we cannot elaborate on these foundations at this point, we can at least give an outline. [Those interested in a more detailed description may consult *Church Dogmatics*, I, 2 (par. 22, sec. 3) II, 2 (par. 36-39), III, 4.]

A free man is one who chooses, decides, and determines himself and who acts according to his thoughts, words, and deeds. The course of his actions is a consequence of the nature of his God-given freedom. It is therefore in order to use interchangeably freedom and commandment. Man does the good when he acts according to the imperative inherent in the gift of freedom. He does the evil when he obeys a law that is contrary to his freedom. But these definitions need to be qualified.

Man's freedom as the directive and criterion for his actions is the gift bestowed upon him in a historical event of the free God's encounter with him. The giver does not retreat behind his gift, nor the lawmaker behind the law, nor divine freedom behind human freedom. It is God who determines how human freedom becomes directive and criterion for human action. Free man is subject to God's most concrete command, for through this command human freedom takes on authoritative form and the imperative whereby man is confronted and measured becomes decisive. God is always man's Creator, Reconciler, and Redeemer. He wants man to be His creature, His partner, and His child. What this means for each of us here and there, today and tomorrow, is decided by the free word of the free Lord in ever-renewed encounter between God and an individual. Measured against the divine commandment, mans action—his ethos—is found either good or evil. If our interpretation of divine and human freedom is accepted, these terms affirm the content and consequence of the imperative and the criterion, and concurrently exclude any arbitrary and accidental characteristics.

Ethics must be understood as the attempt, scientific or otherwise, to cope with the question of good and evil in human behaviour.

Ethics according to our assumptions can only be *evangelical ethics*. The question of good and evil is never answered by man's pointing to the authoritative Word of God in terms of a set of rules. It is never discovered by man or imposed on the self and others as a code of good and evil actions, a sort of yardstick of what is good and evil. Holy Scripture defies being forced into a set of rules; it is a mistake to use it as such. The ethicist cannot take the place either of the free God or of free man, even less of both together. His prescriptions in no way prejudge either the divine imperative or human obedience. On what authority would he prescribe, even though he quoted Bible verses, what a certain human being at a certain time should do or not do? Any such pretence, though well intended, is bound to lead astray. When the divine imperative urges upon man here and now a decision on a course of action, in harmony with the will of God, the ethicist will fail man with even his most realistic prescriptions and leave him utterly alone. Alas, he will be left alone not with God, but rather with himself, with his own conscience, with the *kairos*, or with his own judgment. In this realistic situation the choice between good and evil is made. To offer ethical norms to man in this predicament is to hold out a stone instead of bread.

If only ethics could reveal to man from the very beginning that in wrestling with the problem of his good or evil actions he is not confronted with his conscience, with the *kairos*, with his own judgment, with any visible or invisible law of nature or history, with any individual or social ideals, and, least of all, with his own arbitrary will. If only ethics could tell him that as a free man he is confronted with the will, word, and deed of the free God.

Ethics is a *theory* of human behaviour. This does not speak against the necessary ethical task. It merely emphasises that the ethical theory is not meant to provide man with a programme the implementation of which would be his life's goal. Nor is it meant to present man with principles to be interpreted, applied, and put into practice. Ethics has to make clear that every single step man takes involves a specific and direct responsibility towards God, who reached out for man in specific and direct encounter. This responsibility is lived out in obedience or disobedience, in good or evil, in confirmation or in negation and loss of the gift of freedom. Ethics exists to remind man of his confrontation with God, who is the light illuminating all his actions. It must be man's guide in his discernment of the apparently unlimited possibilities and in his choice of the only true one, existing either now or in the future. It must be man's teacher of evangelical ethics as the ethics of free grace.

Evangelical ethics will leave the pronouncement of unconditional imperatives to God. Its task is to emphasise the reality and the conditioning of human life, lived in the light of the divine imperative. This does not exclude the possibility of conditional imperatives addressed in concrete situations by a person to a brother. It is part of the risk of obedience involved in the encounter and communion between Christian brothers, and it is part of the risk of action according to the God-given freedom, to be called to invite, even to urge, a brother to a concrete action in a concrete situation, and to ask from him a concrete decision. Man will do so with his eyes lifted up to the living God who is also his brother's God. He will do so with his mind set on human freedom given to his brother also. If his courage is nourished by humility before God and his fellow men, this attitude alone may justify such conditional advice. He who takes the risk of counselling must be prepared to be counselled in turn by his brother if there is need of it. Such mutual counselling in a concrete situation is an event. It is part of the ethos which is realised ethics. It is only indirectly or not at all a part of ethics proper. For ethics is theory and not practice, though it is the theory about practice. Its main problem is precisely the question of the ethos, of the right and wrong, in human action. The ethos of the ethicist implies that he refrain from attempting too much and becoming thereby a lawmaker.

Ethics is reflection upon what man is required to do in and with the gift of freedom. The ethicist should not want to attempt too little either. He must want to realise his calling and his talents. It is not enough to insist that human life is to be lived under the divine imperative. Ethical reflection must go further and ask the question to what extent this is so. Neither the freedom of God's commandment nor that of man's obedience is empty form. Human action takes place at the point of contact between these two spheres of freedom. Each of these is characterised by its own content, tone, and extent. Ethical reflection has to concentrate upon these. It has to begin with the recognition that the free God is the free man's Lord, Creator, Reconciler, and Redeemer, and that free man is God's creature, partner, and child. This insight will be gained at the very source of Christian thinking, in Holy Scripture, where ethical reflection will also renew, sharpen, and correct its findings in continuous searching. In addition, ethical reflection may and must consult the Christian community in its past and present history. It must do this in order to be admonished, nourished, enriched, perhaps stirred and warned, by the use which the fathers and also brethren made and still are making of Christian freedom.

Therefore, ethics is not without signposts in its attempt to point to God's authoritative word of judgment. If it is based on the knowledge of God and of man, it will receive its contour. It will not point to a vacuum, but to the true God, the real man, and the real encounter between them. The ethical quest is and remains a quest and yet is not totally devoid of fulfilment. Indirect as it may be, the quest is a witness to God's concrete word. Ethical reflection may and must be genuine search and genuine doctrine, genuine because true ethics does not deprive God, its object, of His due power and glory. It leaves the uttering of the essential and final word to God Himself. But it does not shrink away from the preliminary words which are necessary to focus man's wandering thoughts on the one centre where he, himself free, shall hear the word of the free God, the commandment addressed to him, the judgment falling upon him, and the promise waiting for him.

[IV]

These short and general comments on the foundation of evangelical ethics may suffice. Our discussion afterwards might well centre on the above remarks, so as not to get sidetracked from the central theme by the additional, and perhaps distracting, remarks I would now like to make. Indeed, before concluding, I propose a short excursion into the field of ethics proper, of what we call "special ethics." I shall take as my starting point the above-described presuppositions. We are gathered here under the auspices of the "Gesellschaft für evangelische Theologie" (Society for Evangelical Theology). This is why I shall choose, as an example and merely as an example, a small and often neglected area: the ethics of theology itself and the ethos of the free theologian.

Is not the free theologian also a man and as such a recipient of the gift of freedom? Does not God address him, his thinking, speaking, and acting as well, when He gives man His commandment in and with the gift of freedom? Let it be noted that according to truly evangelical teaching the term "theologian" is not confined to the seminary professor, to the theological student, or to the minister. It is meant for every Christian who is mindful of the theological task entrusted to the whole Christian congregation, and who is willing and able to share in the common endeavour according to his own talents.

We are about to call it a day and are rather tired. I may, therefore, be excused for substituting some isolated remarks for a
systematic development of the problem. And because I belong
to the old guard today, I may be allowed to switch, at least
in feeling tone, from ethics to a sort of admonition. You may
be assured that there will be no deviations into imperatives
of any kind.

(1) A free theologian, free according to our definition, will
be found ready, willing, and able always to begin his thinking
at the beginning. This means his recognition of the resurrection of Jesus Christ as the directive for his reasoning. In his
reflections and statements he will always first proceed from
God's relationship to man and only then continue with man's
relationship to God. There is an abundance of serious, pious,
learned, and ingenious theological undertaking. But lacking the
sky-light and hence serenity, the theologian remains a gloomy
visitor upon this earth of darkness, an unpleasant instructor
of his brethren, whose teachings, at best, compares with the
sombre music of Beethoven and Brahms! The thoughtful
theologian who refuses to begin with God is bound to begin
with misery, individual and corporate, with the chaos which
threatens him and the world around him, with anxieties and
problems. He will turn around in circles and end up precisely
where he started. Cut off from the fresh air, he considers it to
be his bounden duty not to let others breathe fresh air either.
Only the radical turnabout we have been advocating here
could rescue him. Nobody has accomplished this turnabout
once and forever. Man has been set free for this very event,
this act of obedience which calls for repetition every day,
every hour, whenever a new theological task presents itself.
There is no reason for complaint about the impossibility of
such a turnabout. True, this turnabout is not a dialectical trick
to be learned and then used merrily again and again. Without
the invocation, "Our Father, who art in heaven" this turnabout
cannot take place. This is why it is imperative to recognise
the essence of theology as lying in the liturgical action of
adoration, thanksgiving, and petition. The old saying, *Lex
orandi lex credendi,* far from being a pious statement, is one

of the most profound descriptions of the theological method. We cannot do without this turnabout. The free and true theologian lives from it. In the invocation, in the giving of thanks, and in the petition, this turnabout is realised and the theologian is allowed to live out the freedom of thought which he enjoys as a child of God.

(2) A free theologian starts steadily and happily with the *Bible*. Here must be his starting point, but not because any old or new orthodoxy knocked it into him; it is not a law but a privilege to start with the Bible. It is his starting point not because he abstains from reading and appreciating other godly and worldly books—not to forget the newspapers. He starts with the Bible because in the Bible he learns about the free God and free man, and as a disciple of the Bible he may himself become a witness to the divine and human freedom. He does not start with a doctrine of the canon and of the verbal inspiration of Holy Scripture. But he does begin, not without inspiration, with daily searching of canonical writings. They informed and still inform him. He listens to them. He studies them in many ways, not despising the analytical, the historical-critical method, in order to gain a better understanding.

There are two reasons why the analysis, including the so-called "ascertained results" of historical-critical research, or the so-called "exegetical findings," is not the starting point of a free theologian. First, these results have a tendency to change every thirty years and from one exegete to another, and are thereby disqualified as a valid starting point. Secondly, analysis of both Biblical and secular texts, even though a *conditio sine qua non* of attentive listening to their message, does in no way guarantee and presuppose this act of listening. We listen when we read and study synthetically. The free theologian combines in one single act analysis and synthesis in his reading and studies. This is meditation, the secret of which is, again, adoration. The free theologian, taking the Bible as his starting point, is led by the testimony of the Bible, or more precisely by the origin, object, and content of this testimony. Here Christ spoke to him, and he let Him speak, through the medium of this testimony. Does this imply his speaking in direct quotation and interpretation of Biblical texts and contexts? Maybe often, maybe not always. The freedom bestowed upon him by the origin, object, and content of the Biblical testimony can and must be asserted through his attempt to think and to relate in his own terms what he heard in the Bible. As an illustration I refrained in this address from using one single direct quotation from the Scriptures, with the exception of the Lord's Prayer at the beginning. It is only right to exercise this freedom earnestly and repeatedly. It is an excellent yardstick for our knowing what we say when we quote and interpret. In regard to church practice we may ask whether this attempt should not be made consistently in sermons, as contrasted to Bible study. The freedom of theology is both freedom for exegesis and freedom for what we call dogmatics. At least in his endeavour to sum up the content of a book of the Bible or even the variety of Biblical testimonies, the exegete embarks upon dogmatical thinking. Dogmatics is the conscious and systematic account of the common understanding of all Biblical testimonies with due regard for their variety. Only through a formidable misunderstanding can the two functions of theology—exegesis and dogmatics—be set one against the other.

(3) A free theologian does not deny, nor is he ashamed of, his indebtedness to a particular *philosophy* or ontology, to ways of thought and speech. These may be traditional or a bit original, old or new, coherent or incoherent. No one speaks exclusively in Biblical terms. At least the combination of these terms, if not the meaning they assume in his mind and in his mouth, are, willingly or not, of his own making. The Biblical authors themselves, incidentally, far from speaking a celestial language, spoke in many earthly languages. This is why a free theologian, who is not even a prophet or an apostle, will certainly not wish to dissociate himself from his brethren in Church and world by his claim to speak "as from heaven," "according to the gospel," or, if this is synonymous for him, "according to Luther." If he does speak with any such authority, his listeners must sense it without his explicit affirmation. To speak God's word must be an event and not the object

of his assertion. Even then he speaks from within his philosophical shell, speaks in his own cumbersome vernacular which
is certainly not identical with the tongues of angels, although
the angels may utilise him at times. Three characteristics distinguish the free from the unfree theologian. First, he is aware
of his condition. Secondly, he stands ready to submit the coherence of his concepts and formulations to the coherence of
the divine revelation and not conversely. Thirdly, to mention
the inevitable slogan, he is a philosopher "as though he were
not," and he has his ontology "as though he had it not." A
free theologian will not be hindered by traditional conceptions
from thinking and speaking in the direction from God to man,
as affirmed at the outset of this address. His ontology will be
subject to criticism and control by his theology, and not conversely. He will not necessarily feel obligated to the philosophical *kairos*, the latest prevailing philosophy. The gratitude
of the Royal House of Austria will, in any event, not be
showered upon him. And who knows, he may be quite glad
to resort at times to an older philosophy, like the ill-famed
"Subject-Object-Scheme." If we visualise for a moment the
ideal situation of the free theologian, we may foresee the possibility not of theology recognising itself in any form of philosophy, but of free philosophy recognising itself in free
theology. Yet the free theologian knows very well that, like
a poor wretch, he does not live in this ideal situation.

(4) A free theologian thinks and speaks within the *Church*,
within the communion of saints, whose ordinary members
happen to be not just he and his closest theological friends.
In the Church there are *confessions*. Even in the Mennonite
Church there is a confession called after the small Swiss village
of Schleitheim! Why should a free theologian not pay loving
respect to these confessions as guidance in reading, explaining,
and applying the Scriptures? True, he does not owe them the
freedom of his thought and speech. He is not bound by them.
He will listen to them very carefully. He will be free to express
what they already have expressed, to express it better if he
has the talent to do so. He is equally free to acknowledge their
much better formulation of what he wants to say. He is free,

therefore, to say in his own terms what they already have said.

In the Church there are *fathers:* father Luther, father Calvin, other fathers. Why should a free theologian not be their son and disciple? But why should he insist on complete agreement with them? Why should he artificially reinterpret their findings until Luther is in agreement with him and says what he himself so badly wants to say? Why should he not respect the freedom of the fathers and let them express their wisdom and then learn from them what in his own freedom he may and can learn from them?

In the Church there are also *church governments.* Here in Germany they are even embodied in bishops. These have power to speak their mighty word through pastoral letters within the framework of their own theology which may not always be infallible. They have also power to examine, perhaps even to institute or destitute, certainly to recommend or to withhold recommendation. Why should the free theologian not at least tolerate them as they, in their mildness and prudence, as a rule tolerate him? He will certainly not become their spokesman and subordinate. Nor will he disdain the acknowledgment that a leading church figure may think and say at times the theologically right thing. He really does not—or does he?—want to get a complex, to be misled into opposition against the leadership of the Church and to feed upon his hostility until it becomes the principle of his interpretation of half, if not the whole, New Testament. More is at stake than the pro and con of the confessions, of Luther and Calvin, of the, alas, questionable church government. All this is only a sectarian pro and con. A free theologian is not a man of sect. He thinks and he speaks his definite "Yes" or "No." He is a man of action, not of reaction. His freedom is not primarily "freedom from" but "freedom for." He bewares of becoming enmeshed in a friend-foe relationship. The free theologian loves positive tasks. The Christian community, its gathering, nurture, and mission in the world, are at stake, and the free theologian knows this. He does his research and teaching in and for the community, as one of its members entrusted with this particular task and, hopefully, with the gift to carry it through. Private Christianity is not Christianity at all. Private theology is not free theology; it is not theology at all.

(5) A free theologian works in *communication* with other theologians. He grants them the enjoyment of the same freedom with which he is entrusted. Maybe he listens to them and reads their books with only subdued joy, but at least he listens to them and reads them. He knows that the selfsame problems with which he is preoccupied may be seen and dealt with in a way different from his own. Perhaps sincerity forbids him from following or accompanying some of his fellow theologians. Perhaps he is forced to oppose and sharply contradict many, if not most, of his co-workers. He is not afraid of the *rabies theologorum*. But he refuses to part company with them, not only personally and intellectually but, above all, spiritually, just as he does not want to be dropped by them. He believes in the forgiveness of both his theological sins and theirs, if they are found guilty of some. He will not pose as the detector and judge of their sins. Not yielding one iota where he cannot responsibly do so, he continues to consider the divine and human freedom in store for them. He waits for them and asks them to wait for him. Our sadly lacking yet indispensable theological co-operation depends directly or indirectly on whether or not we are willing to wait for one another, perhaps lamenting, yet smiling with tears in our eyes. Surely in such forbearance we could dispense with the hard, bitter, and contemptuous thoughts and statements about each other, with the bitter-sweet book reviews and the mischievous footnotes we throw at each other, and with whatever works of darkness there are! Is it clear in our minds that the concept of the "theological adversary" is profane and illegitimate? From my experience I would say that the Anglo-Saxon theologians, the fundamentalists probably notwithstanding, have a far better grasp of what I would like to call the "freedom of communication" than we Continentals do. They certainly do not all love each other overwhelmingly. But they treat each other as fellow creatures. We do not always act likewise. There is no ground for believing ourselves justified because of our, perhaps only illusionary, greater depth of thought.

These remarks need to be continued and drawn together systematically. Just think of the important issue of the existence and the reflection of the free theologian in his relationship to Roman Catholicism or to the prevailing political climate. Completeness, however, has not been my goal here. I merely wished to let a concrete example guide your reflection about the gift of freedom as the foundation of evangelical ethics. Therefore, I break off and close with a Biblical quotation in spite of what I said. It is an imperative, full of exegetical and other implications. Many of us are likely to have it interpreted and applied more than once with other people in mind. Today we are asked to hear it for ourselves, as theologians, hopefully as free theologians: "Finally, brethren, whatever is true, whatever is honourable, whatever is just, whatever is pure, whatever is lovely, whatever is gracious, if there is any excellence, if there is anything worthy of praise, think about these things . . . and the peace of God will be with you."

PART III / PERSPECTIVES OF EXISTENTIAL THOUGHT

Carl Michalson / Christian Faith and Existential Freedom

CHRISTIAN THOUGHT about the nature and destiny of man owes more to the word "freedom" than to any other word. Yet no word from the lips of philosophers and theologians is more productive of what the Frenchman, Parain, has called "the giddy sensation of the inexactitude of speech." Theology's ambiguous exposition of freedom can largely be attributed to the ill-fitting instruments of definition it has had at hand. Now, theologians have generally turned to philosophy for the tools of definition. The liability in this alliance has been that philosophy designs its words to fit its own concerns. Because philosophy's concerns have not always been theology's concerns, its definitions have not always been theologically ample. It is an intellectual event of major importance that theology is now turning for its definition of freedom to existentialism,

CARL MICHALSON (1915–1965) was Professor of Systematic Theology at Drew Theological Seminary. He was a noted lecturer and teacher, and was author of a number of monographs and studies, including THE HINGE OF HISTORY (1959). This essay originally appeared in RELIGION IN LIFE, vol. XXI (Autumn, 1952) and is reprinted here by kind permission of Mrs. Janet Michalson.

for there philosophical and theological concerns have come together in a way unprecedented in Western thought.

In the Greek tradition, for instance, philosophy defined man's problem as deliverance from the realm of necessity called nature. Plato outlined a solution in a philosophy which built a case for man's independence from nature and called this independence freedom. This freedom was achieved by man's rational affiliation with an abstract realm of essences which were themselves beyond and independent of nature. Only the human body was considered a victim of nature's necessity. The human reason, transcendent of the body, was free from nature.

The reason, however, was not in itself free. To be rational was instinctively to know the essences—the true and the good. Nor was the will free, for it was the necessity of the will automatically to do what the reason knew. That is why in the realm of morals "to prefer evil to good is not in human nature" (*Protagoras* 758 C). Man does no evil voluntarily. Sin stems from an ignorance for which one is not culpable. The body, a foreign agent, subverts the reason. Knowledge is virtue (*Gorgias* 468, *Timaeus* 86, V, 731). Greek philosophy, while it understood that man was free from "doing what comes naturally," nevertheless delivered human nature into another kind of necessity, the necessity for doing what comes rationally. Escape from the causes of nature was achieved by subjection to the necessitarian logic of essences.

To be just to the lively sense of freedom in experience, the Greeks devised a concept of "free choice." In the last analysis, however, "free choice" meant simply the sense for alternative ways of doing what it is finally necessary to do. Free choice, the prisoner of reason, "mimics freedom by pacing round and round in his cell" (Helmut Kuhn).

In the German tradition man's problem was not so much the problem of escape from nature as it was the problem of justifying moral responsibility. Motivated by this shift in the problem, Immanuel Kant took it upon himself to by-pass the thousand-year-old philosophical anachronism which defined freedom as rational determinism. The *will* is free, Kant said.

It is possible for a man to say either "yes" or "no" to what he knows to be the good, the right, and the true, for reason is shot through with will. Descartes had hinted at this. When man acted in his ignorance, Descartes did not blame the body, as Plato did, for disfiguring the reason; he blamed the will for acting in the absence of a clear idea. This was the only basis on which it seemed possible, according to Kant, to keep morality alive. Unless one is free to choose either good or evil, he is not responsible, and no merit or guilt attaches to his choice. Freedom makes man accountable and makes either merit or guilt imputable.

Further to enhance this responsible moral freedom, Kant transplanted the heaven of ethical ideals, with its hierarchical dominion over man, into the human reason. Man, then, could be his own law-giver. Thus in the eighteenth century, autonomy became a synonym of freedom. Autonomy did not mean antinomianism or anarchy, for the law within is as universal and irrevocable as if it were the law above. Autonomy simply avoided the causal and necessitarian implications in an alliance with either nature or a realm of essences. The law is not the cause, of which moral living is the inescapable effect. It is possible for man to obey or disobey it. One ought to note, however, that the law of good, before which the will decides, is as rational for Kant as it is for Plato. The good is the rational. To that extent Plato survives in Kant. The major difference is that for Kant the will, though *obliged* by the rational, is not *compelled* by it. Freedom of the will, a voluntaristic indeterminism, thereby supplanted philosophy's long-standing definition of freedom as rational determinism.

The Kantian philosophy of freedom is the confluence of two intellectual streams. Greek philosophy's concern for the superiority of the rational over the natural merges with medieval Europe's Latin-Germanic concern for moral responsibility. The Christian freedomists, whose major theological concerns were merit and guilt—Pelagius, Thomas Aquinas, Erasmus, and the seventeenth-century Jesuits—are in Kant's philosophical family tree as truly as are Plato, Aristotle, and the Stoics, whose philosophical concern was the rational. The twin requirements of the Kantian moral philosophy were rational insight into moral truth and the deliberate decision of the will. These were the very materials in the making in Western thought since the birth of the Christian movement.

There is another intellectual stream, however, which is represented by Augustine, the voluntarists of the fourteenth century, the Reformers, and the Jansenists. No matter how dependent this stream may have been upon Greco-Roman thinking, when it came to problems involving freedom it found this line too slack to hold the Christian faith. How talk of rational insight into human destiny when the Sovereign of history is the hidden God who reveals himself at will? How talk of moral responsibility in a man whose entire life is under the fate of sin and whose Christian hope is a destiny that lies beyond history, a destiny whose operation is so free that it is unconditioned by the acts of man? The predestinarian categories of the Augustinian tradition clash with both the rationalistic and the moralistic categories of the Greek and Roman traditions. The fact that contemporary theology is built upon this uneven tripod of traditions surely helps to account for "the giddy sensation" in the contemporary use of the word "freedom."

[I]

Meanwhile, a species of philosophy has developed that is rapidly breaking up these unsteady historical alternatives and retooling the instruments for defining freedom. It is a cluster of vitalisms, pragmatisms, and existentialisms. Despite important differences among these new philosophies, they agree on two points: first, that "existence precedes essence"; and second, that this precedence is the rudiment of freedom. Living is given priority over thinking; the whole of one's life, which is existence, is given priority over that partial function of life which is reason. Rational reflection is a delayed reaction to the perpetual forward motion of one's entire life. "Existence precedes essence," and that is basic freedom. As Sartre has said, "The essence of the human being is in suspense in his freedom." [1]

A list of the recent pioneers in the concept of freedom would include Kierkegaard, Nietzsche, and Dostoievsky; Marx, Freud, and Dewey; Bergson and (in a limited way) Whitehead; and a growing list of contemporary existentialists—the so-called atheistic Heidegger, Sartre, Camus, and Simone de Beauvoir; the theistic Jaspers; and the very theological existentialists—Jewish Buber, Roman Catholic Marcel, and Orthodox Berdyaev. All of these philosophers seem agreed at the two points which place them beyond Plato and Kant, beyond rationalism and moralism.

In the first place, these recent philosophers do not fear, as the Greeks did, that nature will thwart freedom. An almost biblical anthropology animates their thought. The human body is believed to be organic with the total self rather than hostile toward it. Moreover, a kind of biological evolutionism is affirmed which sees in nature a continuous process of agile adaptation more suggestive of freedom than of necessity.

The real enemy of freedom, it is believed, is not nature but reason. Reason is an excellent instrument for insight into past necessities, but it falters in what John Dewey calls "foresight into possibility" or what Whitehead calls "advance into novelty." "Transcendence of mere clarity and order is necessary for dealing with the unforeseen, for progress, for excitement." [2] When "existence precedes essence" a new kind of history comes into being in which "the past loses its unique precedence" (Heidegger[3]), and future possibilities overshadow accomplished facts.

Reason, moreover, is an indispensable agent in the analysis of life, but it is the misfortune of reason that when it analyzes it must "*stop* and think" and thereby miss the many-splendored moving scene. Cocteau once complained in a letter to Maritain that he was so busy writing *The Parade* he never got to see one. Van Gogh deplored having to kill the butterfly he wished to paint. One cannot sketch life from death. But it is inseparable from the operations of the reason, so these vitalists believe, to take "a snapshot of the mobility of the inner life" (Bergson). "The letter killeth," and the reason deals in letters. How, then, shall reason live with the spirited mobilities of art, of love, of religion? "We are free," said Bergson, "when our acts spring from the whole personality." [4]

In the second place, these contemporary philosophers are not, as Kant was, enamored of moral responsibility. That is, they have no taste for what Romano-Germanic culture calls responsibility, accountability, and the imputability of moral guilt. Irresponsibility in the newer sense is not a moral or a legal notion, it is a personal notion. It does not denote a fault to be imputed; it is a default of responsibility. One ought not ask, therefore, "Was his act conscious and deliberate?" One ought to ask, "Was his act *whole*?" Wholeness is an attribute neither of consciousness nor of rational deliberation, but of the hidden unity and destiny of the personality. Irresponsibility, then, is a sickness and responsibility is its opposite: personal wholeness and health and responsiveness to one's vocation.

For a fact, the sickness of the personality is often incurred by its very conscious and deliberate effort to conform to the rational and the moral. Nietzsche and Freud contribute stunning evidence of this. The bad conscience, they say, is a disease the personality contracts. It is a "reaction-formation" (Freud) that follows when its instinct for freedom is "forced back, trodden back, imprisoned within itself and finally only able to find vent and relief within itself" (Nietzsche). The bad conscience is the sense of oppressiveness in a life whose proper vitality is stifled by codes that have no necessary relation to the emerging needs of the human spirit but which, for the proprieties and emotional loyalties that surround them, compel the spirit to hypocritical submission. "The soul whose will is cloven in two within itself" says to itself, "I am sick of myself!" "The *sick*, then are the great danger of man," said Nietzsche, "*not* the evil."

Whatever freedom is, then, it is believed there are aspirations associated with man's freedom toward which the reason is unsympathetic. The intellect, as Karl Heim once said, is "an archive director." But man is a history-making, not simply a history-recording animal. Life and desire and the quest for authenticity, better known to religious tradition as faith or salvation—these supersede the restrictions of mere correctness.

You see, gentlemen, reason is an excellent thing, there's no disputing that, but reason is nothing but reason, and satisfies only the rational side of man's nature, while will is a manifestation of the whole life, that is, of the whole human life including reason and all the impulses. . . . Reason only knows what it has succeeded in learning . . . and human nature acts as a whole, with everything that is in it, consciously or unconsciously, and even if it goes wrong, it lives.

So Dostoievsky writes in his *Notes From the Underground*.[5] Ordinarily one's choices will conform to what commends itself to consciousness as rational. But there is a point at which one may even will to be stupid, "in order," as Dostoievsky says, "not to be bound by an obligation to desire only what is sensible."

This Russian wildness is reminiscent of Tertullian's *credo quia absurdum*. The famous phrase is apocryphal, but Tertullian has said what amounts to the same. *Certum est, quia impossibile est.*[6] These words are generally translated to read, "The fact is certain because it is impossible." Actually, *certum* means just the opposite of certain. In Roman law—and Tertullian was a lawyer in the Roman tradition—*certum* means "resolved." It pertains not to a certainty but to the kind of action one must take in the absence of certainty. *Certum* is a rhetorical parallel for *credible* in this very passage. When one does not know "for certain" and the issue is crucial, one must resolve. The faithful man is not the rational man but the resolute man, and resolution takes place in freedom. That which is impossible to reason is possible to freedom.

What, then, shall one say of moral responsibility, should one decide to enter into an affiliation in the absence of rational certainty and transparency? Descartes and Kant would answer, "Immoral, the antithesis of freedom." Tertullian gave an answer in his *Prescription against Heretics*: "There is impunity in erring if there is no delinquency." Tertullian knew what the skeptics of the Middle Academy at Athens knew: significant action ought not to wait upon rational clarity, if in fact the things that matter most cannot be rationally penetrated. The so-called modern Tertullian, Kierkegaard, speaks similarly.

If only the mode of this relationship is in the truth, the individual is in the truth even if he should happen to be thus related to what is not true. . . . The truth is precisely a venture which chooses an objective uncertainty. . . . If I am capable of grasping God objectively, I do not believe, but precisely because I cannot do this I must believe.[7]

Moral responsibility which presupposes the consciousness of clear and distinct ideas is utterly appropriate to matters involving the true and the false, the good and the evil, the right and the wrong. How does it fare, however, where one's whole life is involved, his loves and hates, his loyalties and lies, his humility and his pride, his life and his death? When one's whole existence is at stake, "there is impunity in erring if there is no delinquency." In the spirited resoluteness of freedom there is a talent that ranges beyond the level of conscious and deliberate choice. "The free act is," as Sartre says, "absurd, beyond all reason." [8] "Existence precedes essence" as resolution precedes reflection and love precedes calculation.

[II]

What is this "freedom" which these recent philosophies set up against previous philosophical definitions? Five elements in the existential view can be singled out.

1. Freedom IS the human existence. Man is not a "something" with the attribute of freedom. Man *is* his freedom. There is no attribute or function of man that can be equated with man's very being. It may be said that man thinks, wills, and feels; but it ought not to be said that man IS thought, will, or feeling. As Jaspers has stated it, "In the resolve I experience the freedom in which I decide not merely about something but about myself. . . . *I myself am the freedom of this choice.* Pure choice appears only as a choice between objectivities; but freedom is as the choice of myself." [9] Or, as Kierkegaard has said, when one does not choose, one withers away in consumption.

2. But, according to existentialism, freedom is nothing. One experiences a "vast and pointless sense of freedom" (Sartre)

when contemplating the world about him. Pascal knew the sensation when he contemplated the infinity and absurdity of the universe which seventeenth-century science had uncovered. The seventeenth-century preacher John Donne knew it when he exclaimed of the universe, " 'Tis all in peeces, all cohaerence gone." Wordsworth knew it when he referred to this same universe as a nothing in which one is "forlorn" but for some creed. In the words of Pascal,[10]

> When I consider the short duration of my life, swallowed up in the eternity before and after, the little space which I fill, and even can see, engulfed in the infinite immensity of spaces of which I am ignorant, and which know me not, I am frightened, and am astonished at being here rather than there; for there is no reason why here rather than there, why now rather than then.

Sartre described the sensation in his first novel, *Nausea*. A young man sitting on a park bench contemplates the root of a tree. It blurs, fades, and otherwise illustrates evanescence, and the young man becomes sick. The clue to his sickness is his discovery that existence is radically contingent, that is, that there is no reason for existence. There is nothing *in* existence that explains it. A fundamental difference between the ancient and the modern views of the world is thereby marked. The ancient was alternately annoyed by cosmic necessity and edified by cosmic orderliness. The modern is sickened by cosmic contingency. The more comforting cosmology of antiquity is thus replaced in modern times by an intense life-feeling which Wilhelm Dilthey has characterized as a "feeling incapable of being solved by demonstration," an "insoluble metaphysical void at the bottom of every consciousness." [11] This void, this nothing *is* man's freedom. As Sartre puts it in his novel, *The Reprieve*, "Inside, nothing, not even a puff of smoke, there is no inside, there is nothing. Myself: nothing. I am free, he said to himself, and his mouth was dry."

3. Yet, it is believed that freedom is possibility. The "nothing" of freedom is a "lack" (Sartre), but a "lack" is a possibility. To classical philosophy, "possible" meant "non-

contradictory." To contemporary existentialism "possible" means a lack to be filled. "Nothing" is a possibility in existence, which accounts for the striving, desiring, and seeking by which human life is constantly attempting to fulfill itself. The complement of the sickening sensation of being tied to nothing, of swimming over 70,000 fathoms (Kierkegaard), is the fascinating possibility of going somewhere and being something. Freedom is "a vibrating needle" (Buber), a "viscosity" (Sartre), an urge toward unforeseen possibilities, an indefinable sense of being "for the sake of" something (Heidegger).

4. Hence, freedom is a burden. Man feels "condemned forever to be free" (Sartre). As freedom, the human existence is the one point in all reality where being is most apt to fail. Man can choose himself as nothing or as in relation to some possibility beyond himself. He can reach beyond himself to some relationship which may confer a meaning that is not intrinsic to his existence. "Freedom is not an indifferent will but the possibility of being free for something." [12]

The risk of freedom, however, is that it is possible for one to relate himself to that which itself participates in the nothingness, contingency, and absurdity of existence. Religion calls this idolatry, and philosophy calls it nihilism. Neither atheistic nor theistic existentialism knows of an ultimately secure relationship, though both know that man is haunted by a desire for a fulfillment he is never able to achieve. Atheistic existentialism sometimes leaves the possibility open and remains wistful (as in Heidegger), sometimes rejects the possibility and becomes Stoical (as in Sartre). That one must make this choice is the burden of one's freedom. That he must do it without the certain knowledge that there is any actual basis for his choice makes the burden poignant.

But such a choice is equally burdensome to the theistic existentialist, for when he chooses a relation to the transcendent, noncontingent reality he calls God, he chooses what he does not know but simply believes or hopes. This is his freedom. As Jaspers says, "I am free because I do not know," or as Marcel says, freedom is to "decide . . . without any appeal."

5. Freedom is, then, a terrifying burden, a burden of a des-

perately serious lack, a burden so terrifying it has become the source of an endemic human sickness recognized in life today as *anxiety*. As freedom, man may choose either to be what he is or to affiliate with sources of authenticity beyond himself. This freedom is not simply the ability to choose but the inability not to choose (Simone de Beauvoir). The choice is between contingency and loyalty, between a dying independence and a living dependence, between hopelessness without obligation and hope with obligation. One desires existence on his own terms but fears that if he "bows down to nothing he cannot bear the burden of himself" (Dostoievsky). One fears to pledge himself, yet desires the authenticity which right relationship confers. The collision of fear and desire is the friction in freedom which we know to be anxiety, the rubbing together of nothingness and possibility. Anxiety is a condition that paralyzes action and obscures whatever transparency man has at the very moment he needs it the most—the moment in which his destiny, his very being, his life and death is being determined. The predicament of man is a predicament born of freedom, a sickness, what Balzac called "a tetanus of the soul."

The widespread practice of deploring any reference to sickness as a symptom of pessimism is on the wane. Circles that deal in the therapy of the mind know that nothing so obstructs the therapeutic process as a fictitious sense of health. "Anxiety is the ground of hope" (Jaspers [13]). The *human* ground, to be sure, and of a hope that is by no means determinative: one can learn, as Byron said, "to love despair," for "in despair there are the most intense enjoyments" (Dostoievsky).

Nonetheless, it remains true as Kierkegaard understood it that the possibility of this sickness is "man's advantage over the beast." "It is the greatest misfortune not to have had it," [14] for it is the initial impulse toward recovering health and authenticity. Nietzsche understood it this way when he compared the sickness of the spirit to a pregnancy. You can get over it and have something to show for it beside. John Calvin seems to have understood it this way when he says in the opening lines of the last edition of his *Institutes*, "Our poverty

conduces to a clearer display of the infinite fullness of God.
. . . Nor can we really aspire toward him till we have begun
to be displeased with ourselves."

[III]

The implications of the existential notion of freedom have
already begun to effect a ferment in theology. A few of the
strategic areas must suffice as illustrations.

1. The *image of God* has generally been believed to be some
fundamental likeness man has to God, some such resemblance
as one would expect to see between a father and his son. This
resemblance has usually been located in man's rationality. But
theology has been embarrassed to find the sense of the likeness between God and man inspiring self-satisfaction rather
than filial loyalty and responsibility. Moreover, there has been
a restlessness in theology respecting the way in which affirmations of man's likeness to God disregard the irreversible structure in a relation that exists between Creator and creature.

In protest against this genetic definition of "likeness" the
theologian has urged that the image of God is to be found in
one man only, in God's Son. What, then, of the image of God
in other men than Christ? The image of God in man is the
human possibility for man's relationship to God. That possibility is freedom, and *freedom is responsibility, or the ability
to be at God's disposal.* Not freedom, then, as Aristotle defined
it when he said "a man is free . . . who exists for his own sake
and not for another's." Not even freedom as, for instance,
Philo defined it when he regarded freedom in man as a quality
that most resembles God, the power of interrupting the laws
of nature. Ours is a freedom which is not at all like God's because it is a freedom for dependence, a burdensome and
restless freedom, a freedom which fulfills itself only in dependence upon God. "Existence precedes essence." The doctrine
of the image of God in man means that the desire to relate
oneself to God precedes even the knowledge that there is a
God. He hath made us out of the nothing of freedom, and our
souls are restless until they choose themselves in him.

2. The doctrine of *original sin* has been retained in contemporary theology as a mythological key to the gravity of human life. It is difficult, however, in doctrines of original sin for theologians to satisfy the demands both of morality and of personal realism. Generally, whatever the original sin is, no one is expected to assume personal responsibility for it, inasmuch as it was precipitated without one's own conscious, deliberate choice. It is a Kantian requirement that an accountable act be voluntary and conscious, but this requirement suggests two problems.

The first problem is that our destiny-determining acts are so profound that we cannot subject them to analysis. We can only presuppose them. As Balzac has said of our wounds, "we cannot examine them, they hurt too much." Or, as Sartre has said, "Conscious deliberation is always faked. . . . When I deliberate the die is already cast. . . . The decision has already been taken." [15] Original sin is the spiritual tension at the root of our lives that vitiates all our acts—rational and voluntary— without either our knowledge or our choice. This is what Luther and Augustine meant by the bondage of the will. It does not mean we are not free. Man *is* freedom. It does mean our freedom is sick, an anxious freedom. Ever since the Apostle Paul it has been known by the Christian tradition that the problem of freedom is not the problem of choice but of ability, not legislation but execution, not ends but energy.

The second problem in a moral definition of original sin is that guilt is denied to original sin because such an original act was not freely, that is, consciously and deliberately committed. Hence, responsibility for the declivity in one's life is also abrogated. What if guilt, however, were not something legally imputable, as if the person were a criminal whose aberrations could be traced to specific acts of offense? What if guilt were a condition of being, a condition of deep, personal irresponsibility, a default of vocation? Formally, guilt is the disproportion between what one is and what one ought to be. Actually, what if guilt were not simply the failure to achieve recognized moral ends, but the condition of being at odds with one's spiritual destiny? What if guilt were not a result but a condition of doing wrong? That is, not a doing wrong at all, but a being wrong?

"Being guilty," says Heidegger, "does not result originally from a fault; faults originally become possible on the basis of an original guilt." [16] "Guilt" is no more legal or moral a concept than is "righteousness." "Being guilty" is a sickness of freedom; not a fault to be condemned but a sickness to be cured. There is a responsiblity in sickness, but not a legal or moral one. One is not blamed for being sick, but he is expected to *assume* responsibility for it as the first step to a cure. For a long time now the story of Adam has dawned on men with the abruptness and lucidity that comes when one "suddenly remembers where he left his glasses" (T. S. Eliot).

3. The *grace of God* in Christ is a therapy. It is not the effect of a transaction, legal, moral, or commercial. "Satisfaction" for sins was an expression Luther associated with moral philosophers, jurists, papists, and hangmen. There is no more effective therapy for the sickness of freedom, however, than love. Love casts out anxiety. Love does not blame, it heals; love does not exact, it confers. Love is not weighed, it is received. Love is not subject to bargaining, it is subject only to gratitude. Love has no reason, it can only be trusted. God chooses to love us in Christ, and "we can only choose our being chosen" (Barth). *"Libertas sine gratia nihil est"* (Augustine). Freedom without grace is nothing. But grace is the medicine of salvation; it heals the sickness of freedom. The story of God's faithfulness in Christ is good news for the spiritually sick which makes them whole again, and this wholeness is "the liberty wherewith Christ hath made us free."

To say that the predicament of man is the sickness of his freedom is not to infer that this sickness is a weakness. It is rather an imbalance of one's powers, more often inordinate than weak. Spiritual anxiety expresses itself with a violence which the Christian tradition has long associated with rebellion and pride. In the words of Byron:

> There is a very life in our despair,
> Vitality of poison,—a quick root
> Which feeds these deadly branches . . .

Augustine called it the *libido dominandi*. Luther called it *Anfechtung*, or temptation, by which he meant not the kind of appeal which petty vices have for the morally weak, but the dreadful sense of infinite possibility one gets in the presence of holy things. So deep-seated an illness of the spirit will not yield to just any religious homeopathy. Christian doctrines of the atonement, while they can stand being stripped of their mythological trappings, conserve one persistent element. It is the sense of an almost violent aggressiveness in the love of God, which, in collision with man's own violent freedom is productive of a therapy as though by shock.

4. *Christian ethics*, then, becomes the articulation in action of the spiritual health in one's life. That is to say, Christian ethics is subordinated to no law but the law of liberty. The Christian existence precedes moral essences. As Dostoievsky believed, "the possibility of being able to place the question of right *after* the meaning of one's existence is the greatest and most ultimate freedom of man." [17] Theologically, this means man's freedom is a freedom primarily to choose himself in relation to God, and only secondarily to choose between good and evil. The Christian's ethical responsibility is to evolve the morality consistent with this theological destiny. Satre's phrase, "You are free: choose! That is to say, invent!" if given Christian baptism would read, "Love God and do as you please." The irresponsible man is the man who evades the responsibility of determining God's will by retreating into some pre-established moral structure. To do so is, both in existentialism and in psychoanalysis, to adopt an infantile morality. But "how can we know what is God's word, and what is right or wrong? . . . You must determine this matter for yourself," said Luther, "for your very life depends upon it."

5. *Theism* suffers most at the hands of the maxim, "existence precedes essence," though it probably deserves to suffer. Christian philosophers have expanded the seed of the Christian faith into trees of wisdom in which a man may lodge without existing. Theisms create a world view out of what requires a decision, a science out of a faith.

There is really a quantitative paucity of truth in the Christian gospel. It is, as the Westminster Confession rightly says, sufficient "for salvation," but it is scarcely sufficient for cosmology and metaphysics. The Christian truth is the Christ, to know whom is to be free. There is a life-and-death difference between possessing truths about Christianity and being true in Christ. The one is a technological achievement and the other is a condition of personal freedom.

When contemporary existentialists avow their atheism it is not in hostility toward God but toward Western philosophy's opinions about God. Theistic philosophy has constructed God in man's image without in the first place being correct about man. The effect has been to destroy in man all consciousness of what Camus has called "vertical transcendence." When Augustine finished his treatise on the Trinity he recognized that silence might have been preferable, for the very sound of one's own voice, though he talk about God, is apt to lull one to sleep. Even Nietzsche, when he pronounced that "God is dead," was only informing against God's murderers, not burying God.

Heidegger's philosophy is a philosophy of openness toward the future—which is freedom. But God, who is eternal, is in the future, and freedom is waiting for God. Sartre's atheism is considerably less remediable. There is a stubbornness about it. The Christian God about whom he knows the most is the God of French Catholicism, who, though he is in the future as an eternal God, is in the future only as he was in the past. Literally, he is the same, yesterday, today, and forever, for his essence *is* his existence. His mind is made up. The Roman Catholic theism sponsors the idea of a God who is at once rational and static. Protestantism, with its biblical revolt against this kind of Aristotelianism, avows the God of Abraham, Isaac, and Jacob, the acting and passionate God, the Father of our Lord Jesus Christ. This God is dynamic and irrational: he is free. Even in him, existence precedes essence. There is an "atheism" in Protestantism which repudiates the ideas of God which do not give to God a life as good as man's, a free life. "Even truer than our freedom and truer than the wretched truth of our *servum arbitrium*, is the heartening truth that God is free." [18] And what is freedom? Not the ability to do only what the rational structure of one's nature allows. That is Scholasticism. God is free to do whatever his passionate heart chooses. God is the Creator—even of his own nature. That is to say, he *is* free.

The Christian faith, then, in these and other areas, is being expressed anew with the help of this new notion of freedom. It is a notion which has progressively eluded rational determinism and voluntaristic indeterminism in favor of the consciousness of a spiritual possibility. This sense of freedom leaves man's life dry with the thirst for God. On some other occasions when theologians have asked philosophers for bread, the philosophers have returned them a stone. Today, in the philosophy of freedom, they have given us yeast.

NOTES

1. Sartre, J.-P., *L'être et le néant*, Paris, 1948, p. 61.

2. Whitehead, A. N., *Modes of Thought*. The Macmillan Company, 1938, p. 108.

3. Heidegger, M., *Sein und Zeit*. Halle, Germany, 1927, p. 391.

4. Bergson, H., *Time and Free Will*, tr. F. L. Pogson. Allen & Unwin, 1910, p. 172.

5. Dostoievsky, F., *Short Novels*, Dial Press, 1945, p. 147.

6. *On the Flesh of Christ*, 5.

7. Kierkegaard, S., *Concluding Unscientific Postscript*, tr. David F. Swenson, Walter Lowrie. Princeton, 1944, pp. 178 and 182.

8. *Op. cit.*, p. 559.

9. Jaspers, K., *Philosophie*. Berlin, 1932, Volume II, p. 182.

10. Pascal, B., *Pensées*, No. 205.

11. Dilthey, W., *Gesammelte Schriften*. Leipzig, 1914, Volume I, "Einleitung in die Geisteswissenschaften," p. 364.

12. *Op. cit.*, p. 144.

13. Jaspers, K., *Vom Ursprung und Ziel der Geschichte*. Zürich, 1949, p. 193.

14. Kierkegaard, S., *Sickness unto Death*, tr. Walter Lowrie. Princeton, 1941, pp. 20 and 39.

15. *Op. cit.*, p. 527.

16. *Op. cit.*, p. 280.

17. Lauth, Reinhard, *Die philosophie Dostojewskis.* Munich, 1950, p. 146.

18. Barth, Karl, *Die kirchliche Dogmatik.* Zürich, 1948, III, 2, p. 43.

Sister Mary Aloysius / Freedom and the "I": An Existential Inquiry

HARDLY ANYONE will deny that "freedom" and "self" are terms currently in vogue. So powerful is the lure of freedom that even contemporary totalitarianism is obliged to advance its aims under this alias. And the self, banished from scientific discourse by rigorously "objective" psychologists, has not merely regained respectability but achieved new lustre—a lustre reflected in the growing usage of such compounds as: self-actualization, self-integration, ego-involvement, etc.

But when, as in the title of this essay, "freedom" and "self" are conjoined, a chain of provocative questions comes to mind: Do these terms refer to realities? If they do, are these realities different from one another? If they are, can they be related to one another? If they can be, what sort of relation exists between them? Is it a one-way relation of the type "ordination to"? In this case, is it freedom that exists for the self or the

SISTER MARY ALOYSIUS, S.S.J. (1922–   ) teaches philosophy at Nazareth College in Michigan and has written on Gabriel Marcel as well as studies on sense-intuition. "Freedom and the I" is reprinted from INTERNATIONAL PHILOSOPHICAL QUARTERLY, vol. III (1963) by kind permission of the Editor, W. Norris Clarke, S.J.

self that exists for freedom? Suppose, however, that there are not two realities here but only one. Which is illusory—freedom or the self?

Because Jean-Paul Sartre and Gabriel Marcel submit contrasting answers to these questions, juxtaposing their views should furnish a pointed and stimulating introduction to problems raised by the freedom-self dyad. Knowledge, the ancients were fond of remarking, is best served by the opposition of contraries. But, in addition to their clarifying function, these existentialist antitheses suggest new and promising lines of inquiry. It is with both advantages in view that this essay proceeds to: (1) presentation of the Sartrean and Marcellian analyses of freedom and the "I," and (2) reflection upon them from the precise viewpoint of the new perspectives which they open.

Freedom vs. the "I": Sartre's Phenomenological Ontology

To know the mind of Sartre on the question of self and freedom is not an easy matter. It is true that an early article, "The Transcendence of the Ego," takes a stand, in the name of freedom, unambiguously against the conception of consciousness as self-being.[1] Yet it is no less true that the major work of Sartre, *Being and Nothingness*, not only speaks of consciousness as "self-presence," but even makes of self-presence the "very being of consciousness."[2] Opposition seems basic. There is no avoiding confrontation of the two sets of data. Not until the meaning of the self-structure first denied and then affirmed is clear can it be decided whether Sartre's thought has moved from one contrary to another, whether it is unchanged but beset by internal contradictions, or whether what appear to be contradictions are explainable as differences of formulation.

THE SELF AND CONSCIOUSNESS

In the article on "The Transcendence of the Ego," Sartre contests the thesis that "behind" each consciousness there is a superempirical ego tirelessly, though hiddenly, constructing whatever reality appears to consciousness. Not only, he objects, is there in consciousness no superempirical "I." There is in consciousness no "I" at all. Three reasons in particular urge him to this conclusion: (1) Consciousness needs no "I." (2) If an "I" were to inhabit consciousness, consciousness would be destroyed. (3) In fact, however, inspection of immediate consciousness reveals no "I" whatever.[3]

That the "I" is not necessary to assure the unity of consciousness seems obvious to Sartre. Consciousness is always consciousness *of* something. Why cannot this "something" confer unity upon consciousness? After all, the object of consciousness is an independent unity, and consciousness is nothing but a surpassing of itself toward that independent unity. Why, then, seek a unifying principle apart from the focal point which, at any given moment, concentrates and specifies the regard of consciousness?

It can be objected, of course, that the object may well account for unity "at any given moment," but does not at all account for unity experienced throughout a series of moments. Sartre, however, has a ready answer: Not the synthesizing activity of a self, but a "transversal" activity of consciousness explains the identity-feeling. Consciousness itself, by virtue of a "vertical" movement, continually transmits real and concrete remembrances of past acts to its present act. Nothing more is needed, he insists, to assure the subjective unity of conscious experience.

Nor is there need to go beyond consciousness in order to explain individuality. By essence, consciousness is consciousness *of* something. Now this "something" is perforce a definite thing. By virtue of its object, therefore, consciousness is "finitized." Thus finitized, consciousness cannot but exist individualized. Individuality, like unity, requires no other principle than consciousness itself. The "I," Sartre concludes, is "totally useless."

Not only is it useless. It is downright pernicious. If an "I" were to inhabit consciousness, then consciousness as a type of existence would be undone. Essential to it as a mode of existence which reveals being is absolute translucency. To be sure, the being that it reveals is revealed only imperfectly.

Ultimately, indeed, the object of consciousness is impenetrable opacity. Yet, precisely as revealing, consciousness is purely and simply translucid. It is purely and simply consciousness of its object. Otherwise there would be no object. To situate in consciousness an "I"—an "I" which is, by definition, neither the object of consciousness nor consciousness itself—is to introduce a zone of darkness where lucidity is the law of existence. Such an intrusion could result only in the "congealing" of consciousness. Clearly, a consciousness thus darkened and deadened would no more be what, in fact, consciousness is and what, by right of essence, consciousness must be: absolute, translucid spontaneity. Not merely superfluous, therefore, the "I" is the death of consciousness.

But these reasonings are negative and abstract. To Sartre's mind, there is a positive and concrete warrant for expulsion of the "I" from consciousness. Anyone, he claims, who observes carefully and without prejudice the structure of prereflective consciousness must admit that primitive awareness is without an "I." [4] Take such acts as running after a streetcar, reading a newspaper, looking at a picture. In all these acts, Sartre asks, where is the "I"? It is, in truth, nowhere. There is only the streetcar-to-be-overtaken, the newspaper-to-be-read, the picture-to-be-looked-at. Plunged into a world of objects—objects endowed with attractive and repellent qualities, possessed of dangerous and intriguing possibilities—consciousness is altogether absorbed, utterly fascinated.

Sartre, of course, does not deny that, upon reflection, the "I" can be made to appear. What he denies is the relevance of such an "appearing" for a theory of consciousness. To him prereflective consciousness is primary, absolute, underived. Reflective consciousness is secondary, relative, derived. Hence, there is but one safe guide to the essential structure of consciousness: acts of prereflective awareness. Reflective awareness, precisely as derived, cannot be trusted since whatever is found in its act may have adventitious origins. That prereflective consciousness is without an egological structure is to Sartre, therefore, the decisive point, and the last word of the article on the "transcendence of the ego" is a bold proclamation of the absolutely impersonal nature of prereflective awareness: "This absolute consciousness, when it is purified of the *I*, no longer has anything of the subject." [5]

The major philosophic work of Sartre, *Being and Nothingness*, seems to reverse the judgment that prereflective awareness is impersonal: "Prereflective consciousness is self-consciousness." [6] What is more, the self of self-consciousness is "the very being of consciousness." But opposing the easy conclusion that these words reflect a radical change of mind is the fact that the Sartre of *Being and Nothingness* continues to regard a superempirical ego as a "vicious hypothesis." Whether these expressions of viewpoint are consistent or conflicting obviously depends upon the meaning of the "self" now declared to be the very being of prereflective consciousness. Obviously, too, determination of this meaning waits upon analysis of the Sartrean conception of prereflective consciousness.

Such an analysis yields comprehension, not merely of the Sartrean self, but also of Sartrean existentialism in its depth and breadth. The reason is two-fold: to analyze prereflective consciousness is, in the first place, to analyze the key concepts of this philosophy, for these key concepts—consciousness, freedom, human being—refer, in the end, to one and the same reality. To study conscious being is, in the second place, to study nonconscious being, for neither of these regions of reality—regions which, to Sartre's mind, constitute the whole of reality—can be explained apart from the other.

Why conscious and nonconscious being cannot be understood in isolation becomes clear when the peculiar relation of negation that binds them together is grasped: nonconscious being, as unmarred identity of "dumb-packed-togetherness," is pure positivity and thus resembles an unending "yes." Conscious being, as incorrigible destroyer of identity, is pure negativity and thus resembles an unending "no." Deprived of its "solid" object, the identity-shattering act of consciousness is impossible. Its "no" supposes a "yes."

This relation of negation explains, to Sartre's satisfaction at least, the knowing activity of consciousness.[7] Consciousness knows a table, for example, because it determines itself as *not* the table and the table, in turn, as *not* the rest of the world. Only because it is itself *not* the table is consciousness able to know the table. Only because it is itself *not being* is consciousness able to reveal being.

Sartre insists on this point: consciousness "is not" the being that it reveals. The problem is: what is the "is not" of consciousness?

Sartre first observes that consciousness does not coincide with itself in a full equivalence. Unlike the table which is purely and simply what it is, the believing man is not purely and simply his belief. He is not simply his belief because, and this is Sartre's second point, his belief does not exist in itself but for a "witness." What is more—and this is the third, the decisive point—the witness is not itself a being. If the witness were a positive being, consciousness would no longer be consciousness. The reason is the familiar one: an "interloper" in consciousness which would be neither the object of consciousness nor consciousness itself would undo consciousness as a mode of existence that is "pure regard of an object." Hence, to return to the example of belief, what separates belief from consciousness (of) belief must be the "pure negative." [8]

Concerning the "pure negative," Sartre makes two precisions: (1) The "pure negative" is not absolute nothingness. Because consciousness is never the "negativing" reflection of all being but of a particular being only, it is inseparable from some determinate "fact" of consciousness. In other words, what consciousness denies of itself is always some specific datum of experience: this table, this belief, etc. [9] (2) Yet it must not be imagined that consciousness is a positive being in its own right, a being standing over against the given "fact" and denying its identity with it on the basis of some prior identity with itself. Sartre never tires of repeating: The being of consciousness is *entirely* a borrowed being; it is *merely* a reflector-being. Of itself and in itself, it is "without the slightest sufficiency," a "pure privation," an "absolute lack." Whatever consciousness has of being, of solidity, of consistency, is completely on the side of its object. [10] That the unity of the object is broken and its fullness "decompressed" is entirely the result of the "negativing" act of consciousness.

At precisely the point of this "break" in being, Sartre situates the self: the self is the "nonsubstantial witness" whose regard shatters being. The self is the "fall" of being from the identity of perfect coincidence to a "deterioration of coincidence." As a deterioration of coincidence, the self is nowhere, is nothing. Consider, Sartre directs, the sentence: "He bores himself." Where is the self? What is the self? It is nowhere. It is nothing —neither subject nor predicate. Were it one or the other, the indicated relation would vanish. Hence, "the self represents an ideal distance within the immanence of the subject in relation to himself, a way of not being his own coincidence, of escaping identity." [11]

When, therefore, Sartre speaks of "self-presence" as the very being of consciousness, he means to designate a diminution of being sliding off into absence rather than a plenitude of being overflowing into presence. What prevents nonconscious reality from being perfectly itself is a certain lack of cohesion, a break in its surface, a flaw in its texture whereby it veers off toward nothingness. Precisely this nothingness is what Sartre intends by "self."

Yet "self" has another meaning for Sartre. Not only does it designate the utterly nonsubstantial "witness" rising up out of the ruined identity of nonconscious being, but it also represents an ideal value: the absolute coincidence of consciousness and its object. What consciousness is ever seeking is an ideal self comprising the attributes of conscious and nonconscious reality, i.e., a self having the permanent identity proper to nonconscious being *and* the lucidity proper to conscious being. Although this self is an ideal value, Sartre wants it clearly understood that it is not a universal abstraction. To illustrate its concrete character, he chooses the example of suffering. When anyone suffers, he suffers in the presence of a norm, namely, "suffering-in-itself." Now this norm refers to an eminently particular though hopelessly inaccessible goal: a suffering that would be full, motionless and mute, yet completely conscious.[12] What is aimed at in every here and now instance of suffering is an "in-itself" of suffering that endures like trees and rocks, that overflows and completely seizes the sufferer like a torrent, that coincides with itself at every point like some huge and solidly circular stone, but which, beyond that, is transparent with the transparency of full and perfect awareness.

That this ideal "consciousness-as-suffering-in-itself" is absolutely impossible of realization is the point to be underlined here. Consciousness is, as such, incompatible with the ideal self: As soon as the sufferer is aware of his suffering, he *is* not his suffering. He is merely "present to" it, and this is but a way of saying that he is "absent from" it. What is true of the ideal suffering-self is true of every ideal self, for identity and consciousness are contradictory attributes.[13] The ideal self is an ideal impossibility.

No more than the "witness" of immediate consciousness, then, is the self as "ideal value" a positive being. An "ideal impossibility" is as ontologically empty as "pure negativity." Whether, indeed, the traditional term "self" is appropriately applied to either is a question. In any case, it is by now clear that Sartrean ipseity does not refer to a reality in the usual sense. Moreover, it *cannot* refer to an actual entity, for Sartrean consciousness is constitutionally incapable of *being* anything. If it were something, it could not—on Sartrean premises, at least—reveal being. To reveal being through being itself a nothingness of being—here in lies the paradoxical "reality" of Sartrean consciousness.

As a phenomenologist intent upon reporting human experience, Sartre can scarcely avoid speaking of the self as if it were a reality in the ordinary sense. But this manner of speaking is clearly at odds with his ontological account of consciousness as an unrelieved nothingness of being. To the conflict between the phenomenological and ontological reports, the obscurity of Sartrean ipseity, noted by more than one commentator, may well owe its origin.[14]

What is certain, at any rate, is the thoroughly nonpositive nature of Sartrean ipseity. The self that is "the very being of consciousness" is, after all, only a "hole" in being, an "ideal absence." If, as is commonly assumed, the "I" signifies a positive entity, then Sartrean ipseity cannot but appear absurd.

Yet it is not mere arbitrariness or a will to nihilism that inspires Sartre's effort to read a self-entity out of consciousness. What he believes to be at stake is no less a good than freedom. That freedom and a self-entity cannot co-exist peacefully in his world follows from Sartre's notion of freedom and his notion of being.

THE SELF AND FREEDOM

Sartrean freedom is essentially "negativing." In his free acts the agent judges his present situation as *lacking* in certain respects and *denies* it in view of a *not-yet-existing* situation which would supply its "lacks." Presupposed to this denial is a two-fold "negativing" withdrawal: (1) The free agent steps back, as it were, from the real situation before him to constitute it as a total system and to provide "space" for its valuation, surmounting, and denial. (2) The free agent wrenches himself away from his own past; otherwise he could neither consider the situation before him as *his* situation nor deny it against the background of *his* future projection.[15]

Why this insistence on negativity? Sartre sees no other way of escape from the determinism inherent in positivity. To be remarked here is the equation of positivity and determinism: what is called the "causal series" transpires entirely on the plane of positive existents. On that plane the law is that prior positive entities or events produce posterior positive entities or events according to an order of unyielding determinism. But the causal series cannot subdue negativity, for negativity is outside its grasp. Neither the "negativing" judgment of the present as lacking nor the projecting of the not-yet-existent situation is submitted to the empire of the causal series. How can the present situation, as positive actuality, give rise to the recognition of "lacks"? As positive actuality, the present situation simply is what it is; it refers only to being and not at all to the non-being of "lacks." And how can the present situation, as present, explain the projection of a future situation? As present, it can offer only what it is; it cannot point beyond itself to a not-yet-existing situation. In sum, because the recognition of lacks and the projection of an ideal are negative effects in no way deducible from positive causes, they are free. The point of Sartre's insistence is plain: "negativing" acts are free and free acts are "negativing." [16]

Free or "negativing" acts proceed from consciousness because consciousness is ontologically nothing but a "negativing" of being. Analysis of the Sartrean meaning of self-consciousness reveals, it has been seen, no trace of a positive self-entity: consciousness is altogether on the side of the negative; denying of itself that it is being is its entire "reality." Precisely as ontological negativity, consciousness is free. Fundamental freedom and consciousness are thus ultimately indistinguishable, for they are equally a "being free of being." [17]

Clearly, being is here taken as the archenemy of freedom. It is an "engluing trap," a "snare" of freedom. If, then, one is to be free on Sartrean terms, it is only on condition of escaping the engluing grasp of being. Because human being is, as consciousness, a continuous escape from being, it is inescapably free. Human reality, precisely by virtue of its nonreality, is "condemned to be free." [18]

By the same token, a self-entity is an archenemy of freedom. In direct proportion to its positivity, it prevents the negating escape of consciousness. It "englues" the absolutely fluid spontaneity of Sartrean freedom.

Yet Sartre is aware that consciousness consistently appears as personal and that the self persuades practically all men that it is, indeed, a positive reality. To his mind, however, this state of affairs is nothing less than a "universal deception." The truth is that consciousness cannot stand the anguishing revelation of itself as absolute and, hence, as totally responsible for its choices. To distract itself from a vision of itself too dreadful to endure, consciousness constitutes the "I" as its "false representative." [19] By focusing its attention on a pseudo-reality, it masks from itself its own terrifying reality.

For Sartre, then, there can be no positive relation between freedom and a self-entity. Freedom alone is, and it is in the mode of an "is not." Self-being, if it should exist, could exist

only at the expense of freedom. But self-being is not. Whatever self-being men attribute to themselves is an illusion con-
jured up by a sick freedom unable to stand the vision of itself
as absolute. Yet, Sartre avers, if freedom is to be realized, that
vision must be endured. The fact must be faced that the "I"
is freedom's own creation, a kind of "third party" as much
outside consciousness as any objective fact of experience. Only
by renouncing the dubious comfort afforded by the self-decoy
can freedom flourish.

Freedom for the "I": Marcel's Concrete Approaches

Gabriel Marcel sees in self-being, adequately understood, not
the death but the "for" of freedom. For self-being itself includes a "for": namely, the free moral person. And its "for" is
identically the "for" of freedom: freedom exists to create the
moral person.

FREEDOM AS CREATIVE AND RECEPTIVE

Of first importance is a proper understanding of the creativity
in question. Marcel explicitly warns that it is not to be taken
as *ex nihilo* production.[20] Neither is it to be confused with
the inert submission of pure passivity. Given these negations
of the extremes, the mediating synthesis announces itself:
Properly free activity, as Marcel sees it, is at once creative and
receptive. In the free act there is always something received.
Yet the free agent does not submit to the datum in a merely
passive way. He actively assumes what he receives.

As apt analogues of the creative responsivity that is free
action, Marcel points to sensation and artistic invention. In
sensation, at least as Aristotle understood it, there is receptivity.[21] Yet the sense does not simply undergo a physiological
modification. It actively engages itself with reality in an act
that is best compared to a "welcoming" of being. More to the
point, however, is the analogy drawn from artistic invention.
Like free action, artistic invention involves the exercise of intelligence. But, in addition, the common experience of the
artist indicates an important peculiarity of free creativity:

before he creates his work, the artist cannot know what it will be. In its final form, it may well take him by surprise. Similarly, the self-creative function of the free act is most often known "after the event." [22]

Marcel links this interesting fact of "delayed recognition" to the capital point of his view of freedom: the intimate articulation of freedom and "gift." [23] Because the personal being created in freedom is, in last analysis, received from the hands of another, awareness of the relation between the creative act and self-realization is gradual. It is an "awaking in wonder." Here again Marcel opposes Sartre whose "negativing" consciousness cannot be surprised at anything. Sartre, it will be remembered, distinguishes two movements in the free act. Significantly, both are negative: a present situation is denied as "lacking," and a future situation is projected as not-yet-existing. Marcel also can be said to distinguish within the free act two movements. Significantly, both are affirmative: a gift is recognized by a free subject and is freely "welcomed" by him.

Marcel admits, however, that it is no easy matter to explain this act of recognition. What is it that prompts the subject's recognition of an "ought" as *his* "ought"? What assures him that the value which calls him by name is indissolubly bound up with *his* being? There can be no doubt, Marcel reasons, that an "exigence of being" [24] is at work in the individual, but why the individual feels himself specifically addressed by a particular value as the bearer of *his* personal being remains inexplicable.

THE PERSON AS SOURCE AND END OF FREE ACTION

One thing is certain: the recognition in question is impossible to an impersonal "one." Marcel, like Heidegger, is the foe of anonymity.[25] To the alienated man of technocracy, the faceless mass-man, it is useless to speak of engagement. There is no one to engage. Recognition of value and dedication to it suppose a subject who actively confronts, assesses, and assumes his situation.

When Marcel insists upon the personal subject as source

and end of free action, he once more opposes Sartre for whom the least trace of a personal subject is death to freedom. Not that the personal subject affirmed by Marcel is to be conceived as a "given" entity endowed with attributes and subsisting apart from, or prior to, free engagement. Rather than a "substrate" of free engagement, the person *is* free engagement. Outside free engagement—of which he is, indeed, the alpha and omega—the person does not exist.[26]

But is not Marcel moving in a circle? How can the personal subject be at once source and end of the free act? Further, if the person does not exist outside the free act, what becomes of the subsistent self which assures the fundamental identity of the developing self? Or is the person not the self? Marcel seeks to acquit himself of the charge of circularity by pointing out that free activity is an internal process of development whose point of departure is a self more or less closed in upon itself, but whose term is a self "open" to dialogue with others. Since there is here progression from lesser to greater "openness," the personal subject who initiates free activity cannot be strictly identified with the personal subject in whom this free activity terminates. To the charge that his position represents a denial of the self, Marcel replies that his refusal to hypostatize the person in no way amounts to a denial of the self. On the contrary, free action is precisely the nexus that conjoins the self to itself. That is to say, free action is like a lever whereby a self lifts itself out of the restrictive confines of the "I myself," the egotistical self of exclusivity, to the broad perspectives of the "I-thou," the "available" self of dialogue.[27]

RELATION OF THE SELF TO BEING

Implied in the self-act-person relation are two consequences of metaphysical importance: (1) In its deepest sense, free action refers to the way in which the self realizes itself. Hence, a philosophy of freedom is indissolubly bound to a philosophy of being. (2) That the self is able to create its personal moral being points to the excellence and uniqueness of its mode of being. In somewhat the same way as Sartre, impressed with the negativity of consciousness, asks: what must man be in his being that he should be the being by whom nothingness comes into the world? Marcel, impressed with the positive creativity of free engagement, asks: what must man be in his being that he should be the being by whom self-being comes into the world?

That Sartre correctly grounds free acts in a certain "non-coincidence" of human being Marcel readily admits. Man does not coincide with his being as a stone coincides with its being. What Marcel will not concede, however, is that this noncoincidence is to be interpreted solely in terms of the void. Where Sartre sees "deterioration of coincidence," hence lack of being, Marcel sees triumph over limitative determinateness, hence "superabundance of being."

Superabundance derives from this: the human self is by essence a free and conscious participant in the "being-dimension" of things. To the end of understanding better Marcel's notion of human self-being, three variations on the theme of the self's noncoincident, participative structure are here singled out for summarization: the self as immediately plunged in existence, a life-situation, self-life. With none of these—existence, life-situation, self-life—does the self coincide, for in each of them it "participates." That is to say, each of them contains innumerable possibilities of being; certain of these the self, by its free creativity, makes actual.[28]

To begin with the first of these variations, that of the self's immediate sharing in existence and its "exigence" to participate in being, is to begin with the most fundamental of the three. That Marcel here distinguishes existence and being is evident: By "existence" he intends nonconscious and nonfree reality—reality rigorously restricted to being here *or* there at *this* point in time. By "being" he understands conscious and free reality—reality able to surmount the dichotomy "here *or* there at *this* point in time." But, Marcel adds, no such clear-cut distinction between existence and being is possible where the self is concerned, for human *self-existence* is somehow inclusive of *being*. In the case of its own existence or the existences of those it loves, the self will not consent to the limitation of existing to mere "being here *or* there at *this* point in time." Its and their existences it knows as surmounting the restrictive dichotomy: to be here *or* there at *this* point in time.[29] Precisely this ambiguity of human self-existence points to the participative structure whereby the person is an existent open to being.

It is as if human self-existence were lying on a slope. To the extent that it slides downward toward the base of pure sensible existence, it is not being. To the extent that it mounts up toward the summit of conscious and free reality, it fuses with being. At exactly the moment when existence and being fuse, freedom is on the scene. Freedom is, as it were, the engine that powers existence up the slope. When the self resists, through the exercise of its liberty, the weight which drags it in the direction of things, it takes shape as authentic being.

Given this conception of the relation between existence and being, it is not difficult to disengage what is intended by the claim that the self is essentially a participator: insofar as the self is incarnated, it is immerged in sensible reality. It participates "existence." Insofar as the self is incarnated spirit, it is open to the "exigence of being" that comes to it from within its existential situation, but which transcends infinitely the impersonal or spatio-temporal level of reality. Vermeer's "View of Delft" or Beethoven's "Thirteenth Quartet" can be thought of only as responses to such an exigence. But responses may be far less spectacular. Whenever, in fact, the self answers creatively the exigence of being, it transmutes existence into being. It lifts itself, by an exercise of freedom, from existential to ontological participation.

Taking a different viewpoint toward the self, Marcel analyzes its noncoincidence in terms of being and life. Just as the self is and is not its existence, so it is and is not its life. Regarded either in its pastness or its presentness, its life never adequately represents it.[30] By virtue of the aspirations and potentialities of its spiritual being the self is always beyond the present consciousness that it has of itself. But that the self is more than its life hardly allows the conclusion: therefore, the self is not its life. On the contrary, the self experiences its life as more fully its own in proportion as it narrows the gap between its being and its life. This it does by answering creatively, that is to say, freely, the "exigence" of being rising up out of its own situation.

Emphasis upon the *situation* as an indispensable means to, and inexhaustible mine of, personal development is a singular merit of the being-life variation. Here Marcel makes two important precisions. (1) Within its particular situation and never apart from it, the self finds the ordeal or "test" which its free activity transforms into being. This necessity of non-abstraction from its situation derives directly from the self's embodiedness.[31] Because the self is essentially an *incarnated* existent, it is submitted to the "exigence of incarnation": it must express its self-creation in and through the concrete modalities proffered by its situation. (2) Within the inexhaustible depths of an ingathered [32] self-in-situation, freedom enables a creative recognition constitutive of the new self whose emergence represents, in a sense, the creation of a new being.[33] To be underlined here is the word "inexhaustible." No self ever fully realizes the possibilities of its situation, for at its base is a bottomless depth of potentiality and inspiration and at its summit is an infinite actuality of being. From this it follows that any crystallization of the self in particular incarnations arrests self-actualization. Marcel therefore complements the "exigence of incarnation" with an "exigence of transcendence": the self must base its creative activity on a received nature and order it to a transcendent end. Experienced at first as dissatisfaction with a present self, the "exigence of transcendence" urges the self to realization at ever deeper and purer levels of experience.

Reference to varying levels of experience suggests the third variation on the theme of noncoincidence: the diversity-in-unity of self-being. That self-existence is susceptible of multiple "tonalities" is a fact experienced by every reflective person. Marcel prefers to call these fluctuating self-modalities "existential modulations." [34] Although existential modulations are innumerably varied, they can be divided into two broad categories according as they refer to superficial or profound levels of self-existence. Insofar as this formulation of "superficial" and "profound" refers back to preceding variations, it is readily seen that the superficial self belongs on the side of existence and life, whereas the profound self belongs on the side of being. Insofar as this formulation represents a variation of theme, however, it adds a new note: Marcel assimilates the superficial self to the category of "having" and the profound self to the category of "being." [35] Hence, freedom's task here becomes the transmuting of having into being.

In possessive having Marcel observes a curious dialectic: to the extent that the haver occupies inertly the "space" that lies between his possessions and their utilization, to that extent do his possessions succeed in "having" him. Obviously effective at the level of material objects—one has only to think of the miser and his gold—this boomerang action is subtly operative at deeper levels of reality. Thoughts and opinions petrify and become dead weights upon the shoulders of the one who "has" his opinions in a passively possessive way. Freedom turns against itself when it is centered on the pseudo-ideal of self-management. Life is no more life when it is given over to the goal of an autonomous "having" of life. Whoever would save his life does indeed lose it.

But the dialectic of having is not determined in one direction. To the extent that the haver occupies creatively the interval between his possessions and their utilization, to that extent do his possessions promote the cause of self-being. Thoughts and opinions that are continually put to the test, freedom that engages in liberating communion with others, life that knows itself as a gift for sharing—these translate the self from superficial levels of existence to profound ontological depths where it freely and consciously affirms itself as being.

No longer dominated by the fluctuations of shallow modalities, this free self is *compos sui*. To be *compos sui* is to be oneself. Neither internal nor external forms of alienation can get a grip on the one who is truly at one with himself. Implied here is a kind of interior plenitude. Freedom is achieved on the plane of *super*determination rather than *in*determination. When the free person acts, he has not fewer but more reasons for acting. Of these he disposes with a certain ease and mastery, for he is in fundamental accord with himself and hence able to recognize the reasons that are *his*. Not that anyone ever fully achieves this inner order. As Marcel aptly remarks, the free person is *sursum*, not *sum*.[36] Yet, granted that everyone is "on the road" (*viator*) with respect to its fulfillment, free action intends nothing less than this personal self whose ordination to being is freely assumed and consciously realized.

Upon consideration of the self's noncoincidence from the viewpoints of existence and being, being and life, and varying self-modulations, the "for" of Marcellian freedom comes into the clear. In every case, the self appears as initially immerged in a locus large with innumerable possibilities of being: existence, life, and diverse self-modalities. From out of these there arises an "exigence": the self is urged to *be* being through creative response to values latent in existence, life, and the varied tonalities of self-existence. Whenever the self does so respond in free and effective engagement, it transmutes existence into being. Through its freedom which is at the "juncture" of existence and being, within the "interval" of being and life, and in the "space" between being and having, the self translates itself from existential to ontological participation, from life to being, from superficial to profound levels of personal subjectivity. Despite the diversity of formulation, the underlying theme is one: from an *immergent* participation, that is, a non-free and nonconscious sharing in being, the self is called to an *emergent* participation, that is, a free and conscious sharing in being.

Unlike Sartrean freedom, then, Marcellian freedom is far from being a "lonely god": it is not "outside" being but within it, not a "negativing" of being but an affirmative "welcoming" of it, not a supreme value *in se* whose sovereignty demands the sacrifice of self-reality but a means to it whose precise function is the promotion of self-reality. Yet it would be misleading to draw too heavy a line under these antitheses. Opposition is relieved by agreement at certain critical points: although Marcellian freedom does subserve the vocation of the self as "participator," it does not thereby become subservient. No more than Sartre does Marcel reduce freedom to a mere "means to." With good reason it can be said that the "for" of Marcellian freedom is, in the end, nothing other than freedom. Is not the moral person a self who lives, moves, and has his being in freedom? Again, no less than Sartre does Marcel reject a "self-thing." His "exigence of transcendence" is a protest against that "congealing" of consciousness which Sartre so rightly abhors.[37]

But the primary aim of this essay is neither to enumerate antitheses nor to discover harmonies in the attitudes of these existentialists toward freedom and the "I." Still less, it may be noted parenthetically, is a critique of their attitudes a prime objective. What is intended here is much less ambitious than either design, though not, perhaps, less interesting: namely, inquiry into these attitudes for fresh perspectives on the freedom-self relation.

The Freedom-Self Relation: New Perspectives

To order the inquiry, this tripartite question is posed: what valid new modes, if any, of conceiving the self, freedom, and the freedom-self relation emerge from the existential analyses of Sartre and Marcel? Since each "part"—self, freedom, the freedom-self relation—raises a fairly distinctive question, each requires a somewhat independent treatment. That these "treatments" are presented as introductory indications and not at all as exhaustive penetrations goes without saying.

Very little positive illumination of self-being seems offered by the Sartrean account of the "I." If the self is, as the Sartre of the "Transcendental Ego" essay claims, only a "universal deception," then it would appear that, once denounced as a fiction, it need never be thought of or spoken of again. Or, if the self is, as the Sartre of *Being and Nothingness* insists, so "pure" a negative that it is an "absolute lack" without the "slightest sufficiency," then it would appear that, deprived even of the possibility of being denounced, it need never be thought of or spoken of at all.

But what if the self be proved neither a universal deception nor a pure negative? In that case, the very failure of the Sartrean theses may be positively instructive. What Gilbert Varet observes of the attempted phenomenological ontology of Sartre could then be said also of his attempted demolition of the egological structure, namely, that its greatest merit is precisely its failure.[38]

That Sartre does fail to maintain his theses on self-being is rather easily shown. Let it be supposed that the self is a deception projected by consciousness for the sake of masking from itself its own absolute freedom. One need not be especially acute to observe that there is here presupposed a unity of design, i.e., the masking of freedom, which is inexplicable apart from some kind of self-being. Again, let it be granted that the self of self-consciousness borrows its *entire* reality and *all* its sufficiency from the datum of which it is, indeed, nothing but the "negativing" reflection. How, then, explain the real efficiency evidently implied in the "negativing withdrawal" of free activity? On Sartrean premises the datum is nothing but "dumb-packed-togetherness." It simply is what it is and cannot point beyond itself either to "lacks" or a "not-yet-existing" situation. What, then, is to account for the positive acts of withdrawing, evaluating, recognizing lacks, projecting an ideal situation wherein these lacks are supplied? The fact is that freedom as "negativing withdrawal" entails a series of positive acts which imply, even demand, an egological structure. Unless withdrawal is conceived as a condition attending the realization of the self's free initiative, it is meaningless and becomes, in the end, indistinguishable from passive acceptance of every datum—including withdrawal itself. Only as the expression of a self attending and choosing does the Sartrean notion of freedom as "negativing withdrawal" make philosophical sense.

What Sartre is in theory ever denying, however, he is in practice always affirming: a "finitized" consciousness cognizant of its finitude—what more is required for personal being? A consciousness aware of its continuing identity in time—does it not suppose the unifying "center" proper to personal being? A consciousness existing as present to itself—is this consciousness anything other than self-being? Despite a clever exploitation of language and a masterful handling of phenomenological technique, the inconsistency is observable and it is instructive. Unable to demolish the egological structure without, at the same time, implying an egological structure, Sartre unwittingly but helpfully raises the question: is this inability due to the fact that some sort of self-being inescapably belongs to human consciousness?

But what does it mean to say that self-being "belongs" to consciousness? Certainly it cannot mean that the self is something "had" by consciousness. Sartre is surely a thousand times right when he insists that "consciousness does not possess an ego." A self-thing introduced into consciousness could have no other effect than the "undoing" of consciousness. For establishing the mutual exclusivity of consciousness and a self-object there is hardly a more effective argument than that developed in the essay on the "Transcendence of the Ego." Here again the negative intention of Sartre yields a positive gain in comprehension.

Yet might it be that the self is not that which consciousness *has* because the self is that which consciousness *is*? Sartre, of course, cannot entertain this possibility. Having acclaimed thing-being the paradigm of being, he is compelled to situate consciousness outside being. The least degree of positivity in consciousness would suffice to shatter the aims of his ontology. Hence, also, he is obliged to confine his analysis to the level of prereflective consciousness where the egological structure does not "appear." Within the framework of his ontology, consciousness cannot be self-being for the reason that it cannot *be* anything at all.[39]

Fortunately, Marcel's world of being is not circumscribed by an initial equation of being and thing-being. Not all beings in Marcel's world of being must be object of having. He is therefore free to entertain the possibility that self-being *is* the being of consciousness and that, conversely, the being of consciousness *is* self-being. But Marcel does more than entertain the possibility. By his incisive analysis of having and being, he opens an approach to self-existence that holds much promise.

If the contribution of Marcel to the knowledge of self-being is to be appreciated, however, the difficulty of knowing self-being needs to be underscored: to say that the fundamental self cannot be an object of having is to say that no "objective" knowledge can be had of it. The fundamental "I" is not the empirical ego, Sartre's "ideal unity of psychic states," which can be placed before the "mind's eye." The fundamental "I" *is* the "mind's eye," the "last spectator," which cannot itself be "observed." [40] At this point the world of difference that separates the thinking "I" and the "I" that is thought—the "I-source" and the "I-object"—begins to emerge. It is a world of difference which the *cogito* of Descartes leaves unremarked, and which, remaining unremarked, begets the worst confusions.

In elaborating the opposition between having and being, Marcel is implicitly pointing up this world of difference between the I-object and I-source. What is "had"—in this case, the I-object—manifests these distinguishing characteristics: (1) it exists, to some extent at least, independently of the I-source; (2) it exhibits with respect to the I-source a certain exteriority and foreignness; (3) it is assimilable to things; (4) it is, in principle, disposable; (5) it is, in principle, transferable. Conversely, what is not "had"—in this case, the I-source—does not exist independently, exhibits no exteriority or foreignness, cannot be assimilated to things, and is in no sense either disposable or transferable. Admittedly, these are negative precisions, but they yield positive insight into a reality that cannot be approached "objectively."

On this difficult matter of the nonobjective approach to self-being, Marcel likewise projects new light. Since what one *is*, by virtue of its non-exteriority, cannot be placed before the mind's eye, its grasping requires a unique type of reflection. Marcel calls it "second reflection" and describes it as "ingatheredness": ingatheredness means that self and being are "welcomed" *together* from within, not set "outside" one another.[41] Whereas "objective" knowledge abstracts from the subject-source, second reflection includes the subject-source. But this inclusion, precisely by reason of the subject's nonobjective character, can be effected only indirectly: here, as the poet says, the "side glance" is "craftiest to detect." [42]

To be sure, the analysis of having and being and the introduction of second reflection are merely openings—perhaps, in the long run, but tiny apertures. Yet through them the light falls in a new way and a fresh perspective results: self-being emerges as "subjectivity."

Not that emergence of the self-as-subjectivity is here posited as an absolute novelty. To claim that subjectivity—the I-source —was unknown to the ancients would be rash indeed. When it is asserted that self-as-subjectivity is emerging, it is meant simply that, for the first time, it is assuming a center-stage position. For the first time, self-as-subjectivity is becoming a focal point of attention and exploration on its own merits and on its own terms.

This emergence of self-as-subjectivity promises at least two significant gains: (1) for the most fundamental of human knowledges, metaphysics, the gain is a widened scope and a deepened penetration. Being is subject as well as object. Whatever the difficulties posed by its elusiveness—difficulties by no means minimal—an adequate philosophy of being is obliged to include subject-being.[43] But the subject is not only *a* mode of being. It is a *privileged* mode of being. As the "there" of being, it is the *sine qua non* of object being's "appearing." To grasp object-being in the ground of its "appearing" is to penetrate it at the deep point of its original upsurge. Hence, subjectivity proffers new depth as well as new breadth to metaphysical knowledge. (2) For the social sciences, the gain is nothing less than their humanization. Self-being is central, not peripheral, to human being. Insight achieved with respect to self-being illumines human being precisely as *human*. That the social sciences are in dire need of this humanization is recognized by not a few among the social scientists themselves who, lamenting the failure of mechanical models, are openly raising the self-question.[44] If their questioning results in discovery of the self within the perspective of subjectivity, then a decisive step will have been taken toward successfully weathering the present crisis in the sciences of man.

To discover the self within the perspective of subjectivity is to discover "fundamental freedom." Freedom, seen as fundamental, is cast in a new light. And this change of perspective, as in the case of self-being, merits attention.

But what claim has fundamental freedom to novelty? After all, when it is said that human being is fundamentally free, what is meant if not that man is naturally free? And has not traditional philosophy said the same thing many times over? Has it not consistently maintained that man is a being naturally endowed with the power or faculty of free decision?

Marcel's difficulty with the view of freedom as "attribute" or "faculty" serves two purposes here: it indicates the *fact* of the difference and something of the *nature* of the difference between the traditional view of freedom as faculty and the existential view of freedom as fundamental. In essence, his objection to the notion of freedom as faculty comes to this: it risks assimilating freedom to something "had." Assimilation of freedom to an object of having entails disastrous consequences: (1) it supposes a separation or interval between the possessor-substance and the "had" attribute; (2) it "thingifies" the possessor-substance by conceiving it as an entity "already-made" to which the attribute is attached; (3) it favors the fragmentation of man, i.e., his division among diverse faculties or powers. Yet, Marcel is aware of the danger that inheres in the denial of freedom as faculty. If freedom is not possessed by man then does it not become a power "outside" him—a power whose presence or absence is now largely a matter of caprice? How escape this "ruinous dilemma"? Marcel takes refuge in a distinction that has become classic: the distinction of mystery and problem. Like the being of man, freedom is mystery and, as mystery, surpasses the subject-object dichotomy. Unlike the problem, it is not merely *before* man but *within* him. It is, in fact, man himself: the freedom which is specific to the human mode of being, the ability of self-determination, is *identical* with the human mode of being. To be free in the fundamental sense is to be human, and to be human is to be fundamentally free.[45]

Sartre, too, identifies human reality and fundamental freedom when he describes consciousness as an "original choice."[46] By its very rising up in the midst of being, consciousness carves out a "world." That is, it "chooses" or "selects" aspects of being in terms of the end-projecting upsurge which, as consciousness, it *is*. Concerning the "original choice" or "end-projecting upsurge" which defines the very being of consciousness, Sartre makes these precisions: (1) it causes, not the *being* of being, but the *meaning* of being. Although it is true, therefore, to say that consciousness in its emerging causes the "there is" of the world, it cannot be concluded that consciousness thereby *creates* the world. (2) Its "choice" of the world is neither deliberated nor instinctive. Here Sartre utilizes to advantage his distinction of prereflexive and reflexive consciousness. The "original choice," rigorously identical with prereflexive consciousness, is consciously though not explicitly posited. As a kind of spontaneous *Weltanschauung*, it "solves" without reflective labor the individual's "problem of being." Given these precisions, it becomes clear that human being is inescapably choice of being. Or, put more pointedly, human being exists as choice of being.[47]

Sharp and vigorous, the Sartrean formulation of fundamental freedom has the merit of pointing up unmistakably the significance of the new perspective: namely, illumination of the human mode as *radically* free. Of course, it can be argued that the equivalence of freedom and the human mode of being is by no means an absolutely new discovery. So much is easily granted. What must also be granted, however, is that long habits of meticulously defining and classifying human powers have considerably dulled, if they have not deadened, appreciation of this equivalence. These habits have bequeathed the conception of freedom as something that subsists apart, an entity that is "strong" or "weak," an arbiter that enters on the scene only after reason has pleaded its case. As designedly correcting the illusory simplicity of neat definitions and precise diagrams of interacting powers, the perspective of fundamental freedom reflects a new dimension of depth.

But fundamental freedom is by no means the whole of freedom. To the attentive eye, this perspective reveals human being not only as radically free but as radically incomplete. Being fundamentally free means nothing else, in fact, than existing as "unfinished," as "not-already-made," as "open" to fulfillment. Hence, the perspective "fundamental freedom" refers beyond itself to the perspective "freedom-as-self-achievement."

It is in Marcel's account that freedom-as-achievement takes the foreground. Fundamental freedom is "for" the creation of the moral person. And, since the moral person is pre-eminently free, freedom here suffers no indignity. It is as much "for itself" as it is "for another": fundamental freedom is "for" freedom-as-achievement.

Sartre, too, envisions freedom-as-achievement. In this he is happily inconsistent. Having officially rejected a positive self-reality, he is logically left with no reality to achieve. Having initially equated fundamental freedom with the whole of freedom, he is logically forced to the dead-end conclusion: "In relation to freedom there is no privileged psychic phenomenon. All my modes of being manifest freedom equally." [48] But, impervious to logical canons, Sartre does not hesitate to distinguish "freedom-as-fact" and "freedom-as-value." Freedom-as-fact is equivalent to fundamental freedom and refers to human being as inescapably free by virtue of its negativity. Sartre likes to describe this fundamental freedom paradoxically: to be man is "to be what one is not and not to be what one is." [49] Freedom-as-value is equivalent to freedom-as-achievement and refers to the deliberate assumption and resolute living out of fundamental freedom: to be what one is not is to live engaged, committed to freedom for all; not to be what one is is to maintain the mastery over every enterprise, to be ever fluid and creative.

Endorsement of the Sartrean notion of achievement is not, of course, the point of these remarks. Sartrean achievement is hardly a fish without bones. However, these remarks intend the endorsement of no particular notion of achievement. What they intend concerns rather the achievement-perspective itself: its freshness and its promise.

Emphasis upon freedom as achieving personal being represents a decided shift of viewpoint and brings to light new possibilities of understanding.[50] Traditional philosophy, confronted by the scandal of an apparent breach in the causal order, directed its efforts toward reintegrating free action into the ordered realm of natures and necessity.[51] Nor is the fact of its concern inexplicable. If the free act's defiance of causal order were real, then one of the pillar-principles of this philosophic speculation would collapse. In grappling with the problem posed by the free act as "objective fact," therefore, traditional philosophy reveals an admirable sensitivity to essential issues and an enviable fearlessness in face of a seemingly unresolvable antinomy. But to understand the concern of traditional philosophy with freedom as objective fact is not to deny that its concern permitted freedom as subjective fulfillment to remain in the shade. To have brought this inner intelligibility of freedom—its ordination to the creation of the personal subject—out of the shade and into the light is precisely the merit of freedom-as-achievement.

As achieving subjectivity or effecting liberation, freedom is active. When existentialists envision freedom as "actualizing" or "liberating," they perforce envision it as dynamic. That both Marcel and Sartre direct their attention to freedom-as-dynamism is, therefore, nothing remarkable. What is remarkable is that they view free dynamics from standpoints diametrically opposed and, in so doing, illumine most helpfully both phases of the dialectic of freedom.

By taking the side of affirmation, Marcel points up the "yes" moment of free activity: freedom exists to affirm being and, through its affirmation, to "participate" it. Presupposed to its "yes," moreover, is an initial and positive overture on the part of being: being first offers itself to freedom as gift. From the first, being has a "hold" on freedom. By virtue of the positive hold of being upon it, freedom experiences the "exigence of being." If it answers affirmatively this exigence in creative fidelity, hope, and love, it conjoins the self not to being merely but to Absolute Being.

Mention of fidelity, hope, and love suggests the intersubjective setting of Marcellian affirmation.[52] The being to which freedom says its "yes" is pre-eminently personal. Ultimately, in fact, it is none other than the Absolute Thou. Fundament of every vow of fidelity, source of every spring of hope, attraction of every *élan* of love, the Absolute Thou works unceasingly in the obscure and deep places of human freedom. He it is who prepares the encounter of freedom and freedom, who waits in the windings and at the turnings of human relationships and who, in the ripening of these relationships, reveals himself as their ground and end.

But intersubjective affirmation, though the first and fundamental moment in the dialectical advance of human freedom, by no means suffices. Advance means surpassing, and surpassing means negation. To allow no "engluing" or ensnaring of human freedom, but to maintain its spontaneous and fluid mastery—this is the function of negativity. The Sartrean perspective of "negativing withdrawal" highlights it well.

Superbly well also does the Sartrean perspective reveal the blocking of freedom by pseudo types of intersubjectivity. For there are degraded forms of human relationships whose effects are exactly opposed to the liberating effects of authentic intersubjective communion. Submitted to the hostile stare of the Other, freedom is "frozen," its fluid spontaneity "thingified," its self-awareness darkened.[53] Conquered, whether by seduction or force, freedom disappears in the aggressor and only the shell of self-being remains. In the dialectical advance of freedom, therefore, stern refusal of enslaving modes of interpersonal attachment is not less important than loving acceptance of liberating modes of interpersonal communion.

Precisely as focusing upon affirmative and negative aspects of free action, the Marcellian and Sartrean perspectives complement each other in a quite remarkable way.[54] Taken together, they allow a by no means negligible advance in the understanding of freedom as dialectically creative of self-being. To advance toward freedom as self-creative is to approach both self and freedom in their inner intelligibility, for freedom and self are not independent entities: the self *is* self to the extent that, by virtue of the freedom which it fundamentally is, it lifts itself to higher and higher reaches of personal being. Viewed apart from the relation constitutive of them, neither self nor freedom is seen truly. Its freedom-dimension obscured, self-being is liable to all sorts of distortions—not the least of which is the "homunculus" so rightly derided by psychologists. Its self-creative function ignored, freedom is likewise liable to perversions—not the least of which is the Sartrean "caricature of aseity" so justly denounced by Marcel.[55]

For the same reason, i.e., the relational character of self and freedom, the perspectives of self-as-subjectivity and fundamental freedom require the comprehensive setting: freedom as dialectical progression toward self-achievement. For the self-as-subject is at once fundamental freedom and creative freedom. And creative freedom is at once grounded in fundamental freedom and pointed toward the subject as free moral person. Nor is the subject as free moral person other, in the end, than creative freedom rising up out of fundamental freedom. Yet, to acknowledge these "convergings" is not to assert the merging of all perspectives. True, the reality is one. Nevertheless, the perspectives must emerge and "play" successively, for this one reality is also multiform.

So complex a unity is it, in fact, that it lends itself to innumerable points of view. Those suggested by the Marcellian and Sartrean analyses—subjectivity, fundamental freedom, freedom as dialectical tending toward self-achievement—scarcely represent an exhaustive enumeration of possible perspectives. Neither are they, as presented here, exhaustive penetrations. It is by now only too obvious that they are, as remarked at the outset, "introductory anticipations." As such, they are hardly more than invitational.

But they are invitations of more than passing interest. It may even be that acceptance or rejection of them is decisively important. That man, possessed now of the power of planetary destruction, should come to see something more of himself as subject and something more of himself as freedom may, in the end, make all the difference.

NOTES

1. "La transcendance de l'égo: Esquisse d'une description phénoménologique," *Recherches philosophiques*, VI (1936–37). English translation: *The Transcendence of the Ego*, trans. Forrest Williams and Robert Kirkpatrick, New York: The Noonday Press, 1957).

2. *Being and Nothingness: An Essay on Phenomenological Ontology*, trans. Hazel Barnes (New York: Philosophical Library, 1956), p. 76.

3. *Transcendence of the Ego*, pp. 37–42.

4. *Ibid.*, pp. 45–49.

5. *Ibid.*, p. 106.

6. *Being and Nothingness*, p. 76.

7. *Ibid.*, pp. 24, 67, 175–176.

8. *Ibid.*, pp. 74–75. Sartre encloses the "of" in parentheses in order to indicate that the preposition satisfies only a grammatical requirement and is really incompatible with the unity of consciousness and its object.

9. *Ibid.*, pp. 618, 630.

10. *Ibid.*, pp. 77–79, 84.

11. *Ibid.*, p. 77.

12. *Ibid.*, pp. 91–94, 566.

13. *Ibid.*, p. 615.

14. Alfonse de Waelhens suggests that the fundamental difficulty of Sartrean existentialism is the conflict between the phenomenological report and the ontological framework: *Une philosophie de l'ambiguité: L'existentialisme de Maurice Merleau-Ponty* (Louvain: Publications Universitaires de Louvain, 1951), pp. 2–3. Similarly, Gilbert Varet locates the basic weakness of Sartre's philosophy in the failure to distinguish intentionality as methodological principle and intentionality as ontological thesis: *L'ontologie de Sartre* (Paris: Presses Universitaires de France, 1948), p. 158. Some commentators who have remarked the unsatisfactoriness of Sartrean ipseity are: Jean Hyppolite, "La Liberté chez J.-P. Sartre," *Mercure de France*, 312 (1951), 397; Wilfred Desan, *The Tragic Finale: An Essay on the Philosophy of Jean-Paul Sartre* (Cambridge, Mass.: Harvard University Press, 1954), p. 150; Gilbert Varet, *op. cit.*, pp. 84, 137, 139–140, 158–159, 160–162.

15. *Being and Nothingness*, pp. 443–447.

16. *Ibid.*, p. 435.

17. *Ibid.*, p. 437. It should be noted that Sartre distinguishes, implicitly at least, between a fundamental freedom that is the *fact* of man's being and an acquired freedom that is the *liberation* of his being. The latter freedom is achieved in the act of assuming

fundamental freedom as supreme value. Francis Jeanson, a disciple of Sartre, makes the distinction explicit: *Le problème moral et la pensée de Sartre* (Paris: Editions du Myrte, 1947), pp. 294, 308.

18. The ultimate grimness of Sartrean freedom is, perhaps, best expressed by Mathieu, philosopher-hero of Sartre's novel, *Le sursis* (Paris: Gallimard, 1945), p. 285. Upon discovering his freedom, Mathieu says: "Dehors. Dehors, hors du monde, hors du passé, hors de moi-même: la liberté c'est exil et je suis condamné à être libre."

19. *Transcendence of the Ego*, pp. 100–101.

20. Marcel often inveighs against the absolute creativity of Sartrism. His critique reduces to three points: (1) Man experiences himself, not as creating values absolutely, but as *recognizing* them. (2) Sartre himself cannot consistently maintain his thesis for, when he is not consciously theorizing, he invokes certain values as inherently desirable, e.g., courage and truth. (3) If, *per impossible*, absolute creativity were a fact, then freedom as a properly human perfection would disappear and in its stead there would reign a mere "anarchical disposition." *Les grands appels de l'homme contemporain* (Paris: Editions du temps présent, 1947), pp. 160–167.

21. The Aristotelian account of sensation is, to Marcel's mind, in accord with human experience, whereas the Kantian account is not. Kant, it is true, did see the necessity of a datum, but he assumed too hastily that any receptivity of the datum must be detrimental to the subject's spontaneity. *Le mystère de l'être* (Paris: Aubier, 1951), I, 134–135.

22. *Ibid.*, II, 118.

23. *L'homme problématique* (Paris: Aubier, 1955), pp. 68, 71.

24. The expression "exigence of being" refers to a basic point of Marcel's philosophy. It receives various formulations: it is the "presentiment" or "forefeeling" that guides the concrete approaches to being, the "blinded intuition" that sustains philosophic reflection, an "appeal" or "call" of being, an "exigence of transcendence." In the chapter, "L'exigence de transcendance," *Le mystère de l'être*, I, 47–66, Marcel comes closest to specifying its meaning: the exigence is experienced as dissatisfaction and as an urge for "vertical" transcendence. That is, the satisfaction of this exigence does not lie in things outside the self, objects of what Marcel calls "horizontal" transcendence, but in an inner enrichment of the self. Thus, the exigence of being arises out of the depths of the self and seems to be a presentiment or forefeeling of, an appeal or call for, the fullness of selfhood.

25. Marcel himself suggests the comparison: *ibid.*, II, 9. For a more extended discussion of the anonymous "one" and its opposition to the person, see: *Du refus à l'invocation* (Paris: Gallimard, 1940), pp. 146–150.

26. *Ibid.*, pp. 151–157.

27. These precisions were made in a letter to the writer: April 18, 1959.

28. Because Marcel's work is exceedingly diffuse, the writer invented this synthesis of variations to serve as a kind of "conducting thread" for his reflections on the self-structure. It is submitted with some assurance, however, since Marcel has expressed to the writer his approval of the arrangement.

29. *Le mystère de l'être*, II, 29–30.

30. *Ibid.*, I, 163–185. In this chapter, titled "Ma vie," Marcel develops at length what is merely indicated here.

31. Marcel opposes strenuously an intellectualism that disdains the empirical situation as only incidental to the self's "true being" of "pure reason." *Ibid.*, pp. 146–147.

32. "Ingatheredness" refers to a special type of reflection which Marcel sometimes calls "recollection" but more often calls "second reflection." Unlike "first reflection," which is a directing of the mind outward toward objects of scientific knowledge in disregard of personal experience, "second reflection" is a regrasping of the self and an easing of the mind through a free consent to being that is not only *before* the self but *within* the self: *Man Against Mass Society*, trans. G. S. Fraser (Chicago: Regnery, 1952), pp. 68–69.

33. The self-creation in question here evidently refers to man's development as a moral being and not to an auto-creation of the self's substantial being.

34. *Le mystère de l'être*, I, 145–146.

35. Being and having are important and recurring themes in Marcel's meditations. What is here summarized is developed in his essay, "Esquisse d'une phénoménologie de l'avoir," *Etre et Avoir* (Paris: Aubier, 1935), pp. 223–255.

36. *Homo viator* (Paris: Aubier, 1944), p. 32. Marcel confronts the difficult problem of the human person's metaphysical status at greater length in the chapter, "Remarques sur l'acte et la personne," *Du refus à l'invocation*, pp. 139–157.

37. "Ce que j'ai voulu dire, c'est simplement que la personne ne se réalise que dans l'acte par lequel elle tend à s'incarner (dans une œuvre, dans une action, dans l'ensemble d'une vie), mais qu'en même temps il est de son essence de ne jamais se figer ou se cristalliser définitivement dans cette incarnation particulière. Pourquoi? Parce qu'elle participe de la plénitude inépuisable de l'être d'où elle émane." *Homo viator*, p. 32.

38. *Op. cit.*, p. 3.

39. Sartre, *Being and Nothingness*, pp. 118–119. That Sartrean consciousness cannot *be* anything derives from its very being which

"has to be always beyond that which it is." Sartre suggests that, from this point of view, a more appropriate formulation of the *cogito* might be: "I think; therefore, I was."

40. "No matter what I think, represent to myself, or imagine, I will always be this unique individual existence which is 'there,' together with the represented, thought, or imagined object, as the one to whom these objects 'appear.' Whether I think of the origin of the terrestrial globe or the air traffic in the year 2000, I am always 'there with it' as the singular ego. Somehow I am present, not as a person called by this or that name, who is a father of a family and a citizen of this state. I am present neither as a personal nor as a social ego, but as the anonymous and primordial ontological center, i.e., as the subject which faces the different objects, and quasi-objects in an objective or quasi-objective way. . . . The 'last spectator' necessarily escapes from every kind of 'world nihilation.' " Stephan Strasser, *The Soul in Metaphysical and Empirical Psychology* (Pittsburgh: Duquesne University Press, 1957), p. 105.

41. Ingatheredness is "essentiellement l'acte par lequel je me ressaisis comme unité: le mot même l'indique, mais ce ressaisissement, cette reprise affecte l'aspect d'une détente, d'un abandon. *Abandon à . . . détente en présence de . . .* sans qu'il me soit en aucune façon possible de faire suivre ces prepositions d'un substantif qu'elles commanderaient." Marcel, *Position et Approches Concrètes du Mystère Ontologique* (Paris: J. Vrin, 1949), p. 63.

42. Rosamond Haas, "The Listener," *This Time This Tide* (New York: E. P. Dutton, 1950), p. 37.

43. Robert O. Johann, S. J., makes this point: "Subjectivity," *The Review of Metaphysics*, 12 (1958), 290.

44. Thus Gordon Allport writes: "Up to now the 'behavioral sciences,' including psychology, have not provided us with a picture of man capable of creating or living in a democracy. These sciences have in large part imitated the billiard ball model of physics, now of course outmoded. They have delivered into our hands a psychology of an 'empty organism,' pushed by drives and moulded by circumstance." *Becoming* (New Haven: Yale University Press, 1955), p. 100.

45. *Du refus à l'invocation*, pp. 152–157.

46. *Being and Nothingness*, p. 439. "It [freedom] is not a quality added on or a property of my nature. It is very exactly the stuff of my being."

47. *Ibid.*, p. 444.

48. *Ibid.*, p. 445.

49. *Ibid.*, p. 67.

50. The pointing up of this perspective is to be credited to Robert O. Johann, *op. cit.*, pp. 200–234.

51. Quite understandably, therefore, traditional philosophical psychology is bent upon showing that free action is the expression of a tendency to *bonum in genere*, and traditional natural theology is bent upon assuring the peaceful coexistence of human spontaneity and divine causality: Johann, *op. cit.*, pp. 228–229. It is true that these efforts leave something to be desired; Paul Ricœur, for example, notes certain difficulties raised by the notion of "will as nature": *Philosophie de la volonté: Le volontaire et l'involontaire* (Paris: Aubier, 1949), pp. 180–186. But it is also true that no solution of a philosophical problem leaves nothing to be desired.

52. Intersubjectivity is the dominant theme of Marcel's philosophy. The interested reader is referred to his incisive analyses of these intersubjective phenomena in particular: fidelity (*Du refus à l'invocation*, pp. 192–225) and hope (*Homo viator*, pp. 39–91).

53. Sartre write a luminous, though somewhat depressing, page on the Other as threat to freedom: *Being and Nothingness*, pp. 252–302. The Other as liberating Thou seems not to appear to his phenomenological eye, however. The two forms of conjunction which he does describe—the "us-object" and the "we-subject"—are hardly positive. In the former case, two or more conflicting consciousnesses feel themselves collectivized by the petrifying gaze of a third man who despises them. In the latter case, two or more conciousnesses arrive at a highly dubious, essentially unstable, group-feeling by reason of certain superficial types of sharing: using, for example, the same staircase, corridor, or subway.

54. It cannot be said that Marcel stresses affirmation to the point of excluding negation in the way that Sartre stresses negation to the point of excluding affirmation. The "exigence of transcendence" referred to above indicates appreciation of the negative "moment" in free action. Moreover, Marcel explicitly recognizes the need to include in an account of freedom the note of distance as well as presence, of negation as well as affirmation: *L'homme problématique*, p. 66; "L'existence et la liberté humaine," pp. 158–159. But he does not emphasize negativity. Temperamentally, it seems, he is little inclined to such emphasis.

55. To make of freedom a supreme value—an end in itself—is to make of it a "caricature of aseity": "L'existence et la liberté humaine," p. 162.

PART IV / PERSPECTIVES
OF NEO-TRADITIONAL THOUGHT

Dietrich Bonhoeffer / Responsibility

and Freedom

Initial Considerations

RARELY HAS ANY generation shown so little interest as ours
does in any kind of theoretical or systematic ethics. The academic question of a system of ethics seems to be of all questions the most superfluous. The reason for this is not to be
sought in any supposed ethical indifference on the part of our
period. On the contrary it arises from the fact that our period,
more than any earlier period in the history of the west, is
oppressed by a superabounding reality of concrete ethical
problems.

Today there are once more villains and saints, and they are

DIETRICH BONHOEFFER *(1906–1945) dedicated not only his mind but his life
to Christian freedom in responsibility and discipleship. He was the author of a number of writings in theology and ethics, including* THE COST
OF DISCIPLESHIP.
EDITORS' NOTE. *This "essay" has been developed by the present editors
from the English version of Dietrich Bonhoeffer's* Ethics *using material
from the pages of that work as indicated: 3, 5, 6, 7, 8, 112, 113,
137, 138, 139, 140, 194, 195, 196, 197, 216, 217, 218, 219, 220, 221 (nonitalicized)
pages were used entirely. The title and three section heads were added.
Reprinted with permission of The Macmillan Company from* ETHICS *by
Dietrich Bonhoeffer. Copyright 1955 by The Macmillan Company.*

not hidden from the public view. Instead of the uniform gray-ness of the rainy day we now have the black storm-cloud and the brilliant lightning flash. The outlines stand out with exag-gerated sharpness. Reality lays itself bare. Shakespeare's char-acters walk in our midst. But the villain and the saint have little or nothing to do with systematic ethical studies. They emerge from primeval depths and by their appearance they tear open the infernal or the divine abyss from which they come and enable us to see for a moment into mysteries of which we had never dreamed. What is worse than doing evil is being evil. It is worse for a liar to tell the truth than for a lover of truth to lie.

But if someone sets out to fight his battles in the world in his own absolute *freedom*, if he values the necessary deed more highly than the spotlessness of his own conscience and reputation, if he is prepared to sacrifice a fruitless principle to a fruitful compromise, or for that matter the fruitless wis-dom of the *via media* to a fruitful radicalism, then let him be-ware lest precisely his supposed freedom may ultimately prove his undoing. He will easily consent to the bad, knowing full well that it is bad, in order to ward off what is worse, and in doing this he will no longer be able to see that precisely the worse which he is trying to avoid may still be the better. This is one of the underlying themes of tragedy.

Yet our business now is to replace our rusty swords with sharp ones. A man can hold his own here only if he can com-bine simplicity with wisdom. But what is simplicity? What is wisdom? And how are the two to be combined? To be simple is to fix one's eye solely on the simple truth of God at a time when all concepts are being confused, distorted and turned upside-down. It is to be single-hearted and not a man of two souls. Because the simple man knows God, because God is his, he clings to the commandments, the judgments and the mer-cies which come from God's mouth every day afresh. Not fettered by principles, but bound by love for God, he has been set free from the problems and conflicts of ethical decision. They no longer oppress him. He belongs simply and solely to God and to the will of God. It is precisely because he looks only to God, without any sidelong glance at the world, that he is able to look at the reality of the world freely and without prejudice. And that is how simplicity becomes wisdom. The wise man is the one who sees reality as it is, and who sees into the depths of things. That is why only that man is wise who sees reality in God. To understand reality is not the same as to know about outward events. It is to perceive the essential nature of things. The best informed man is not necessarily the wisest. Indeed there is a danger that precisely in the multiplicity of his knowledge he will lose sight of what is essential. But, on the other hand, knowledge of an apparently trivial detail quite often makes it possible to see into the depths of things. And so the wise man will seek to acquire the best possible knowledge about events, but always without becoming dependent upon this knowledge. To recognize the significant in the factual is wisdom. The wise man is aware of the limited receptiveness of reality for principles; for he knows that reality is not built upon principles but that it rests upon the living and creating God. He knows too, therefore, that reality cannot be helped by even the purest of principles or by even the best of wills, but only by the living God. Principles are only tools in God's hand, soon to be thrown away as unserviceable. To look in freedom at God and at reality, which rests solely upon Him, this is to combine simplicity with wisdom.

No man can look with undivided vision at God and at the world of reality so long as God and the world are torn asunder. Try as he may, he can only let his eyes wander distractedly from one to the other. But there is a place at which God and the cosmic reality are reconciled, a place at which God and man have become one. That and that alone is what enables man to set his eyes upon God and upon the world at the same time. This place does not lie somewhere out beyond reality in the realm of ideas. It lies in the midst of history as a divine miracle. It lies in Jesus Christ, the Reconciler of the world. Whoever sees Jesus Christ does indeed see God and the world in one. He can henceforward no longer see God without the world or the world without God.

Freedom and Bodily Life

Bodily life, which we receive without any action on our own part, carries within itself the right to its own preservation. This is not a right that we have justly or unjustly appropriated to ourselves, but it is in the strictest sense an "innate" right, one which we have passively received and which pre-exists our will, a right which rests upon the nature of things as they are. Since it is God's will that there should be human life on earth only in the form of bodily life, it follows that it is for the sake of the whole man that the body possesses the right to be preserved. And since all rights are extinguished at death, it follows that the preservation of the life of the body is the foundation of all natural rights without exception and is, therefore, invested with a particular importance. The underlying right of natural life is the safeguarding of nature against intentional injury, violation and killing. That may sound very jejune and unheroic. But the body does not exist primarily in order to be sacrificed, but in order that it may be preserved. Different and more exalted considerations may give rise to the right or duty of sacrificing the body, but this in itself presupposes the underlying right to the conservation of bodily life.

The life of the body, like life in general, is both a means to an end and an end in itself. To regard the body exclusively as a means to an end is idealistic but not Christian; for a means is discarded as soon as the end is achieved. It is from this point of view that the body is conceived as the prison from which the immortal soul is released for ever by death. According to the Christian doctrine, the body possesses a higher dignity. Man is a bodily being, and remains so in eternity as well. Bodiliness and human life belong inseparably together. And thus the bodiliness which is willed by God to be the form of existence of man is entitled to be called an end in itself.

The preservation of bodily life involves protection against arbitrary infringement of the liberty of the body. The human body must never become a thing, an object, such as might fall under the unrestricted power of another man and be used by him solely as a means to his own ends. The living human body is always the man himself. Rape, exploitation, torture and arbitrary confinement of the human body are serious violations of the right which is given with the creation of man, and what is more, like all violations of natural life, they must sooner or later entail their own punishment.

Rape is the use of the body of another for one's own purposes, enforced by the application of a power which is not rightful. In opposition to it there stands the right of the human being to give or to refuse his body in freedom. In special circumstances the bodily strength of the individual may rightfully be set to work for the sake of the common good even under compulsion, but human sexuality remains exempt from any such constraint. Any attempt to bring about particular marriages or other sexual relationships by coercion, whatever the reasons may be, is quite clearly an infringement of the bodily liberty of the human being, and it conflicts with that underlying fact of sexual life which, as a natural mode of defense, marks the limit beyond which no alien interference may pass, namely the sense of shame. In the natural feeling of shame, expression is given to the essential freedom of the human body in its sexual aspect. The destruction of the sense of shame means the dissolution of all sexual and conjugal order, and indeed of all social order in the widest sense. Certainly the sense of shame assumes various forms and can be cultivated in various ways. But this unchanging essence, which is founded in nature, is the safeguarding of the freedom of the human body against any sort of violation. This freedom watches over the mystery of human corporeality.

We speak of exploitation of the human body in cases where a man's bodily forces are made the unrestricted property of another man or of an institution. We call this state of affairs slavery. But this does not refer simply to the system of slavery in antiquity. There have been historical forms of slavery which have preserved the essential liberty of man more effectively than do certain social systems in which the concept of slavery is itself rejected but the men who are said to be free are in fact totally enslaved. To this extent there is good reason for the attitude of many of the Church Fathers, including St.

Thomas Aquinas, who condemn not the name but the fact of slavery. And this fact exists wherever a man has, in fact, become a thing in the power of another man, wherever a man has become exclusively a means to another man's end. This danger is always present in cases where a man has neither freedom to choose his place of work nor the possibility of exchanging his place of work for another, or even of determining the amount of work that he is to perform. This means that in the end the bodily forces of the workman are utilized without restriction; at best this utilization is limited by the need for conserving the man's usefulness, but on occasion even this limit may for some particular reason be overstepped and the consequence is total exhaustion. A man is thus robbed of his bodily strength; his body becomes wholly the object of the stronger man's exploitation. The freedom of the human body is destroyed.

Torture of the body is to be distinguished from that retributive punishment through which one who is guilty of a base crime against the body of another has his dishonor brought home to him by the injury done to his own body. By torture of the body we mean in general the arbitrary and brutal infliction of physical pain while taking advantage of a relative superiority of strength, and in particular the extortion by this means of some desired admission or statement. In such cases the body is misused, and therefore dishonored, exclusively as a means to the achievement of another man's purpose, whether it be for the satisfaction of his lust for power or for the sake of acquiring some particular information. The innocent body's sensitiveness to pain is cruelly exploited. Torture is, in any case, generally an ineffectual means for discovering the truth; though, of course, this argument can have force only in cases where it is really the truth that is being sought for. But, quite apart from that, any physical torture inflicts the most extreme dishonor on the human being, and consequently engenders an intense hatred and the natural bodily impulse to restore this wounded honor by the application of bodily force. Bodily dishonor seeks to avenge itself on the body of the infamous tormentor. In this way the violation of man's bodily freedom once again destroys the foundations of society.

Arbitrary deprivation of liberty, such as the seizure of defenseless and innocent people (for example when African negroes were hunted, captured and transported as slaves to America) and other forms of arbitrary imprisonment, constitutes a violation of the liberty which is given with the human body. When a man is forcibly and wrongfully separated from his home, his work and his family, and is prevented from exercising all his bodily rights and treated as though he were guilty of some crime, then he is being deprived of the honor which is associated with bodily liberty. And if the innocent man is robbed of his freedom and his honor, then the guilty man must remain exempt from punishment and from public dishonor, and that means that the whole order of society will be undermined and that a restoration of the rights of natural life must sooner or later necessarily ensue.

Responsibility and Freedom

The structure of responsible life is conditioned by two factors; life is bound to man and to God and a man's own life is free. It is the fact that life is bound to man and to God which sets life in the freedom of a man's own life. Without this bond and without this freedom there is no responsibility. Only when it has become selfless in this obligation does a life stand in the freedom of a man's truly own life and action. The obligation assumes the form of deputyship . . . freedom displays itself in the self-examination of life and of action and in the venture of a concrete decision.

The fact that responsibility is fundamentally a matter of deputyship is demonstrated most clearly in those circumstances in which a man is directly obliged to act in the place of other men, for example as a father, as a statesman or as a teacher. The father acts for the children, working for them, caring for them, interceding, fighting and suffering for them. Thus in a real sense he is their deputy. He is not an isolated individual, but he combines in himself the selves of a number of human beings. Any attempt to live as though he were alone is a denial of the actual act of his responsibility. He cannot evade the responsibility which is laid on him with his paternity. This reality shatters the fiction that the subject, the performer, of all ethical conduct is the isolated individual. Not the individual in isolation but the responsible man is the subject, the agent, with whom ethical reflection must concern itself. This principle is not affected by the extent of the responsibility assumed, whether it be for a single human being, for a community or for whole groups of communities. No man can altogether escape responsibility, and this means that no man can avoid deputyship. Even the solitary lives as a deputy, and indeed quite especially so, for his life is lived in deputyship for man as man, for mankind as a whole. And, in fact, the concept of responsibility for oneself possesses a meaning only insofar as it refers to the responsibility which I bear with respect to myself as a man, that is to say, because I am a man. Responsibility for oneself is in truth responsibility with respect to the man, and that means responsibility with respect to mankind. The fact that Jesus lived without the special responsibility of a marriage, of a family or of a profession, does not by any means set Him outside the field of responsibility; on the contrary, it makes all the clearer His responsibility and His deputyship for all men. Here we come already to the underlying basis of everything that has been said so far. Jesus, life, our life, lived in deputyship for us as the incarnate Son of God, and that is why through Him all human life is in essence a life of deputyship.

Responsibility, as life and action in deputyship, is essentially a relation of man to man. Christ became man, and He therefore bore responsibility and deputyship for men. There is also a responsibility for things, conditions and values, but only in conjunction with the strict observance of the original, essential and purposive determination of all things, conditions, and values through Christ (John 1:3), the incarnate God. Through Christ the world of things and of values is once more directed towards mankind as it was in the Creation. It is only within these limits that there is a legitimate sense in speaking, as is often done, about responsibility for a thing or for a cause. Beyond these limits it is dangerous, for it serves to reverse the whole order of life, making things the masters of men. There is a devotion to the cause of truth, goodness, justice and beauty which would be profaned if one were to ask what is the moral of it, and which indeed itself makes it abundantly clear that the highest values must be subservient to man. But there is also a deification of all these values which has no connection at all with responsibility; it springs from a demoniacal possession which destroys the man in sacrificing him to the idol. "Responsibility for a thing" does not mean its utilization for man and consequently the abuse of its essential nature, but it means the essential directing of it towards man. Thus that narrow pragmatism is entirely excluded which, in Schiller's words, "makes a milch-cow of the goddess" when that which has value in itself is in a direct and short-sighted manner subordinated to human utility. The world of things attains to its full liberty and depth only when it is grasped in its original, essential and purposive relevance to the world of persons; for, as St. Paul expresses it, the earnest expectation of the creature waits for the manifestation of the glory of the children of God; and indeed the creature itself shall be delivered from the bondage of corruption (which also consists in its own false self-deification) into the glorious liberty of the children of God (Romans 8: 19–21).

Responsibility and freedom are corresponding concepts. Factually, though not chronologically, responsibility presupposes freedom and freedom can consist only in responsibility. Responsibility is the freedom of men which is given only in the obligation to God and to our neighbor.

The responsible man acts in the freedom of his own self, without the support of men, circumstances or principles, but with a due consideration for the given human and general conditions and for the relevant questions of principle. The proof of his freedom is the fact that nothing can answer for him, nothing can exonerate him, except his own deed and his own self. It is he himself who must observe, judge, weigh up, decide and act. It is man himself who must examine the motives, the prospects, the value and the purpose of his action. But neither the purity of the motivation, nor the opportune circumstances, nor the value, nor the significant purpose of an intended undertaking can become the governing law of his action, a law to which he can withdraw, to which he can appeal as an authority, and by which he can be exculpated and acquitted. (This makes it unnecessary to raise the fallacious question of determinism and indeterminism, in which the essence of mental decision is incorrectly substituted for the law of causality.) For in that case he would indeed no longer be truly free. The action of the responsible man is performed in the obligation which alone gives freedom and which gives entire freedom, the obligation to God and to our neighbor as they confront us in Jesus Christ. At the same time it is performed wholly within the domain of relativity, wholly in the twilight which the historical situation spreads over good and evil; it is performed in the midst of the innumerable perspectives in which every given phenomenon appears. It has not to decide simply between right and wrong and between good and evil, but between right and right and between wrong and wrong. As Aeschylus said, "right strives with right." Precisely in this respect responsible action is a free venture; it is not justified by any law; it is performed without any claim to a valid self-justification, and therefore also without any claim to an ultimate valid knowledge of good and evil. Good, as what is responsible, is performed in ignorance of good and in the surrender to God of the deed which has become necessary and which is nevertheless, or for that very reason, free; for it is God who sees the heart, who weighs up the deed, and who directs the course of history.

With this there is disclosed to us a deep secret of history in general. The man who acts in the freedom of his own most personal responsibility is precisely the man who sees his action finally committed to the guidance of God. The free deed knows itself in the end as the deed of God; the decision knows itself as guidance; the free venture knows itself as divine necessity. It is in the free abandonment of knowledge of his own good that a man performs the good of God. It is only from this last point of view that one can speak of good in historical action.

It must seem at first sight as though everything we have said about free responsibility is applicable in practice only when a man finds himself in what we call a "responsible position" in life, in other words when he has to take independent decisions on the very largest scale. What connection can there be between responsibility and the monotonous daily work of the laborer, the factory worker, the clerk, the private soldier, the apprentice or the schoolboy? It is a different matter already with the owner-farmer, the industrial contractor, the politician or statesman, the general, the master craftsman, the teacher and the judge. But in their lives, too, how much there is of technique and duty and how little of really free decision! And so it seems that everything we have said about responsibility can in the end apply only to a very small group of men, and even to these only in a few moments of their lives; and consequently it seems as though for the great majority of men one must speak not of responsibility but of obedience and duty. This implies one ethic for the great and the strong, for the rulers, and another for the small and the weak, the subordinates; on the one hand responsibility and on the other obedience, on the one hand freedom and on the other subservience. And indeed there can be no doubt that in our modern social order, and especially in the German one, the life of the individual is so exactly defined and regulated, and is at the same time assured of such complete security, that it is granted to only very few men to breathe the free air of the wide open spaces of great decisions and to experience the hazard of responsible action which is entirely their own. In consequence of the compulsory regulation of life in accordance with a definite course of training and vocational activity, our lives have come to be relatively free from ethical dangers; the individual who from his childhood on has had to take his assigned place in accordance with this principle is ethically emasculated; he has been robbed of the creative moral power, freedom. In this we see a deep-seated fault in the essential development of our modern social order, a fault which can be countered only with a clear exposition of the fundamental concept of responsibility. As things stand, the large-scale experiential material for the problem of responsibility must be sought for among the great political leaders, industrialists and generals; for indeed those few others who venture to act on their own free responsibility in the midst of the pressure of everyday life are crushed by the machinery of the social order, by the general routine.

Yet it would be an error if we were to continue to look at the problem from this point of view. There is, in fact, no single life which cannot experience the situation of responsibility; every life can experience this situation in its most characteristic form, that is to say, in the encounter with other people. Even when free responsibility is more or less excluded from a man's vocational and public life, he nevertheless always stands in a responsible relation to other men; these relations extend from his family to his workmates. The fulfillment of genuine responsibility at this point affords the only sound possibility of extending the sphere of responsibility once more into vocational and public life. Where man meets man—and this includes the encounters of professional life—there arises genuine responsibility, and these responsible relationships cannot be supplanted by any general regulation or routine. That holds true, then, not only for the relation between married people, or for parents and children, but also for the master and the apprentice, the teacher and his pupil, the judge and the accused.

But we can go one step further than this. Responsibility does not only stand side by side with relationships of obedience; it has its place also within these relationships. The apprentice has a duty of obedience towards his master, but at the same time he has also a free responsibility for his work, for his achievement and, therefore, also for his master. It is the same with the schoolboy and the student, and indeed also with the employee in any kind of industrial undertaking and with the soldier in war. Obedience and responsibility are interlinked in such a way that one cannot say that responsibility begins only where obedience leaves off, but rather than obedience is rendered in responsibility. There will always be a relation of obedience and dependence; all that matters is that these should not, as they already largely do today, leave no room for responsibilities. To know himself to be responsible is more difficult for the man who is socially dependent than for the man who is socially free, but a relationship of dependence does not in any case in itself exclude free responsibility. The master and the servant, while preserving the relationship of obedience, can and should answer for each other in free responsibility.

The ultimate reason for this lies in that relation of men to God which is realized in Jesus Christ. Jesus stands before God as the one who is both obedient and free. As the obedient one He does His Father's will in blind compliance with the law which is commanded Him, and as the free one He acquiesces in God's will out of His own most personal knowledge, with open eyes and a joyous heart; He recreates this will, as it were, out of Himself. Obedience without freedom is slavery; freedom without obedience is arbitrary self-will. Obedience restrains freedom; and freedom ennobles obedience. Obedience binds the creature to the Creator, and freedom enables the creature to stand before the Creator as one who is made in His image. Obedience shows man that he must allow himself to be told what is good and what God requires of him (Micah 6:8); and liberty enables him to do good himself. Obedience knows what is good and does it, and freedom dares to act, and abandons to God the judgement of good and evil. Obedience follows blindly and freedom has open eyes. Obedience acts without questioning and freedom asks what is the purpose. Obedience has its hands tied and freedom is creative. In obedience man adheres to the decalogue and in freedom man creates new decalogues (Luther).

In responsibility both obedience and freedom are realized. Responsibility implies tension between obedience and freedom. There would be no more responsibility if either were made independent of the other. Responsible action is subject to obligation, and yet it is creative. To make obedience independent of freedom leads only to the Kantian ethic of duty, and to make freedom independent of obedience leads only to the ethic of irresponsible genius. Both the man of duty and the genius carry their justification within themselves. The man of responsibility stands between obligation and freedom; he must dare to act under obligation and in freedom; yet he finds his justification neither in his obligation nor in his freedom but solely in Him who has put him in this (humanly impossible) situation and who requires this deed of him. The responsible man delivers up himself and his deed to God.

Mark John Farrelly / God's Sovereignty and Man's Freedom

THE HARMONY taught by Scripture and tradition to exist between God and free will refers not only to the relation between
grace and free will, but also to that between the divine plan
and free will. In the first part of this study we presented what
seems to us to be the teaching of Scripture and tradition on
this harmony. In the preceding chapter we advanced a philosophical analysis of God's causality of the creature's free will
act for the purpose of explaining to some extent and defending this harmony as it refers to grace and free will. In the
present chapter we shall advance a philosophical analysis of
God's providence, knowledge, and will in their relation to free
will to help to explain and defend the harmony we found expressed in Scripture and tradtion between God's plan for the
salvation of the free creature and the acts of the free creature.

We shaʌi not, then, in this chapter attempt to show once
more what Scripture and tradition do teach on this matter.

MARK JOHN FARRELLY *(1927–   ), of St. Anselm's Abbey, Washington, D.C.,
is the author of* AUTHORITY IN THE CHURCH *(1966). The present essay is
Part I of Chapter VI of his* PREDESTINATION, GRACE AND FREE WILL *(1964) and
is reprinted by permission of The Newman Press.*

We have already seen that for exegetical reasons both Banez and Molina understood God's predestination to be an absolute divine intention for the salvation of the individual. In the dilemma this posed Banez held that predestination was the first of God's intentions for the one to be saved, while Molina held that it was the last. The former accordingly held that God predestined the individual antecedent to his foreknowledge of his merits, while the latter held that God predestined him only consequent upon foreknowledge of his merits. We have already shown in our analysis of Scripture and tradition that in our opinion the dilemma that is at the origin of this divergence between Thomists and Molinists is not necessitated by the doctrine of revelation. For reasons previously advanced it seems to us that the predestination taught by St. Paul is one that is conditioned on man's fidelity to God in this life and thus one that can be frustrated by man's bad will. Hence, we can say both that God's predestination is antecedent to man's merits and that God does not have an absolute unconditioned intention for the salvation of the individual while he is still in this life. The reasons from Scripture and tradition on which our opinion is based have already been presented and will be taken as the basis for what follows in this chapter.

What we have already written, however, does not adequately explain or defend the harmony between God's will in the order of grace and man's free will. By the philosophical analyses they presented, Banez and Molina seem to call into question our interpretation of the harmony expressed by Scripture. They do this, not simply through their philosophical explanations of God's causality of the free will act, which have been examined in the preceding chapter, but also through their opinions on the relation between the uncreated source of God's created causality and the free will act of the creature. Their explanations of the infallibility of divine providence, the divine foreknowledge of the created free will act, and the efficacy of the divine will seem to present philosophical difficulties to our understanding of predestination as a conditioned divine intention. Thus, to defend our understanding of predestination, we must see whether, in fact, natural, philosophical considerations invalidate it. Moreover, predestination is included within God's providence for the rational creature; and so to understand the supernatural mystery to some extent, one must make an analysis of providence in the natural order and of God's will and knowledge that providence involves, all in their relation to the free act of the creature. We are restricting ourselves to the considerations about these matters that are necessary to show the nature of the harmony that exists between God and free will, and we in no way intend to give an exhaustive treatment of any one of them. With this intention we shall analyze successively the relation of God's will to the created free act, the relation of God's infallible knowledge to the created free act, and the relation of God's providence to the movement of man to his perfection. At appropriate places we shall show the relevance of these philosophical analyses to the supernatural mystery that is our central concern.

The Divine Will and the Creature's Free Will Act

TEACHING COMMONLY ACCEPTED AND THE PROBLEM

As a basis for our analysis of the natural relation between God's will act and that of the free creature, we must recall the relevant truths that all theologians accept. In himself God is infinite, and thus he is a personal being [1] endowed with intellect and will of unmeasured perfection, and possessed of supreme happiness that is incapable of intrinsic addition or subtraction.[2] Whatever being exists outside of God is caused by his intellect and will [3] by the causality through created acts which we described in the preceding chapter, and exists as a participation in his being. Since God has need of nothing outside himself for his perfection and happiness, his will to create is wholly free.[4] And since this will to create is a will to communicate a share of his goodness and perfection to creatures, it is properly speaking an act of divine love. All creatures, then, have the perfection and the measure of perfection they do have as a result of God's love and the measure of His love for them. One creature is better than another because it is loved more than another.[5] The ultimate purpose of God's will in creating is neither a divine need to be fulfilled (since his inner perfection is infinite) nor the created good loved for its own sake (since this is infinitely below him). Rather the uncreated divine goodness is the ultimate purpose in creating,[6] as the object of the love of friendship is the purpose of action. God creates to express the value of his infinite goodness and his love of this goodness. So all good intrinsic to creation and particularly that good that is the fulfillment of the creature is caused by divine goodness through the mediation of God's will, and is a sign of his goodness and his love of his goodness.[7] Hence the intrinsic actualization or good of creatures is his purpose in creating and acting in the world, but it is a purpose ordained to the ultimate one of his own uncreated goodness.

As the love of the divine will and the exemplary causality of the divine intellect is the first cause of the goodness and nature of every creature, it is the first cause, too, of the morally good free will act and every aspect of it. Since the created act by which God causes is causally antecedent to that of the free creature, God's intellect and will as first cause premove the creature to its particular good act; his act does not follow the initiative of the creature or simply concur with its act. Moreover, this divine causality and the intention of God's will and intellect that is its source is one that bears intrinsically upon the created free act; it is not limited to the extrinsic determination of circumstances or the conferral simply of power to act rather than the free act itself, for the intrinsic created act within the free will that actualizes and determines it is a participation in the act of the divine will and intellect. Since these attributes of God's causality and hence of his divine intention relating to the free act of the creature were examined in the last Chapter, we need not delay on them here.

Concerning the relation between the divine will and the sinful act of the rational creature, all theologians agree that God in no way wills the sins of the free creature, but simply permits them. St. Thomas shows that this follows from the nature of moral evil and the object of the divine will. Evil is the privation of the good that should exist in a being or in an act.

Death is the privation of the life of the being, and sin is the privation of the right order in human acts. Since the proper object of any appetite—whether it be natural, animal, or intellectual—is the good, no appetite can desire evil for its own sake. While nothing can desire evil for its own sake, it may desire some good, the acquisition of which demands the sacrifice of another good. For example, when the lion wants food, it desires secondarily the death of the deer; the man who seeks the pleasure of an immoral act wants incidentally the privation of the right order in his acts. A desire of evil in this way, the only possible way, is an incidental or accidental desire of evil rather than a desire of it for its own sake or an essential desire of evil. And even such a desire of evil is only possible when the agent wants the good he is directly seeking more than that which he sacrifices in the evil attached to his pursuit of the good. This is true of the divine will, since it is essentially ordained to divine goodness, and so St. Thomas concludes this analysis by writing:

> God wants no good more than his own goodness, although he wants some particular good more than another particular good. Hence God wills in no way the *evil of sin* which is a privation of the order to the divine good. But he wills the *evil of a natural defect* or *the evil of punishment* by willing some good with which such an evil is conjoined. Thus by willing justice he wills punishment, and by willing to preserve the order of nature he wills certain things to be corrupted in accord with their natures.[8]

Since, then, God loves no good more than his own goodness, he cannot will sin even accidentally, since this is a privation of the right order to his goodness. Some have thought that God does will sin to exist, since it results in a greater perfection of the universe; the Romans' persecutions of the Christians led to the patience of martyrs. But this does not show that God willed this sin of the Romans even accidentally; it simply shows that he is so powerful that he can make their sin serve his own purpose. God does not will the sin of man in any way. But as his governance of the world shows, he does not, as he could, prevent sin from taking place. Hence, he permits or tolerates sin in the world.[9]

The question central to the problem of the nature of the harmony between God's will and the free acts of the created will can now be posed. Granted that the particular good free act of the creature is due as to its first cause to an intention of the divine will which in its desire that the creature perform this particular act both precedes the act of the creature and intrinsically and causally affects the free power and act itself, is this divine intention as antecedent to the good free act of the creature frustrable? Is it in its condition as antecedent frustrable by the resistance of the created free will or is it infallibly effective of its result, the good act of the creature that follows? Note that when we ask whether God's antecedent intention is frustrable or not, we refer simply to its relation to the particular good free act of the creature, and not to its relation to the larger purpose to which God ordains that particular created act. A similar question can be asked of the morally evil act in the natural order. This is only permitted by God, as all theologians agree, and not willed by him. But what is the nature of this permission in its condition as antecedent to the sinful act that takes place in history? Is it such that, antecedent to its actual occurrence, the particular sinful act in history is absolutely certain to occur? Or is it such that, antecedent to the actual occurrence of the sinful act, there is no basis for certainty that it will occur? In this question we restrict ourselves to the nature of God's permission of the first formal sin of a particular rational creature. If the creature has already sinned seriously against God, God can in justice withdraw his sustaining power from the creature in punishment for the previous sin and thus allow him to fall into further sins; if he does not, it is simply due to his divine mercy. Theologians generally are agreed on this; the critical problem is the nature of God's permission of the first sin of the rational creature.

Before we present our own answer to these two critical questions, we shall recall the opinions of Banez and Molina. As we saw in the first chapter, they are in essential agreement in their answers to these questions, though for different reasons. Both held that the natural good free act is due to the divine will in such a way that, antecedent to the free choice of the creature in time the divine will's intention that the act take place is infallibly efficacious.[10] Their difference was on the nature of this efficacy; their philosophies agree in holding the fact of this efficacy. We have shown in the first chapter the reasons that motivated such a conclusion, so here we need only recall the main ones. Banez thought that, since the choice of the created will was a movement from potency to act, it must be preceded by a physically predetermining premotion which by a priority of nature determined the act of the will. The first source of such a created causality is a divine intention that is also effective antecedent to the act of the created will. Moreover, he thought that the whole goodness of the free created act could not be attributed to God as its first cause unless the act were due to an antecedently effective divine intention. Also the decree of the divine will was for Banez the medium by which God has eternal knowledge of the free act of the creature; he held, therefore, that it must be intrinsically effective of itself to give certain knowledge of the free created act.[11] Molina's explanation of God's causality and knowledge differed from this, but he arrived at this conclusion he held in common with Banez from different premises. Granted his interpretation of God's causality of the free act and his theory of *scientia media*, God has knowledge of what the free will would do given any circumstances in which it could be placed, and he has this knowledge before he actually determines the particular circumstances in which to place the individual. The intention of the divine will by which God places the free creature in the circumstances he knows will eventuate in its good act is in its condition as antecedent to the actual choice of the created will in time infallibly effective in bringing about the good act. It is extrinsically effective because of the fact that God's intention follows *scientia media*, but it is infallibly effective.[12] Other considerations have seemed to support this philosophical conclusion of Banez and Molina and have been adduced at various times. For example, God's omnipotence, his immutability, the eternal and causal antecedence of his will act to that of the creature, and the infallible efficacy of his providence—all have seemed to necessitate such a conclusion.

Banez and Molina explain God's permission of the first sin of a particular rational creature in an analogous manner. They hold that God's permission of the first sin of a rational creature is such that, antecedent to the actual free choice of the creature in time, it is certain he will sin. Before the actual sin that occurs, God's permission is such that the sin is certain to follow. Such a permission is necessary in Banez's opinion to explain how God has infallibly certain knowledge of the future free sinful act of the creature, and he is explicit in holding that the first sin of the rational creature is preceded by a divine permission in his sense.[13] Moreover, this is implied as the converse of his doctrine that the good act of the rational creature must be preceded by an infallibly effective divine intention if it is to take place. Hence, the same or similar considerations motivated his explanation of the one and the other. He defended his explanation against attacks upon it by affirming that God has no obligation to prevent all sins or to sustain the free creature in the practice of the moral good. Moreover, he held that in the order of the execution of God's providence the bad will of the free creature preceded God's denial of the help to sustain it in good.[14] Molina's doctrine of God's intention following *scientia media* implies that the creature's sinful act is preceded by a divine permission in the sense of a choice of circumstances that give adequate helps to avoid the sin, but which in fact God knows will be followed by the sin. Molina held that God's permission of the first sin of the rational creature in this sense was not due to any previous sin on the part of the creature.[15] The responsibility for the sin is completely the creature's and not God's, since it is due to the self-determination of the creature foreseen in *scientia media*. God's part is simply the determination of the circumstances.

Our opinion is that the divine intention or desire that a particular good free act of the rational creature in the natural order take place is not infallibly effective of this particular act or infrustrable antecedent to the cooperation of the free will of the creature. It is conditioned, and thus can be rejected by the creature. We also think that God's permission of the first sin of a rational creature in the natural order is that contained within a frustrable intention that the creature do good, and is not such that it is certain to be followed by the sin of the creature. We shall present our reasons for this opinion and try to answer difficulties that may be raised against them. Later we shall use this philosophical analysis we give here to explain to some extent the message of revelation concerning God's will in its relation to the morally good act or sinful act in the order of grace. And we shall conclude by considering some arguments from fittingness that have been used in this matter.

GOD'S WILL AS ANTECEDENT TO THE GOOD FREE WILL ACT IN HISTORY
How can we know whether the divine intention or desire by which the individual good free act of the creature in the natural order is anticipated is frustrable or infrustrable? We cannot know it by the fact that the good act follows at times and does not follow at other times, because we are asking this question specifically of the good act that does in fact take place. And we are asking, not whether the created causality, but whether the uncreated causality or intention of the divine will that is the first cause of the created free act is frustrable or not antecedent to the cooperation of the free will. It seems that our knowledge of the nature of this uncreated divine intention is gained as our knowledge of other divine attributes is gained, namely, through the created effects of God. Thus from the nature of the act of the free will and the created cause that brings it about, we can induce the nature of God's antecedent divine intention that it take place, unless such an induction would be incompatible with God's perfection. This is based on the fact that the divine will in its causality of creatures and their acts is guided by divine wisdom. In its desire of the act of a creature, the divine will is not autonomous, unrelated to, or opposed to the order of divine wisdom. It is specified by divine wisdom so that it desires that order of things that is determined by divine wisdom. And we know the

order of things that divine wisdom has established in the world through the things of the world. The natures of creatures and thus the manner of acting proper to various creatures is the result of the first causality of the divine mind, and hence these natures show the order that is established by divine wisdom and imposed by it upon the world and upon the divine will to direct its causality of the things of the world. Hence the activity of creatures shows us, not only the nature of the created causality that brings it about, but the nature of the uncreated causality of the divine will that is its source.

In the last chapter, we examined the nature of the rational appetite or will of the creature, the manner of acting proper to it in this life, and the created causality by which God brings about its act. It is a power the proper object of which is the good presented to it by the intellect. Its act is an *actus perfecti* or a self-movement and self-determination in virtue of the causality exercised upon it by its object. And in this life the good presented to it does not and does not appear to satisfy its desire completely. So we found that under God's causality that is exercised through the object presented to it, the will is completely free to act or not to act. That is, antecedent to its act the premovement and predetermination that God exercises upon it through its object is frustrable, conditioned, and can be rejected. The good free act that takes place is anticipated by a causal influence of the good that is not antecedently infallibly effective in eliciting the act. From this it would seem that the desire or intention of the divine will that is the source of the good act of the creature through the causal influence of the good is also frustrable, conditioned, and subject to rejection by the will of the creature if it so desires. It seems, in other words, that it is not antecedently infallibly effective or infrustrable as it is related to the particular free good act of the rational creature.

It also seems to us that such is the philosophical teaching of St. Thomas. There are, it is true, some texts that seem opposed to such an opinion. For example, when we examined St. Thomas' doctrine in our study of tradition, we saw that he thought that predestination was an absolute divine intention for the salvation of the individual rational creature. But St. Thomas adopted such a position because of his interpretation of revelation, and not because of his philosophical principles. Moreover, he said at least once that the effect of such a predestination was gained "from the concurrence of many causes that are contingent and able to fail in gaining their effect." [16] It is difficult for us to see how he could say this if he thought that philosophical principles demanded that the divine intention antecedent to any particular good act of the free creature must be infallibly effective of that particular act. Another statement that may seem opposed to our opinion is his teaching that if God moves the free creature to act, it is impossible that the creature not act.[17] This, however, is a conditional statement and does not distinguish God's premovement from his simultaneous concurrence with the created free act, so it does not prove or indicate that the good free act of the creature is, according to the order God has established, anticipated by an infrustrable divine intention. St. Thomas also writes that God wants some effects to occur necessarily and for these fits necessary causes, and he wants some to take place contingently and for these adapts contingent causes.[18] But this leaves unanswered the question whether God in his ordinary providence wants individual good free acts of the rational creature to exist by a will that is antecedently infallibly effective or not.

The following passage of St. Thomas is more difficult to explain.

> God indeed moves the will immutably because of the efficacy of his moving power which cannot fail. But because of the nature of the will that is moved, which is related indifferently to different objects, necessity is not induced but liberty remains. So also divine providence operates infallibly in all things; and yet effects proceed from contingent causes in a contingent way, since God moves all things proportionately, each according to its own manner.[19]

This is written in answer to the objection that since movement by an extrinsic principle results in the inner necessity of the appetitive acts of animals, God's movement of the rational appetite results in the inner necessity of its acts. In the first part of his answer, St. Thomas shows that, while the animal's appetitive act follows a particular form that necessitates it, man's rational appetite is related indifferently to different objects, so his act is not necessitated. But in the same answer St. Thomas asserts that God preserves his divine attributes when he moves man's will. God "moves the will immutably because of the efficacy of his moving power which cannot fail"; and "divine providence operates infallibly in all things." Does this mean for St. Thomas that the good acts of free creatures are anticipated by a divine will and causality that could not in fact be resisted by the will of the creature? If we had only this passage, it would appear that this is what he means by the efficacy of God's power that cannot fail and the infallibility of divine providence. But even so our interpretation to this effect would be a deduction from his teaching, and perhaps it would not be a necessary deduction, since these divine perfections can, it seems, be preserved, even though the human will rejects an antecedent divine movement to the good.

There are, in fact, other statements of St. Thomas that more explicitly treat the question we are studying and that seem to correct the impression one may receive from some of the texts indicated above. These statements are found particularly in his various treatments of the question of God's knowledge of the free acts of the creature. We will examine in the next section St. Thomas' explanation of this knowledge; here we restrict ourselves to what is immediately relevant to our present question. In his first treatment of God's knowledge of free created acts, St. Thomas recalled the objection forwarded by some that God, who causes man's acts, is a necessary cause, and as a result man's acts are also necessary and not contingent. His answer is that when an act is caused by a first cause that is necessary and by an immediate cause that is contingent, the act is contingent, since the immediate cause can defect from the movement of the first. Although the sun is a necessary cause, a tree exposed to its light may not flower owing to some defect within it. In applying this to God and free will, he states that it can be that the created contingent cause will not act under the antecedent influence of God who is the first and necessary cause, since the will can defect or fall short of God's causality. And so he concludes that "the knowledge of God cannot exist together with the defection of the second cause. For it cannot be that at the same time God knows this man will run and this man will fail to run. And this is because of the certainty of his knowledge and *not because of his causality.*" [20] St. Thomas teaches here that it is not the causality of God that accounts for the infallibility of his knowledge of a contingent or free created act, for the second free cause can fail to act even when the first and necessary cause has exerted its influence upon it. If St. Thomas had thought that the good act of the created free will was anticipated by a divine intention or causality that was antecedently infallibly effective of this particular act, it seems to us that he would have affirmed, and not denied, that God's causality was the reason for the infallibility of his knowledge of the free created act. For indeed, if the divine intention is infallibly effective of this particular created act causally antecedent to the free choice of the free created will, it is of itself a medium of infallible knowledge. It is very difficult to draw any other conclusion from St. Thomas' denial that it is such a medium than that he did not think the divine intention and causality were infallibly effective of the particular free act antecedent to the choice of the free will.

What, then, does he mean when he writes that the first cause cannot fail to achieve its effect? It seems to us that he means that it is some larger divine purpose such as the divine glory, and not the particular free good act of the creature that takes place in time, that God wants with an antecedent infallible efficacy. Whether the free creature cooperates with God's providence or not, his purpose will be gained; and if the particular good free act fails to take place, this failure is due, not to the failure of God's intention or causality, but to that of the creature. Thus there is a compatibility between the unfailing power of God and the failure of the free act that he antecedently wants to occur. St. Thomas writes:

> . . . although the first cause exerts a more powerful influence than the second, still the effect is not completed unless the operation of the second cause come about. And hence if there is a possibility of failing in the second cause, there is also the same possibility of failing in the effect, although the first cause cannot fail . . . [21]

Therefore it seems to us that the teaching of St. Thomas is in agreement with the opinion we have presented. We find it very difficult to harmonize the statements we have just quoted from St. Thomas and others like them with the teaching of either Banez or Molina on this matter. Moreover, since their explanations of the relation of the intention of the divine will to the free act of the creature are dependent upon their understanding of the nature of the free act and the way that it is caused, we find the same difficulties against the former as we did against the latter in the preceding chapter.

GOD'S PERMISSION OF THE FIRST FORMAL SIN OF A
RATIONAL CREATURE

The second question that we have to answer concerns the nature of God's permission of the first formal sin of the rational creature in the natural order. When such a sin occurs in time, it has been preceded by a divine permission; for unless God permitted it, it could not take place. But what is the nature of this permission as antecedent to the free act of the creature? Is it one that, as antecedent to the free choice of the creature in time, can be a basis for certain divine knowledge that the creature will sin in this particular act? Is it of such a nature because the divine permission involves either a determination of circumstances in which God knows by *scientia media* that the creature would sin or a lack of the intrinsic sustaining divine help necessary for the creature to do good? Or is it, on the other hand, simply the permission involved in the frustrable character of the antecedent divine intention that the creature act in accord with the moral good as we have described it above? In our opinion it is the latter. The reason for this opinion is the nature of sin. Sin, as we have seen, is the privation of the right order of human acts; and the right order of human acts is that to which God has ordained man through the nature that he has given him. It is of the nature of man to be ordained to God as his last end and to achieve that end through free acts in accord with the moral norm. To elicit the morally good act, man has an absolute need of God's premoving divine intention and causality, as we have seen; and without this premovement to the good it is absolutely impossible for man to elicit such an act. This condition of man is the effect of the divine wisdom which is the source of the nature of creatures and the manner of their activity. Thus it seems that God's will is to give to man what is necessary to achieve the end to which God ordains him, and hence the premovement to the good without which man cannot do what is morally good.

It seems, moreover, that God would never lack an intention to give this premovement to the good to the rational creature in the natural order antecedent to its first sin, and in such a way that formal sin would result. For divine wisdom has ordained man to act in accord with the moral norm, and "it is impossible for God to will save what is contained in the plan of his wisdom. This indeed is like the law of justice according to which his will is right and just." [22] Since divine wisdom has given to the rational creature the nature that demands a premovement to the good if it is to avoid formal sin, such a premovement and the divine intention that is its source is owed to the creature, for "this is owed to each thing, that is ordained to it according to the order of divine wisdom." [23] It is not improper for God to owe the creature such help since the creature does not by this have a claim upon him of which God himself is not the ultimate source and end. Such help is owed to the creature ultimately to achieve the end God has in creation, namely, the manifestation of his divine goodness; and God has freely taken this obligation upon himself by the fact of creation. Since God has, therefore, an obligation to the creature and more properly to himself to give the premovement necessary to avoid formal sin, for him, antecedent to the creature's rejection of his help, not to give this would be, it seems, to act contrary to his own wisdom and justice. And since such a lack of an intention to help the creature would be a privation of the order of his justice, the sin of the creature would be imputed to God. For these reasons we cannot think that in the natural order the divine intention that the creature perform the good act and the premovement to the good necessary for the creature to avoid formal sin are ever lacking before the creature's resistance to God's will. The first formal sin of the creature is permitted by God, in our opinion, only in the sense that the antecedent divine intention and premovement to the good free act can be frustrated by the free will of the creature and thus not achieve their purpose.

In our opinion this is the philosophical doctrine of St. Thomas. It is true, as we pointed out when showing St. Thomas' place in tradition,[24] that because of his interpretation of revelation he understood predestination to be an absolute divine intention antecedent to God's foreknowledge of man's merits. As a result of this he taught that God's reprobation of man was not ultimately because of man's sins. And he did not always teach that man's personal sin was the reason for God's refusal of grace. But these views are due to his interpretation of Scripture and of St. Augustine, and not to his philosophical analysis of the relation of created free acts to God's will. Hence, it does not seem to us that they can be used against the opinion we have presented above. And for the same reasons it does not seem to us that Banez's understanding of God's permission of the first sin of the rational creature can be identified with that of St. Thomas. Banez's conception of the nature of this permission applies to the natural order as well as to the order of grace, since it is dependent upon his understanding of the antecedent efficacy of God's causality and intention with reference to the free will act of the rational creature, and it is the means whereby he explains God's certain knowledge of the sinful acts of the rational creature. We need not delay further in pointing out what appear to us to be weaknesses in Banez and Molina's explanations of God's permission of the sinful act of the creature. Let us now turn to answer certain objections that may be posed to our explanation. Objections related to the consequences of this explanation for the infallible divine knowledge of free created acts and the infallible efficacy of divine providence for the world in general will be treated later.

SOME DIFFICULTIES CONSIDERED

In the first place, the objection may be raised that God's will that a particular free act of the creature take place is eternal, and so his causality which is identified with the act of his will precedes that of the free created will. Hence, because of God's eternity, what the act of the creature will be is determined before the creature itself acts. To this we answer that time differs from eternity as the succession of the acts of material beings from the single infinite act of God.[25] Thus the fact that God's causality of the free created act is eternal, while that of the creature is temporal, does not mean that God's act takes place before that of the creature. The one act of God is of a different order from the acts of creatures and is present to all that he causes, as the soul is of a different nature from the body and is present throughout it. So the fact that God's act is eternal does not demand that his causality be infallibly effective and infrustrable antecedent to the act of the creature.

It may be said that God's divine intention that an act of the created will take place is the first cause of this act and hence has a causal antecedence to it. Moreover, God's intention and causality is omnipotent as well as antecedent; hence it seems that it is infrustrable in its condition as antecedent to the act of the creature. To this we answer that, of course, if God wishes his antecedent intention and causality to be infrustrable, it can be resisted by no created will. But the omnipotence of God does not mean that he is unable to present to the will of the creature an antecedent causality which the creature can frustrate or resist. God's omnipotence in his antecedent intention and causality is exercised in accord with the order established by his divine wisdom, which we have examined above. Hence God's intention that the rational creature act in accord with the moral norm can be resisted by the creature. If God, in a particular case, draws a particular rational creature to a good free act by an intention and causality that is antecedently infrustrable, he is acting beyond the order he has established, for a special good he wishes to gain in this particular case. Such an incident, however, does not prove that God's ordinary intention or causality of the free created act was antecedently infrustrable. It simply proves that this particular incident went beyond God's ordinary providence.

St. Thomas teaches, it may be argued, that God wants some events to take place contingently, and so he adapts contingent causes for them. His will is so effective that it causes, not only the free act, but the freedom of the act. And in the same passage he states that "no defect of the second cause can prevent the will of God from producing its effect." [26] To this we say that St. Thomas' interest in this passage is to give the *first* cause of the contingency of created free acts. The first cause is not the contingent character or the created cause since, if it were, the contingency of its acts would not be the result of the divine intention and will; it is God who is first cause of the very contingency or freedom of men's free acts. Man's freedom is a participation in God's love. Moreover, the defect of the contingent cause cannot prevent God from achieving what he wants. So the first cause is the efficacy of the divine will that wants some things to occur contingently and hence makes contingent created causes for these effects, and brings about these effects contingently. Does this mean that antecedent to the creature's act God wants it to come about with infallible efficacy, but in accord with its freedom? It does not appear to us to mean this, for this is another question which St. Thomas does not treat here. He here gives the first cause of the contingency of created free acts. The question whether, in fact, God causes such acts by an antecedently infallibly effective divine decree and causality depends upon the order of wisdom established by God. This order, as we have shown, indicates that God leaves the rational creature in this life free to reject his antecedent intention or desire that it act in accord with the moral norm.

It would appear to some, however, that an antecedent conditioned divine intention that the free creature do well is incompatible with the divine omnipotence, because such a divine intention leaves the creature free to escape from the divine power. To this we say with St. Thomas that, while a thing can escape from a particular cause, it cannot escape from a universal cause that embraces all particular causes.

> Since therefore the will of God is the universal cause of all things, it is impossible that the divine will not achieve its effect. Hence what seems to withdraw from the divine will in one order falls back in to it in another. For example, the sinner who withdraws from the divine will as far as it lies within him by sinning falls under the order of the divine will when he is punished by his justice.[27]

The sinner, then, does not escape the divine power or prevent the divine will from being fulfilled save in a particular order, and so God's will is always fulfilled either through his antecedent will that the free creature do well and thus participate in God's goodness or through his consequent will that the sinner be punished and so manifest God's holiness and justice.

But it seems, it may be said, that such an antecedent will that is conditioned upon that of the free creature is opposed to the immutability of God and his will, since it would mean that God changes his will upon a change of the creature's will. To this we answer that it is one thing for God to change his will and it is another for him to desire a change in creatures.[28] Only the former is contrary to immutability, for God can desire with an immutable will that now one thing occur and later its contrary. In his desire of the manifestation of his perfection, he may antecedently want a man to do what is morally good and then, consequent upon the man's resistance to God's help, that he not have the aid necessary to do what is morally good. What is a fitting means to gain God's glory in the one case may not be in the second. Hence, the conditioned antecedent divine intention we speak of does not imply a change in the divine will, but a divine will that there be a change in the creature if it does not submit itself to the divine will's desire for its good.

God, an objector may continue, is the author of all good; and it is due to him that one man is better than another. Thus if two men face the same temptation and one overcomes it while the other does not, the conquest by the one can only be reduced to God's greater love for him than for the other if the divine intention that preceded the act was infallibly effective. For if in both cases the antecedent divine intention were the same, then God would not have loved one more than the other, and the conquest by the one would not be due to a greater divine love. To this we say that the antecedent love and help God gives to both may be of the same degree. But while the one loses this help through his resistance, the other through God's help overcomes the temptation. And so he overcomes through a greater divine help than that possessed by the other, for he has God's concomitant aid as well as his prevenient aid, and not because he had a greater prevenient aid than the one who failed.

GOD'S WILL AND MAN'S ACT IN THE ORDER OF GRACE

The analysis we have presented of the relation between the divine will and the morally good or sinful act of the free creature has great relevance to the parallel relation in the order of grace. Concerning the supernatural mystery, we found in Scripture and tradtion that man's salutary act was a free gift of God's love to him and in no way a basis for pride, since there was nothing in it that was not given to him by God. Moreover, in examples from the Old and New Testaments, such as God's will of Abraham's obedience and the Christian's fidelity, we found that God's antecedent will of the salutary act was, according to his usual providence, not infallibly effective or infrustrable, but rather conditioned upon the cooperation of the free creature. And finally in the examples of God's permission of the sins of Adam, of Pharaoh in refusing to release the Jews from Egypt, of the Jews' rejection of Christ, and of the infidelity of Christians we saw that the total initiative in sin was man's and not God's, and that God did not desert man unless he had already been deserted by man. It seems to us that the natural analysis we have presented shows that no argument from the natural relation of God's will to the act of the free creature can be advanced to disprove our understanding of Scripture and tradition. In fact, it seems to us that the natural analysis we have presented helps to explain the revealed mystery of God's desire that man believe and perform the other acts of the order of grace. What is true in the natural order in this matter is true in the supernatural order unless the norms of revelation indicate otherwise, as what is true of human nature is true of the human nature of Christ, so the natural analysis we have presented helps us to understand how God's will is related to man's salutary act or omission of it.

What is true of man's dependence upon God for his naturally good act is true of his dependence for his salutary act. The latter, like the former, results from God's love freely given and is the measure of God's love upon which man wholly depends. In fact, because of its supernatural character, the salutary act manifests a greater freedom of the divine will, a greater love, and a greater dependence on the part of the creature. The freedom in God's will that the creature have such a good is over and beyond the freedom of God's creative act, since the supernatural is not owed to man's nature. The greater love that is the source of the salutary act is evident in the fact that by it God ordains man to an end that transcends what he can achieve by his nature, and it is even more evident when it is given to mankind turned away from God by original and personal sin. Also, since such an act transcends man's natural ability and the power of his nature wounded by original sin, man depends upon God's power in eliciting it even more than he does in eliciting a natural act.

What we have said of the antecedently frustrable character of God's will of the naturally good act of the free creature explains to some extent the conditioned divine will of man's salutary acts expressed by Scripture and tradition. In the supernatural, as in the natural order, God may ordain a person to a more perfect act than another or he may ordain one more forcefully than another to a good act, but the order established by his wisdom is such that his antecedent will that the creature perform the act is frustrable. He acts beyond this economy at times in the order of grace, as is apparent in Christ, in the Blessed Virgin to the extent that she was confirmed in grace, in God's intention that Peter's faith not fail, and in those saints who have been confirmed in grace during part of their lives. But in these cases God acts beyond the order established by his wisdom as his normal providence. As miracles are divine acts beyond the order God has established in creation and do not establish or change God's normal providence, so too in the cases we have mentioned God acts beyond the order he has established for mankind generally for the purpose of achieving some special good.

Finally, the analysis we have given of God's permission of man's first formal sin in the natural order helps us to some extent to understand the nature of his permission of an individual's first formal sin in the order of grace. It does not seem that God's permission of the sin of the angels who fell and of Adam's was antecedently certain to be followed by the sins that took place. Of course, God did not have to ordain all of the angels to heaven as a supernatural goal; he could have ordained some to a supernatural and others to a natural end. Thus he would not have sustained the latter in a movement to a supernatural goal, but in that case the fact that they did not ordain themselves to God with a supernatural love would not have been a sin, since it would not have been a privation of an order willed by God. Nor would it seem that the first formal sins of men in the order of fallen and redeemed humanity are preceded by a divine permission that is a negation of the prevenient grace necessary (as we explained in the preceding chapter) to avoid formal sin. It is with reference to fallen humanity that God has revealed the universality of his salvific will, and such a permission does not seem to us consistent with this universal salvific will. Moreover, we have seen that the Church teaches that the punishment due to original sin is the pain of the loss of the beatific vision, while that due to personal sin is the pain of sense.[29] If God's permission of fallen man's first formal sin antecedent to his foreknowledge of that sin were an absence of a divine intention that man have the grace necessary to avoid it, and if the motive for this were original sin, it would seem that the pain of sense also is the punishment for original sin. For on this theory the pain of sense inevitably results from original sin through the medium of the formal actual sin that is permitted in this manner. Other matters pertinent to God's universal salvific will shall be treated in a later section, but from what we have said here it seems to us that God's permission of the first formal sin in the order of grace is only that permission that is implicit in the frustrable character of God's antecedent intention and grace moving man to a salutary act. The sin of man in the order of grace, as in that of nature, is wholly due to man's initiative, and it is in no way the result of God's intention not to sustain him in the practice of the moral good. Some men are more guilty than others in rejecting grace and the act to which it moves them, but in no case does God do more than will to permit or tolerate man's rejection of his antecedent grace before man has actually rejected it.

THE QUESTION OF FITTINGNESS

In conclusion of this study of the relation of God's will to the act of the free creature in the natural and supernatural orders, we shall consider certain reasons that have been advanced to show that some order other than the one we have presented is more fitting to man's free act or to God's attributes. For example, it has been argued that it is more fitting for man's freedom that his self-determination within the free act be due to him as to its exclusive cause since it is this that is most distinctive of him as a free being. But to us the very reason advanced to support this opinion seems to demand that the self-determination of the free act be due to man only as its second cause and to God as its first cause, as we explained in the preceding chapter, since what is noblest in the act, more than any other aspect, must be due to God's causality. Man's self-movement and self-determination in his free act is a participation in God's own love of himself.

Others have argued that because of the very weakness and dependence of the free creature upon God, it is fitting that its good acts be anticipated by an infrustrable divine intention and causality, for this presents to him a greater help to avoid evil and do good. But to us it seems that the explanation we have advanced concerning the frustrable character of God's antecedent intention and causality more fittingly accounts for freedom as it is actually experienced in the world. Our experience, as well as the philosophical analysis of the will, shows how liable we are to fail even when we are anticipated by helps powerfully inclining us to do good. The order we have described is one that gives to man everything that is due to him in virtue of the nature God has given him. And it is a much greater gift to have been given the possibility of the achievement of the perfection of human nature than not to have received it, even though there is attached to human freedom the possibility, too, that man will reject God's antecedent intention for his perfection. Moreover, it is a far greater thing to have received the gift of grace than not to have received it, even though grace leaves man free to reject its antecedent movement to eternal beatitude and the salutary acts that merit it.

Some have thought that it would be unfitting for the divine transcendence and dignity to call man to what is good through an antecedent divine intention and movement which man has it in his power to reject since this would make the divine dignity subject to man's choice. To this we answer that that is exactly what sin is, a dishonor and insult offered to God as far as it lies in the power of the creature to do so; but God has created the free creature and has tolerated this possibility and reality of sin. In fact, for his wisdom to have established an order in which the antecedent divine desire that the free creature submit to him is frustrable shows clearly that the ultimate intention of God in his activity with man is not to gain man's submission. God's ultimate purpose is simply to give man a share in his divine goodness out of his divine benevolence and love for his uncreated divine perfection. Whether man accepts or rejects God's antecedent desire, he cannot really add to or diminish the ultimate purpose of God in creation, since the ultimate glory which God's activity in creation gives to him is contained within that divine act itself and the love for the divine goodness and the benevolence to creatures it manifests. Hence, man's rejection of the divine benevolence does not really detract from the divine transcendence or dignity.

Some have thought that it was fitting to divine justice for God to permit some men to sin in the sense of not wanting for them their natural or supernatural perfection antecedent to his foreknowledge of their sins, for creation should manifest the justice of God as well as his mercy. To us it seems that such a permission in the natural order would manifest, not the justice of God, but his injustice, since in our opinion the antecedent divine help necessary to avoid formal sin is owed to the rational creature. And such a permission means that God does not want to give this antecedent help to some creatures. Moreover, it seems to us that such a permission of formal sin in the order of grace, once God has manifested the universality of his salvific will, is incompatible with the expressed divine intention. We think it fitting that, on the understanding of God's permission of sin as we have explained it, those who reject God's antecedent help and sin be punished and thus manifest divine justice. We know from Scripture that if men do not repent their sins they experience this punishment partially in this life through a growing blindness to what is for their welfare and a growing moral hardness, but also that this life is a period of God's patience that holds out to men till death the means of repentance. Only in the next life will unrepented sin merit its final reward, and it is fitting that those who deliberately refused to glorify God's mercy glorify his justice through punishment.

Some have thought that it was not fitting to God's power that men be able to frustrate his desire that they do good. We know that some early Christians were scandalized by the fact that the Jews rejected Christ, and in turn were rejected by God, for this seemed to indicate a weakness in God and an inability to bring his desires to completion. But, as St. John and St. Paul explained, God's toleration of this rejection of Christ by the Jews was not due to God's weakness and did not obstruct the fulfillment of his ultimate goal. God's toleration of their disbelief showed clearly that he was not in need of their cooperation to gain either his purpose in the world or his own glory. The fact that they did not believe did not mean that they escaped God's power, for the sufferings they merited as a result proved that they were still in God's power and that they glorified his justice now that they had rejected his mercy. Moreover, their rejection did not prevent the fulfillment of God's intention in making the Jews his chosen people, namely, the extension of his kingdom throughout the world, for this was fulfilled essentially in Christ, and other instruments were raised up to spread Christ's message throughout the world. In fact, as St. Paul showed, God used the very resistance of the Jews to spread Christ's message more effectively throughout the world. For God to achieve his purposes in the world, within those who cooperate with him and in spite of the opposition of those who resist him, by a divine intention and causality that can be resisted by the individual seems to manifest the divine power in a more striking way than the use in God's common providence of an infrustrable divine intention and causality.

It has seemed to some more in accord with divine mercy that God's antecedent desire that man do good, and his grace by which it is brought about, be infrustrable. But since such a view of God's common providence is associated with the interpretation of his permission of sin as a lack of help to do good, it seems to us that this view reduces man's good acts to God's mercy in such a way that it reduces his sins to God's lack of mercy. Moreover we think that the explanation we have given of God's antecedent intention and grace shows clearly that the motive of God's gifts is his mercy. It seems to be a decisive proof of God's mercy that his grace is extended to men within the uncertainty of their response and the possibility that they will reject it. This seems to show that God is liberal and merciful out of his own divine generosity, and not out of an expectation of man's return of his love.

Finally, it has seemed to many that it is not fitting for God to permit evil, and particularly the evil of sin, if he can avoid it. If he can't avoid it, he is not omnipotent, if he can and does not, he is not the supreme good. To this we answer that the problem of evil is a great mystery which we in no way intend to treat at length here, so we shall restrict ourselves to several considerations that indicate there is nothing unfitting to God in his permission of sin as we have explained it. By the very fact that, out of love for his divine goodness and his desire to communicate a share of it, God creates, beings that are limited and defectible come into existence. Created being is of metaphysical necessity limited, since it depends on another for its bing; but this limitation is an indication of the measure of the creature and not of God's omnipotence; and it is not an evil, for it is not a privation of being the creature should have. Like limitation, defectibility, in the sense of an intrinsic ability to fall into evils in the physical and moral orders, and actual evils in the physical order follow the nature of created and material being. It is the nature of things lower than man to sacrifice their being for man; it is the nature of man to die; and it is his nature on this earth to be able to turn away from God by free choice. The *physical evils* man must endure involve the sacrifice of immeasurably lesser goods than the good for the sake of which he must sacrifice them, namely, the acquisition of God and God himself, so it is not unfitting for God to ordain man to himself in a condition where he must sacrifice such goods to attain him. In fact, such a condition is the result in history of original sin, but such a condition can be the occasion for an ultimately greater perfection than man would have otherwise reached. It is true that this does not seem to justify all physical evil, since some, such as infants, are not in a condition to gain this benefit from such evils. However, even here we can say that if the infant is baptized, the possession of God to which he is ordained makes it far better for it to have life, even one that involves suffering, than not to have it. We do not know adequately the condition of the unbaptized infant in the next life to assert that there is no value for it in the life and sufferings it received. Much mystery remains when this is said, but this much seems to be true, namely, that one cannot say that the physical evils an individual suffers involve the sacrifice of his essential personal good without culpability on his own part, or that the personal good does not more than compensate for the physical evils the individual endures. Moreover, there is a greater good than that of the individual, the good of creation as a whole and the uncreated divine good, that adds further light to this mystery of suffering. And by faith we know that God would not allow an evil from which he could not draw a greater good.

In creating a being morally defectible, God accepted the possibility that some would sin; and he gave permission for this, not in the sense of a lack of his divine intention to sustain man in the practice of the moral good, but in the sense of allowing him to reject the antecedent divine intention and inclination to this good. Is it unfittting for God, then, to communicate this goodness of created being, as he has done, because some men will reject his antecedent intention for their perfection? Should the good that is given to such a vast number of created beings and the glory that is given to God not be given because some free creatures, in culpable rejection of the limited nature of their goodness, sin? The fact that some men will make a sinful use of created goods is, of course, in no way a reason for God not to create; for if it were, evil would overcome good through preventing the existence of the great good realized in the creation of the free creature and the glory God thereby gains. In fact, it is an indication of the transcendence of God and his mercy that he has created the world in the midst of the possibility of this evil, as the measure of the evils a man is willing to suffer for love of God and service of him is a sign of the measure of his sanctity.

NOTES
1. See *ST,* 1.29.3.
2. See *ibid.,* 1.26.1–4.

3. See *ibid.*, 1.19.4.

4. See *ibid.*, 1.19.3. God's creative act can be called necessary only in a meaning that detracts in no way from the freedom of the act. Because of divine immutability, granted that God has freely chosen to create, he cannot on that supposition now do otherwise.

5. See *ibid.*, 1.20.1–4.

6. See the Church's expression of the purpose of God's creative act in the First Vatican Council, Ses. 3, c. 1. See also *De pot.*, 3.15. ad 14; *ST*, 1.19.2; 44.4.

7. *See De pot.*, 3.15. ad 5.

8. *ST*, 1.19:.9. See also *De pot.*, 6.1. ad 8.

9. See *ST*, 1.19.9. ad 1; ad 2; ad 3.

10. See ch. 1, pp. 33 ff.

11. See ch. 1, pp. 5 ff.

12. See ch. 1, pp. 24 ff. and footnote 53.

13. See ch. 1, footnotes 16–18, 32–33.

14. See ch. 1, footnote 33.

15. See ch. 1, pp. 27–28.

16. *De ver.*, 6.3. ad 3. See above, ch. 4, pp. 115 f.

17. See *ST*, 1–2, 10.4. ad 3; 112.3; *De ver.*, 2.12. ad 1; ad 2.

18. See *ST*, 1.19.8; 22.4.

19. *De malo*, 6. art. un., ad 3.

20. 1 *Sent.*, 38.1.5.

21. *De ver.*, 2.14. ad 5. See also *ibid.*, ad 3; 2.12.c. and ad 1; ad 2; *CG*, 1.67; *ST*, 1.14.13. ad 1.

22. *ST*, 1.21. ad 2.

23. *Ibid.*, ad 3.

24. See ch. pp. 115–121.

25. See *ST*, 1.10.1 and 2.

26. *ST*, 1.19.8.

27. *ST*, 1.19.6. See in the same sense *ibid.*, ad 3; *ST*, 1.103.7 and 8.

28. See *ST*, 1.19.7.

29. See ch. 4, footnote 27. See also G. Dyer, "Limbo: A Theological Evaluation," *Theological Studies*, 19 (1958), 32–49 where it is shown that recent theologians are unanimous in denying that infants who die unbaptized experience the pain of sense.

PART V / PERSPECTIVES

OF RATIONAL THEOLOGY

Karl Rahner / On the Theology
of Freedom

A BRIEF TREATMENT of the theology of freedom must forgo historical survey and extended scriptural exegesis. It must content itself, instead, with, at the most, a synthesis of relevant matter from Revelation. One should note, further, that only very gradually do certain ultimate and indelible aspects of the nature of freedom crystallize in philosophical statement, even though they are lived, before such examination, in every one of our acts and in the course of our personal and collective history. The history of salvation and revelation, which includes the history of Christian theology, is thus a history as well of man's philosophical examination of himself as a free being. This is not to say that man always knows with adequate explicitness what human freedom is, nor, on the other hand, to deny that he alters and deepens his concept of freedom when he uses the language of revelation and theology to express it.

KARL RAHNER, S.J. *(1904–   ) has for many years been Professor at the University of Innsbruck. Author of many significant theological studies originally published in German, a number have fortunately been translated, including* THEOLOGICAL INVESTIGATIONS, *Vol. I (1963). "On The Theology of Freedom" is reprinted from John C. Murray (ed.),* FREEDOM AND MAN *with the permission of P. J. Kenedy and Sons.*

For the history of revelation is also essentially the history of man's coming to his full heritage as man—and therefore it is the history of his freedom. This freedom, moreover, is a natural reality pre-existing the history of man's reception of it.

In Jesus Christ the history of salavation has arrived at its definitive and unsurpassable eschatological state. The fact that there can now be no going beyond this position in the context of our world history cannot be taken as an arbitrary disposition by God, as if He simply does not wish to reveal any more to us. It must be, rather, something in the very nature of this eschatological condition, to be, by definition, surpassed now only by the immediate vision of God. When we reach the highest point of revelation in Christ, we reach at the same time the highest point of the self-realization of human freedom. Freedom, understood as communicated to man by God in permanent creation, is freedom to accept absolutely the absolute mystery we call God. We engage in this acceptance in such a way that God is not merely one of the objects for which we have, along with others, some neutral freedom of choice. On the contrary, God is rather the one who "dawns on" man, first of all in this absolute act of freedom, and in whom alone the nature of freedom itself comes to its complete realization.

Freedom in the theological sense is freedom that derives from and is directed toward God. It would be a complete misapprehension of the nature of freedom if one were to regard it as the mere capacity to choose between individual objects given *a posteriori,* among which God would then be placed along with many others. It would be equally fallacious if one were to hold that God, among these objects, plays a special role in the actual choice made by this freedom only because of His own peculiar nature and not because of the nature of freedom itself. Freedom is possible only because there is spirit as transcendence; this point is explicit in St. Thomas. Unlimited transcendence to being as such and, hence, indifference in regard to any particular finite object within the context of this absolute transcendence are to be found only in such a way that this transcendence, in every particular act concerned with a finite object, is always related to the basic unity of being as such: that is, to God.

Further, this is so only in so far as this act of transcendence —which is the basis of every categorial relation to a finite object and for that matter, to the infinite, too, in relation to finite concepts—is supported by a permanent self-disclosure and self-presentation of the context of this transcendence. In other words, freedom has a theological character, not under a concept regarding God explicitly in terms of categorial objectivity along with other objects, but always as part of the nature of freedom itself. God is to be found, unreflected on, in every act of freedom, as its supporting ground and ultimate term. When St. Thomas says that God is known in every object and not in a reflective way but nonetheless really, this surely applies equally to the case of freedom. God is willed in every act of freedom, not in a reflective way but nonetheless really. Conversely, it is only in this way that we experience what is really meant by God: the term, beyond the reach of mind and heart and therefore essentially mystery, of the single basic transcendence of man which is analyzable into knowledge and love.

What is decisive for the Christian understanding of freedom, however, is not that this freedom is empowered by God and related to Him as the supporting context of categorial freedom of choice, but that freedom, in a sense, withstands God. This is the terrifying mystery of freedom in the Christian sense. When one regards God in purely categorial terms as one reality along with others, as one of the many objects of freedom of choice understood as a neutral capacity which occupies itself arbitrarily now with this and now with that, the statement that freedom of choice is freedom of choice even with respect to God offers no special difficulty. The extreme statement about the nature of freedom which, in its radicalness, leaves ordinary categorial indeterminism far behind, is that freedom is freedom even with regard to its supporting ground—that it can thus culpably deny the condition of its own possibility in an act which necessarily affirms this condition once again. What is decisive for the Christian doctrine of freedom is that this freedom involves the possibility of consent to or refusal of its own horizon, and that it is this possibilty which properly constitutes freedom.

Of course human freedom, being freedom mediated in terms of the world, is always fredom as regards a categorial object, freedom as regards something in the world, even where it sets out to be immediately and explicitly freedom with respect to God. The reason for this is that even such an act as explicit consent to or refusal of God cannot be related immediately to the God of the basic transcendental experience, but only to the God of thematic categorial reflection—to God as a concept, not immediately and solely to the God of transcendental presence. But it is nevertheless part of the specifically Christian experience of freedom that this freedom is freedom not solely with respect to some object of categorial experience within the absolute context which is God, but that it is a freedom, if always only mediated, with respect to God Himself and turned toward Him: a freedom to accept or to reject God Himself. It follows, therefore, that it is not this alone or primarily where God is to be found and is conceived reflectively in categorial concepts, but where God is to be found prereflectively, but basically, in the transcendental experience which is a condition and constituent of every personal activity directed to our environment and our fellow men. In this sense we meet God in a most radical way everywhere, as the most authentic challenge to our freedom in everything in the world and—as the Bible says—above all in our neighbor.

To put the problem more exactly, one may ask why the transcendental context of freedom is not only the condition of its possibilty but also its proper object. Or to put it another way, one wonders why it is not enough for us to act in freedom with respect to ourselves, our environment, and our fellow men. It is understood, of course, that the result of such free action, whether fulfilling or negating, lies always within that infinitely large horizon of transcendence from which we confront these objects of our free act. Finally, there is the question of why this horizon itself is also the *object* of this freedom, in the acceptance and rejection of it, when by definition this horizon remains the condition of the possibility of its own rejection. This condition inescapably requires that in this rejection the horizon is necessarily and inevitably affirmed as the condition of the possibility of freedom, and at the same time denied as unreflected-on object. Thus in this act of negating freedom we find the real and absolute contradiction in which God is simultaneously accepted and rejected. This ultimate enormity is at the same time reduced and relativized into the temporal, in the sense that it is necessarily objectified in and mediated through the finite substance of our life in its being spread through time.

We have to insist on the real possibility of such an absolute contradiction in freedom precisely because this possibility is the object of dispute and doubt. This happens in popular theology when people say that it is inconceivable that the infinite God in His objectivity can assess the tiny deformity of some finite reality, the offense against some particular, purely finite thing, except in terms of what it presently is: something *finite*. The argument runs that therefore God cannot evaluate it in terms of some absolute prohibition and infinite sanction, or describe it as directed against His own will as such. The "will" against which the offense is really directed in such a sin would be the God-willed finite thing, and an offense against God's will over and above this would be making God's will illegitimately into a particular categorial thing alongside the thing willed. Nevertheless, the possibility exists of a rejection, through freedom, with respect to God Himself. Otherwise real subjectivity in freedom would be impossible, for its specific quality is a matter of the subject, because it is transcendence.

If the particular things in the world which we meet within the horizon of transcendence are not occurrences in a space which remains unaffected by what it encloses but rather the materialization in history of the self-presentation and accessibility for encounter of this source of our transcendence which supports our subjectivity, then freedom with respect to the particular things we meet is also always freedom with respect to the horizon, the ground, the "abyss," which allows them to meet us and become the inner constituent of our receptive freedom. Inasmuch as the term and source cannot be a matter of indifference for the subject as knower, but are explicitly or implicitly what this cognitive transcendence has to do with even when it does not have this term as explicit object, the subject has the *freedom* to concern itself with God Himself, basically and inescapably, even when this freedom is always realized and mediated in the concrete particularity of experience.

Basically, freedom is freedom to accept or reject God, and is thus freedom of the subject in regard to Himself. If the subject as such is supported precisely by his transcendental immediacy to God, then truly subjective freedom, such as finally orders the subject as a whole, can take place only in accepting or rejecting God, because only there can the subject as such be met with at all. Otherwise, freedom would be some indifferent freedom to choose this or that; it would be an infinitely perpetuated repetition of the same or of the opposite (only a kind of the same); it would be a freedom of the eternal return of the same wandering Jew. The alternative must be the freedom of the subject in relation to himself in his definitive status, and hence freedom as regards God; however little this ground, this most proper and basic object of freedom may be reflected on in the particular act of freedom.

Another consideration brings to light the ultimate theological ground of freedom as freedom before God. If the grace-informed materialization in history of our transcendence is supported by the *self*-communication of God offered to us; if our transcendence as spirit is never to be found as something purely natural but is always embraced and supported by a grace-informed impulse of our being as spirit toward absolute nearness to God; if, in other words, God never becomes present only as the constantly elusive and retreating context of our transcendence but offers Himself as such for immediate possession in what we call divinizing grace—then freedom receives, in transcendence and in accepting or rejecting its ground, a certain immediacy to God through which it becomes in the most radical way the capacity to accept and reject God as such. This capacity is not found in the abstract, formal concept of transcendence to God as merely the remote and elusive context of our existence.

From the Christian point of view, as we said before, freedom cannot be regarded as a neutral capacity to do this or that in any order one prefers and in a condition of time which could be interrupted only from outside, although time could run on indeterminately so far as freedom is concerned. Freedom is rather the capacity to realize oneself once and for all, the capacity which of its nature involves the freely achieved, definitive status of the subject as such. This is obviously what is at issue in Christian language about man and his salvation or damnation, when he must answer, and be able to answer, as one who is free, for himself and for the whole of his life, before the judgment of God. The eternally valid verdict over his definitive salvation or damnation is passed, according to his works, by a judge who does not look upon the mere surface of life, on the "face," but who looks rather on the center of the person over whom he freely disposes, on the "heart." It is true that man's formal freedom to decide and choose is more taken for granted in Scripture than made the theme of conscious reflection. The explicit theme of Scripture, especially in the New Testament, is rather the paradox that the freedom of man, while remaining answerable and without being annulled, is nevertheless enslaved under the demonic powers of sin and death, and to some degree under the Law. It must be freed by the grace of God in an interior inclination for the Law. Thus it cannot be doubted that for Scripture the sinner and the justified man are answerable before God for the deed that sums up their life, and that they are also free to the extent that freedom is a permanent constituent of human nature.

But the authentic nature of this freedom, for Christian revelation, emerges only in so far as it is the basis for absolute salvation or damnation—really definitive and before God. In ordinary, everyday experience, freedom of choice may well look like a feature of some particular human act which can be imputed to a man to the extent that it had been actively performed by him, without this having been causally fixed in advance, and in this sense being forced by some interior condition of the man or by some outside situation which preceded the active decision. Such a concept of freedom of choice, however, atomizes freedom in exercise because it divides it up into nothing but someone's particular acts which are then held together only by some neutral substance—like identity of the subject who performs them all, and of his capacity to do so, and by the single exterior space time in which life is lived. Freedom would thus be nothing but freedom of *action;* it would be the possibility of imputing some particular act to a person who would remain neutral in himself and therefore always able to determine himself to something new, so long as the exterior conditions are given.

Yet from the Christian point of view man can determine and dispose over himself as a whole and for good and all through his freedom. Thus he does not perform acts which are to be qualified purely and morally and which then turn out to be entirely passing—acts which are charged to him only juridically or morally. On the contrary, by his free decision, at the heart of his being and in all truth, a man really *is* good or evil, and in such a way that his definitive salvation or damnation is already to be found in this decision, even if it is still hidden. The freedom in which one must answer for oneself is thus transformed and deepened in a terrifying fashion. Freedom is above all freedom of *being.* It is not only the quality of an act occasionally performed in fact or of the capacity to perform it. It is a transcendental "marking" of the human being itself. If man is really to be capable of disposing over himself for good and all, if eternity is thus to be the act of his own freedom, if this act is to be capable, in certain circumstances, of pulling something permanently good against its own goodness into a ruin which could make this man good or evil in the very ground of his being, and if this being good or evil is not something that hits a man from outside—then freedom must be regarded above all as freedom of being. That is to say, man is the being in whose being being itself is at issue. Man is that being which always has a relationship to itself—one of subjectivity, not simply of nature. Man is always a person; he is not simply "there" but is always *aware* of being there.

Nothing happens to this being in disregard of its relationship to itself; or if anything does so happen to it, then it is subjectively and savingly significant for it, to the extent that it is freely "understood," subjectively accepted, by a free subject as such in a wholly particular way. The "I" of this being cannot be overlooked or objectified. It can never be replaced or explained by another, not even by its own reflective conception of itself. It is pure source, not dependent on anything else, and therefore not capable of being derived from anything else or of being founded on anything else. Its relation to its divine source should not be interpreted in terms of causal and functional relations of dependence such as prevail in the realm of our categorial experience, in which the source retains and binds down instead of setting free, and in which being autonomous, and having a source, grow not in equal but in converse proportion. Through his freedom of being, man is always incomparable. He never fits adequately into any system; he can never be adequately subsumed by any idea. In a basic sense he is unassailable, yet at the same time he is alone and in danger. He is burdened with himself; he has no way of "absolving" himself from having to be himself, alone and once and for all; he has no way of shifting responsibility for himself on to somebody else.

In freedom, it is not a matter of choosing this or that, or of something which can be done or left undone. Basically, freedom is not the capacity to choose some object or to behave in some particular way with regard to this or that. It is the freedom of self-understanding, the possibility of saying yes or no to oneself, the possibility of decision for or against oneself. This possibility corresponds to the self-appropriation in knowledge, to the cognitional subjectivity, of man. Freedom never takes place as a purely objective process, as a mere choice "between" particular objects. On the contrary, it is the *self-realization* of the man who is choosing objectively, and it is only within this freedom in which man has power over himself that he is then also free with regard to the raw material of his self-realization. He can perform a certain act or abstain from it in regard to his own self-realization, something that is inescapably laid upon him. It is his inescapable task, and whatever the variation in the raw material of this self-realization, it is always a self-fulfillment directed toward God, or a radical self-refusal in face of God. For the salvation or damnation in the winning or losing God, something which is fixed in freedom, should not be regarded as a sheer external reaction of a judging or rewarding God. On the contrary, it is itself already achieved in this freedom.

Thus freedom is the capacity for something total. If it is to be able to bring about salvation or damnation, and thus to determine the whole man, it brings the whole man into play, in his past and in his future, in all the complexity of his self-world-God relationships. Freedom is always the self-realization of man choosing objectively in regard to a total realization, a total disposal over his existence in the sight of God. Thus it is easy to see that this basic feature of freedom is exercised in time. At any given moment the total project of existence to which we have referred, one's own total self-understanding, one's *option fondamentale*, remains empty in a multitude of ways, and objectively unrealized. The same actual depth and radicalness of self-disposal are not to be found in every individual act of freedom. All individual acts of freedom, although each of them means to engage in the venture of total and definitive self-disposal, are inserted into the whole of the one whole deed of freedom which recapitulates the one human, temporal, finite life. This is so precisely because each of these acts is performed within the context of the whole of existence and thereby receives its weight and proportion.

Accordingly, in the biblical and Augustinian concept of the heart, in the concept of subjectivity in Kierkegaard, in that of action in Blondel, and so on, there is always appreciation of the fact that there is this basic act of freedom, embracing and marking the whole existence. Of course this act is realized by means of man's particular acts, by means of acts which may be localized in space and time, and which may be objectified in their motives; it cannot be performed in any other way. But it cannot be simply identified in objective reflection with any such individual act. Neither does it represent the pure moral result of the sum of these individual acts, nor is it to be identified simply with the moral quality of the last of one's freely performed individual acts. The concrete freedom of man in which in the sight of God he disposes of himself as a whole in procuring his own definitive status in the sight of God is the unity in difference (no longer capable of being reflected on) of *option fondamentale* and of one's individual free acts, a unity which is the concrete being of the free subject who has realized himself. Thus, to insist upon the point once more, freedom is not the capacity of being always able to do the opposite, of infinite revision. It is the capacity to do something for good and all, the capacity to do something which is valid forever precisely because it is done in freedom. Freedom is the capacity for the eternal. Natural processes can always be revised again and altered; this is why they are indifferent. The result of freedom is the true necessity which remains forever.

Freedom is mystery because it derives from and is directed to God alone, and God is essentially the incomprehensible mystery which as such is precisely the source and term of freedom as such. The ground of freedom is the "abyss" of the mystery, which can never be regarded as something not yet known but which one day will be comprehensible. It is the most basic datum of our transcendental experience in knowledge and love. In its manifest and permanent incomprehensibility it is the ground of the possibility of comprehending everything which is encountered as an individual within its context.

We must forgo putting the epistemological question about how far freedom can really be known. Freedom is not a datum of any empirical psychology, because this discipline can do no more than observe functional connections between particular data within the context of experience, while freedom is always experienced before any such objective experience, as a modality of any transcendental experience. The subject freely knows himself *as not* objectifiable. This radical mysteriousness of the freedom of the subject is thus inserted into the free act of this subject as such. The particular act of freedom shares in the mystery of his origin and future in so far as it is never absolutely objectifiable in its freedom and thus in its moral quality. Of course this peculiarity derives immediately from the strict subjectivity of freedom, but it is also insisted on explicitly in Revelation. It is to be found there that freedom and the concrete free decision are ultimately unobjectifiable. That total decision in which one disposes forever and ever over the whole of one's being and which fixes this wholeness itself in its freely determined definitive state—and only insofar as this happens can a particular act really be called fully free—is submitted, according to Revelation, to the sole judgment of God.

Man brings about his definitive status in freedom and therefore as a *conscious* subject, but he cannot objectify for himself this product of his freedom. That is to say, he cannot judge himself or anybody in his total quality in the sight of God. It is the Catholic doctrine of faith that *homo viator* is denied an absolutely certain judgment about his state of justification or his eternal salvation. The Protestant doctrine of justification—in spite of a tradition of controversy—does not disagree on this point, because even in the Lutheran doctrine of justification, faith regarded as absolute trust can still be tempted. This means that man cannot reflect his free decision with objective adequacy or with absolute certainty. Freedom is truly subjectivity, and subjectivity in itself and in its self-assimilation objectifies a more basic experience than the purely material, the present at hand, and the objective; and it can be unambiguously defined by a precedent and more basic system of coordinates made up of general concepts. In the act of his freedom man knows who he is in freedom and who he wants to be. But this very knowing is really nothing but himself, and therefore he cannot remove it from himself as something objective and manipulable and say as clearly to himself that he declares himself for God in his freedom. This declaration, which is himself, disappears from his sight, in a certain measure, into the mystery of God. An absolutely certain declaration about a man's exercise of freedom in a particular act which could be localized in space and time is fundamentally impossible for this man himself and all the more so for other people.

Of course this does not mean that freedom and responsibility are not things which are to be found in the realm of human experience and reflection and among human beings. Freedom, even in the form of concrete, total self-disposal of the free subject over himself for good and all, still takes place in some given particular categorial materials: subjectivity is always realized in nature. That shows the creatureliness of human freedom. It is equally clear that, without prejudice to the impossibility of any adequate self-reflection, man is always the one who reflects, the one who objectifies himself, the one who places himself under norms of general validity. It is Catholic teaching and—if one considers the morality present materially in the Bible—also thoroughly biblical teaching, that what is developed is more than purely formal principles of the subjective exercise of freedom of the subject with regard to its rightness or wrongness. Developed thoroughly also are material norms of an objective and generally valid kind with regard to right or wrong exercise of this subjective freedom in the categorial material of the nature of man and his world. This result makes it obvious that man is no less authorized than obliged to make a certain reflective and objectified self-judgment of his moral state and thus a judgment with regard to the givenness, rightness, or wrongness of his exercise of freedom in a particular material act.

This knowledge about oneself, which one can tell oneself, which one can examine critically, with regard to which one can arrive at some valid result, is characteristic precisely of the peculiar nature of the pilgrim existence of man in this life, in which freedom is still always at work, and in which every examination is itself still an act of freedom not adequately examined or examinable in a reflective way. It is real knowledge; it gives a "certainty"—the kind of certainty that can be found in the realm of history and freedom—that is to say, the demand to subject freedom itself, once more and necessarily, to norms. One has the right and the duty to include this knowledge of oneself—and eventually his knowledge about other people as well—in the calculus of one's life and one's active deciding and behaving, because otherwise one cannot exist at all. In any case, complete abstention from such a judgment does not escape the risk of such a judgment. On the contrary, it would be itself merely another free and risk-laden decision. Yet this knowledge of freedom, judging, deciding, venturing, and objectifying is not to be regarded as something definitive, absolutely certain, beyond appeal. In this objectified knowledge man accepts himself in his own reflective mode of self-understanding, which is itself just another act of unreflected freedom. Precisely as the one who understands himself in some way or another, man surrenders himself to the mysterious judgment of God, which takes place secretly in the unreflected act of his freedom. Freedom is mystery.

Man's freedom is, in fact, free self-realization into a definitive state. But despite its authentically creative character, it is nonetheless a created freedom. That this freedom is created is apparent for two reasons. This freedom is lived and experienced above all in its transcendental being as supported and empowered by its absolute context, something it does not constitute, but something by which it is constituted. The transcendentality of spirit should not be understood either in knowing or in the free act of living, in the sense that spirit projects and fixes its term and its goal. This goal discloses itself to the knowing and willing spirit in a particular mode of retreat—this is not ontologism. The goal is experienced in the act of spiritual existence itself in terms of the authentically moving cause. The active self-projection of spirit toward its goal, toward its future, is experienced as supported by the self-disclosing goal, over which the spirit does not dispose, because it does not comprehend this goal. On the contrary, in being and in operation it is constituted by it as that which lies beyond it. The specific nature of the transcendentality of freedom, as something supported and empowered by its goal, itself points to the createdness of this freedom, which is immediately experienced as posited.

The character of created freedom is strengthened and clarified by the empowering self-disclosure of this goal. This strengthening occurs because the empowering of freedom for the absoluteness of being is experienced as grace-informed empowering for absolute nearness to this goal in immediate self-communication of this goal—that is, divine grace—even if this experience can be clearly objectified only by its interpretation in supernatural revelation and faith. Grace as nearness to God radicalizes the experience of the createdness of freedom. There is further confirmation of the character of created freedom, as the subject's self-disposal over himself for good and all, is necessarily mediated by an environmental and a community which are given *a posteriori*, uncontrollably, ultimately unplanned. Man accomplishes his basic freedom toward himself always only in going acceptingly through the course of his own given history, something which is given in advance, something which is imposed as a task. Freedom is free to answer to necessity, in acceptance or rejection. Thus its createdness emerges once again.

Creaturely freedom is conditioned by a situation in the sense that it comes to itself only in so far as it goes out into the world. According to Christian doctrine, contained above all in the implications of the doctrine of original sin and of concupiscence, this state of being conditioned by a situation is distinguished by the fact that this situation is always and inescapably determined to some extent by guilt. In other words, the doctrine that there was sin at the beginning of man's history and the doctrine of concupiscence together mean that there is never a situation or any raw material of freedom for the freedom of man—if situation and raw material are seen adequately and without arbitrary abstractions—which would not be partly determined in advance by the guilt in the history of mankind to the particular positive or negative moral decision. Further, it is never possible, before the end of history, to succeed wholly in eliminating this mortgage of guilt which is objectified in the situation. Insofar as freedom must always objectify itself in some alien material, in order to find itself, it is always alienated from itself. It can never see itself so clearly in what it has done in the raw material of the situation in order to be itself that it can recognize in it exactly and with absolute certainty what it is: the acceptance or rejection of itself and of God. That is already clear from the fact that there is no objectification of which one could say with absolute

certainty that it could arise in its concrete form out of freedom alone and not out of nature.

Since it is mediated in created terms, this freedom becomes
unavoidably ambiguous, in an ultimate sense, in its objectification. Thus it becomes a mystery, and as such it must surrender
itself to God. This ambiguity of the objectifications of freedom
for its reflection on its basic nature is now made sharper by
the circumstance that the material which is given in advance
to freedom and which enters into its concrete exercise is
always to some extent determined and shaped by the guilt
from the beginning of the history of the spirit. Of course the
freedom of the individual can always regard this material,
which is partly determined by the guilt of others and which
does not remain outside the act of freedom, in the sense that
it ratifies the guilt-determinedness of this material as embodiment of its own refusal of God, in the sense that it makes it
the objective manifestation of its own guilt. On the other hand,
it may understand it in the sense that it suffers it and overcomes it in consent to God by participating in the cross of
Christ. But this very ambiguity of the given situation and of
its material for the exercise of freedom once again makes the
basic act of freedom a mystery that is ultimately not absolutely open to reflection and not finally soluble—a mystery
for freedom itself. It conceals the meaning and the quality of
the history of mankind as a whole in the unsearchable judgment of God.

Insofar as freedom is always, in every act, freedom for the
mystery of God himself, the mystery by which it is supported
and empowered, the act of freedom is always essentially the
act of man's self-surrender to the uncontrollable disposal of
God, and in this sense it is essentially a trustful risk. In the
history of this freedom's self-experience it becomes evident
only very gradually how God gives Himself to this freedom
which, if it does not want to avoid Him, must trust itself to
Him unconditionally in the venture of freedom into what cannot be controlled. This history of the experience of freedom—
what we call the history of salvation and revelation—is the
experience accomplished in Jesus Christ. God, in what we call

divinizing grace, has given Himself into the possession of the freedom of man, in absolute nearness, and as basis of the free acceptance of this nearness. God in His inmost divinity has delivered Himself to the freedom which delivers itself into the uncontrollable mystery of God. God is not merely the remote context in which, as something always more removed, man projects his free self-understanding. On the contrary, God has become the realm and object of this exercise of freedom in absolute immediacy.

Thus it has become manifest in this experience of freedom that the rejection of God by man, which affects the whole of the history of human freedom, was allowed by God only in the divine consent to His own self-communication to creaturely freedom and that it remains embraced by this consent of God, which is what remains for everyone victorious in the whole history of salvation. The freedom of man is freed into immediacy to the freedom of being of God Himself. It is empowered to its highest possible act, the act which involves its formal nature but which is not demanded by it. The freedom which is directed toward God and derived from Him as origin and future of freedom, freedom as the capacity for dialogue possessed by love, is exercised in the highest conceivable modality of this aspect. It is freedom which is supported by God's self-communication in personal love and which embraces God Himself. The context and the object of love freely bestowed have become indentical.

Austin Farrer / Liberty

and Theology

Existential and "We Think" Philosophies

THE TIME has come to survey the question of voluntary freedom with a wider sweep. We have done what we could do in
the hand-to-hand fight with deterministic misconception. Let
us stop arguing about the freedom of the will, and ask ourselves why, after all, it matters. Let us beg the question of
liberty, and say: Supposing that we have a voluntary freedom,
what is the use of making the fact clear, or stripping away the
sophistries which obscure it? For, as even determinists admit,
men must be allowed to think as though they were freely inventing, and to make choices as though they were freely deciding. Will not the libertarian and the determinist, therefore,
live and act in an identical way? If there is a difference between them, it is that the determinist hopes to perform a feat

AUSTIN FARRER *(1904–   ) is Warden of Keble College, Oxford and is
author of a number of important works in both rational and biblical
theology, including* FINITE AND INFINITE *(1953) and Saving Belief (1964).
"Liberty and Theology" is reprinted with the permission of Charles
Scribner's Sons from* THE FREEDOM OF THE WILL *by Austin Farrer. Copyright © 1958 Austin Farrer.*

of which the libertarian despairs. For the determinist thinks that, reflecting after the event on his neighbour's conduct or his own, he should be able to descry in it the structure of reason, the lineaments of necessity; whereas the libertarian renounces any such hope. And so it may seem that the practical value of libertarianism is nil; it makes a metaphysical fuss about deciding and inventing, things which the sensible man does as he goes along, with no fuss at all. Whereas the practical value of determinism is tangible; it holds before us the hope of causal explanation; it gives us a programme to work upon.

The determinist claim which we have just stated contains an implicit admission, which the counter-argument will seize. What is determinism? It is not a hypothesis, it is a hope. Whatever patterns or regularities are to be found in human behaviour, a libertarian is just as free to recognize, study and profit by them, as a determinist can be. The determinist is in no position actually to plot out the most part of human conduct, as the simple exemplification of established uniformities, whether before or after the conduct occurs. He is singular merely in holding the hope, the pious hope, that under ideal conditions it could be done. Now where we have a general and pious hope entertained about what can be done, we may postulate, as the counterpart to it, a pious faith about the way things are. If some form of action or achievement is held to be in general an ideal possibility, it is surely held to be so in consequence of the general nature of things. If we hope that we will reduce conduct to causal explanation, we believe conduct is such as to be causally explicable. The hope and the belief belong together, and they share the same pious character. If the hope is a pious hope, the belief is a pious belief; not the sort of belief I have when I believe Viet-Minh to be a republic, but the sort I have when I believe the Yellow Race to be a messianic people.

Once it has been seen that determinism is a faith, the way is open to consider libertarianism as a faith also. Now the determinist attack which we were just now considering, amounted to saying that bare libertarianism is an empty faith; it makes a fuss over assuring people of their freedom to do what they will do in any case—contrive, invent, decide. The point ought to be conceded. Bare libertarianism is an empty faith; and if we cast fate out of liberty-hall only to keep the rooms empty, swept and garnished, the demon will return with reinforcements. For the patterns of necessity play so large a part in our thinking, they will always encroach on empty ground. Bare libertarianism is an empty faith; but then libertarianism need not be, and commonly is not, held as an isolated conviction. It is supported by other beliefs, beliefs which both give it significance, and themselves borrow significance from it. We will recall two of them: about creativity, and about responsibility, the believer in freewill has his own way of thinking. We will take the two terms in order.

It may be true that, for practical purposes, the doctrine of necessity concedes the felt freedom of our acts; but it teaches us, when we reflect on them, to view them as the expressions of a natural inevitability. And (the libertarian complains) such a teaching cannot but undermine in us the seeming importance of what we do. For it tells us that there is some nature of things, or of ourselves, in accordance with which we are bound to act; whose tendencies our decision merely applies to the case, and, as it were, precipitates. To employ again the gross metaphor we have used—the statute-laws of our universe, or of our kind, are fixed; our decisions are, at the best, those of judges; our discretion is limited to an application of law to instance. By contrast, the libertarian may see himself as making law. Within the limits which physical and psychological facts prescribe, man may have the sheer liberty to make himself the sort of creature he chooses to be, by adopting a certain sort of life, and building up the customs and aptitudes required for it. No doubt our power to make ourselves is much restricted; by the time we take the task in hand, our elders have done so much to us already. But they have done it, and we shall do the like to our children, pupils or charges. The fact that man-making by men is exercised on others, not on one's self, does not diminish the portentousness of the undertaking. Any one of us, it is true, will over-estimate his importance, if he supposes that he alone, in independence of other individuals or of the social mould, can shape any single soul, his child's or his own. Nevertheless, according to the libertarian belief, the total moulding force will be a function of the number (whatever it be) of free agencies; whether aware, or unaware of their freedom; whether employing it to carve a destiny, or asleep on it, in a nest of convention.

Certain existentialist thinkers on the Continent have carried self-creation to the limit, and have boldly proclaimed (without, in their own eyes, discrediting their doctrine) that liberty is so absolute, it topples over into an absurdity. It may amuse us to compare Sartre's estimate of our condition with Pope's mockery of man. "Go, wondrous creature," says the poet to the featherless biped, "teach Providence to rule; then drop into thyself, and be a fool." Yet, according to Pope, we need not resign ourselves to cosmic folly, for we need not undertake to play providence. We can play the fool in a corner, and it will not be calamitous; *dulce est desipere in loco*. Whereas according to the existentialist philosopher, the sceptre of Providence is forced into our fingers; if we do not play providence to ourselves, no one will; there is no other God. The ordeal of Phaeton is ours; the reins are in our hands, the doors of dawn are open, and we must guide the chariot of the Sun. We must —but it's absurd; our ignorance, our liability to passion, the mutual frustration of our aims, present the spectacle of forty Phaetons drunk, driving wild on the Place de la Concorde.

"Now, my child," they used to say to me, marking the end of a penal silence, "Now you can say what you like." My young lips were struck dumb by so portentous an option; and so it is, when existentialism throws my life into my lap, and says "Be yourself, my boy, and make it up as you go along." The effect is like a paralytic stroke. I come to again, however, at last, and begin to remember—with what consolation to remember—my responsibilities. There will, no doubt, be occasions for sheer personal option, but thank heaven I have not to meditate *in vacuo* on what to make of myself, as the God of Leibniz meditates on what to make of the world. Thank heaven I have this lecture to write, and beyond that, my pupils to see to; and ah, beyond that, if I dare to look, there is Lazarus on the doorstep, covered with sores.

What is it, then? I must, by my effort, and invention, and fidelity, make my life; but always responsibly. Now we talked of responsibility in a previous chapter. We saw that the notion derived from the law-court, and might, even in morals, have a very limited application. The flattest determinism could allow that we are, through the operation of fairly obvious motives, swayed by a social code, for the keeping of which we feel responsibility. But we suggested in our discussion that the most interesting extension of the notion is that which stretches it furthest, and makes us responsible for acting or not acting on our basic valuations; and it is this extended sense of responsibility that we shall consider in the present chapter.

Here, then, is our trinity of notions, our libertarian battle-cry, Liberty, Creativity, Responsibility—or death! We are free, and free to make our lives, but always in response to claims; claims which we may be psychologically free, but are not morally free, to ignore. What is it, then, that ultimately exerts these claims upon us? The philosophy of "How we think" may point out with complacency that we do not commonly trace our responsibilities to a higher source than the custom of our kind, or cite an authority superior to the American way of life. And doubtless a Gallup poll, say of the Civil Service and other black-coated workers, would do much to support the contention; especially if the questionnaire were suitably framed. *Vox Gallupi vox Dei;* still, we must be careful not to misinterpret so august an oracle. It may be that people are content to find their authority in custom; but authority for what? Not, ultimately, for what they should do, but for what they should prize. The man who follows the American way of life does not see in the customs of the tribe obligatory performances, which are their own justification; he takes them both to express, and to be inspired by, a respect for humanity.

The citizen is found, then, to have two objects of respect; and he can easily be reduced to that bewilderment produced by Socratic queries in the common breast, if we ask him which is supreme, humanity, or the American way of Life? Let

Socrates clear up the confusion Socrates has caused. It is plain to the philosopher that humanity, and the American way of life, are not objects of respect on the same level, or so as to be possible rivals to one another. We may respect the American way of life as a sound indicator, pointing out to us what there is in humanity most deserving of respect, as well as how that respect may in practice be paid. Humanity we respect absolutely, if once we can see it straight; and this respect obliges us; we hold ourselves responsible for acting, or failing to act, in accordance with it.

We say that our respect is payable to humanity. The word is almost too convenient; indeed, to the modern ear it is an actual equivocation. It means mankind, and it means the characteristic excellence of human nature. Both are objects of respect, or of regard. But so far from coinciding in practice, they are inclined to tug us in different directions, and, on occasion, to tear us apart. To regard mankind is to accept men as they are, to spare them frustration, to give them their will and pleasure. To regard humanity, in the other sense, is to look for what a believer calls the divine image in us, and the unbeliever the human ideal. It is to censure vice or folly, and push against the tide of appetite, as well in other men, as in ourselves.

To all working moral systems, or ways of life deserving the name, some respect for humanity in both senses is common ground. All direct us to accept mankind as it is, and all uphold a standard of what it should be. And all, no doubt, have their practical ways of dealing with the tension which results; of squaring (if we are to take the Christian example) the law Christ delivers on the Mount, with the indulgence he manifests to sinners. The perplexity is a practical perplexity; it cannot be exorcised by logical analysis. It is no use telling us that there is no rivalry between our two aims; that the human ideal, or divine similitude in us is no concrete entity, let alone person, capable of competing for our attention against John Robinson or Robert Jones; that it is merely a way of conceiving what either of these characters has it in him to aspire after. Such philosophical solutions offer no practical consolation, because the perplexity concerns our action. We have either to accept our children as they are or (however tactfully) edge them towards what they should be.

The modern world has not even yet got over the antique method of reconciling our two aims; a method reflected in that equivocation in the word "humanity," on which we have just remarked. To the Greek philosopher it was no equivocation at all. Just, as to the old-fashioned botanist, a spotted orchid was simply a specimen of the kind, more or less perfect, the teleology of nature being single-mindedly bent on making it as typical as circumstance allowed; so equally, to the Greek thinker, human individuals were simply specimens of mankind, in each of whom the form of the species was, as it were, doing its best to realise itself. To the great scandal of the modern student, everything distinctive of a person, all that makes the individuality of a character, was written off by the Greek as accidental to the essential man, and irrelevant to the teleology of existence. "Be human, my son" was the supreme moral injunction; "Be a Man with a large M." What we call the pull of the ideal was simply the self-realisation of the natural species *man*, on all the levels of being or action; and especially, of course, on the highest. A bad man was a bad specimen, limited, frustrated, warped, unhappy. The art of felicity and the art of virtue were one, and to respect men as they are was the same thing as to respect what they should be. For what are they, it was asked, what have they in them capable of moving respect, beside their human nature, struggling to be itself? Who could seriously respect in a man what was accidental to his being?

Ideal humanity was to the Aristotelian a timeless form of natural substance, a typical object of natural science, engraved in the order of the world, and unalterable as long as heaven revolves. It was conceivable—though God forbid!—that a concentration of disastrous accident might exterminate us, like the dodo; but nothing could change our essence. Had dodos survived, they would have remained incurably (or, I suppose we should say, triumphantly) dodonian. While men survive, they will be as human as ever.

How hopelessly the Greek position has been shot to pieces

is a thrice-told tale: shot to pieces by individualism in ethics, historicism in sociology, and evolutionism in biology. It is not this that we wish to dwell upon, but upon the fact that the Greek did at least know what he was regarding, and towards what he held himself responsible, when he set up the common human essence against the trivial claims of individual deviation. He was respecting a form of nature, timeless and virtually divine. He and his metaphysical faith are gone into limbo, never to return. But what do we, we Anglo-Saxon intellectuals, respect, when we balance regard for the human ideal against our regard for mankind?

The answer of "We think" philosophy to this question is not always mere academic mumbling. There are the forthright prophets who declare: "We learn to have confidence in our volitions," our aspirations for the future of mankind. It is too hasty a dismissal which rejoins: "And did not Stalin have confidence in *his* volitions, when he collectivised the farms, and several million farmers died?" For Stalin's trouble was practical miscalculation. The Socialist utopia was only just round the corner, when the Germans began engaging him in an arms-race—was not it a pity? Otherwise the tears of the peasants would soon have dried, in the dawn of a glorious day. Anyhow, we are not marxist doctrinaires—we have not got ideas into our heads; we keep them at arm's length, and scrutinise them. So we may have confidence in our volitions, our directives for the moulding of mankind; as, according to an ancient myth, God had confidence in his volitions, when he made us this being that we are, and surveying it, called it very good.

Let us pause for a moment, and see what has happened to us. Alarmed by the existentialist predicament, unattracted by the task of being Phaeton and running amok with the horses of the Sun, we took refuge in responsibility. We would create our lives, perhaps, but responsibly, in answer to the claims of mankind, and the truth of our nature. But has not responsibility proved a broken reed? If we are responsible, after all, to our own volitions, are we not back in the car with Phaeton, making up our minds which way to drive? What advantage

have we over the most self-intoxicated existentialist, except a
sort of cautious collectivism? We are not Stalin, we are the
Civil Service; *we* are to have confidence in *our* volitions; not
I in *mine*. And the volitions in which we have confidence are
not the dramatic decisions which existential novel-writing, and
historical disaster, throw into relief, they are policies somehow
settled, and acquiesced in, by a communal complacency. It is
this that does duty for "the truth of human nature," when the
philosophy of "we think" expands into the field of "we ap-
prove" and "we decide."

Positivism and Natural Faith

We have been moving too rapidly and shouting too loud. Let
us sit down and consider carefully what is at stake. Our
philosophers will point out to us that whether we believe in
Aristotle's truth of human nature, or whether we put our
confidence in their and our volitions, there is no getting round
the sheer fact of approval and disapproval, in either case. It is
on this indicator that we must rely, for determining what belongs to the human good, and what does not. We have seen
that Aristotle himself, however, confident in nature as providing the rule of right, defined "good" as "whatever any sort of
being is after." The definition is general, covering the good for
animals and plants, and even, to our amused delight, the good
for stones; they find it in cuddling down as near as they can
to the earth's centre. If we are speaking of man, and his moral
good, we may wish to specialise the verb, and say that "being
after" on our level has the name of "aspiration." So what
human nature aspires after is determined, according to Aristotle, by the lineaments of nature herself; but that is only a
metaphysical belief. In practice there is no way to discover
what humanity aspires after, but experiencing or observing
the aspiration. If our good is that towards which aspiration
naturally jumps, there is no way of knowing what it is, save
by dropping the cat on the floor, and seeing in what direction
it does jump.

Even then, merely to observe in what direction our neighbours' aspiration jumps, will not convince us of the good. After learning all we can from others, and sympathising with them as much as we are able, we may still wonder whether they are not the victims of a common perversity, so long as our aspiration fails to jump with theirs. No good can convince us, that does not win us; the good being defined as what attracts, it cannot be seen as good unless it is felt as attractive; always bearing in mind that we are not now talking of any and every attraction, but of that serious attraction only which can draw our total aspiration.

Well then (say our philosophers) since in practice the human good is known as that which we aspire after, why not leave it at that, and cut away the dead wood, the metaphysical part of Aristotle's doctrine? What use does it serve, to allege that the direction of a healthy aspiration is laid down in the unalterable nature of things, if all we can in practice do is follow our aspiration whither it leads? Why regret the collapse of Aristotelian dogmatism, as though some other dogmatism were needed in its place, which we cannot supply? No substitute is needed, when a chimera has been exploded.

Those who are familiar with this type of debate will see immediately to what issue we have brought the question down: the issue between positivism and natural faith. Not in this question only, but over a whole range of questions, positivists have wished to restrict belief to what a practical test can verify. As with morals, so (for example) with physics. We have no way of discovering physical being outside us, except through its interferences with our bodies, or our instruments; and a strict positivism would reduce physical doctrine to a systematisation of such interferences, actual or potential. But natural faith, including the natural faith of physicists, rebels. It may be (we protest) that we do not know the physical world, except as that which we sound by our interferences with it. But we believe that what we are sounding is a mass of energies carrying on business out there in space, on their own account and, as it were, under their own names, whether any soundings of them are taken or not. There is no circumventing or bypassing the soundings, to reach a direct acquaintance with the physical-in-itself; yet we believe it is something in itself, and if we are theological as well as physical believers, we attribute to God a simple knowledge of it.

It is much the same with natural faith and positivist reduction, in the matter of the good. We cannot bypass aspiration, so as to grasp the good after which it aspires; we can only grasp it through aspiring after it. Yet we cannot cease to believe that there is a true or proper good after which aspiration "feels, if perchance she may find it." For aspiration is always endeavouring to be right aspiration, and to respond to objects, or pursue aims, intrinsically meriting it. Divorced from this endeavour, aspiration is no longer aspiration. If we have confidence in our aspirations, or, in the phrase we previously took up, confidence in our volitions, it is that they are sound, healthy or right; that is to say, that they are after the proper objectives. There is, of course, a striking difference between our natural faith in physical realities, and our natural faith in genuine goods. Physical things would be ideally definable without reference to any soundings of them; goods would not, even ideally, be definable without reference to any aspirations after them; the good being nothing but the proper object of aspiration.

Let us be clear, anyhow, of this: that what Aristotelianism offered, and what positivists have rejected, was a metaphysical, not a directly practical, conviction. Aristotle did not tell us, even if he sometimes thought he did, any other means of descrying the good than approval, aspiration, love. He claimed to tell us what, in its general bearings, that good was, to which these sentiments or attitudes were the natural pointers. It was all that served or expressed the due expansion of an eternal essence, human nature. "Well," it may be asked, "and what was the use of the metaphysical belief, even while men could still believe it? It did not direct their aim." No; but it grounded their faith. To reverence, to worship our own volitions, though backed by those of the Civil Service, is flat idolatry. Whereas nature was divine perfection to the Greeks; and even to Christian Hellenists she was a divine ordinance.

Well, but (we shall be told) this is scarcely news. Who does not know that metaphysical belief, the world over, supplies men with something to adore? But our philosophers will tell us that the wish has everywhere been father to the thought; the pathetic, the essentially childish or recessive desire for an object of unqualified reverence, disappointed by every empirical reality, creates a metaphysical one. The Greeks virtually deified an immanent perfection, supposed to be working itself out in the transience of event. Christians have set their divine perfection further back, a creative will behind, rather than within, the cosmic process. If you want something to worship, this is the sort of thing. We deny ourselves the childish luxury.

"We deny ourselves. . . ." Such language is damaging, if it is not ironical. We cannot take seriously men who talk as though they were free to entertain metaphysical beliefs, or not to entertain them; to say (in the extreme case) "No, I don't think we will have God, thank you" or to say "Yes, let's have him." For either we believe or we do not. What pattern of conviction about the basis of action can we in fact entertain? If we have wrestled with the sophistries of determinism, it was only to clear or to liberate an actual conviction of our power, in some measure, to make ourselves. But if we indeed have the conviction, have we a conviction complementary to it—the conviction of our responsibility for the exercise of this power? The questionnaire proceeds: Responsibility to what? And desiring to voice a common agreement, and to steer clear of metaphysics, we answer, Responsibility to mankind, in others and in myself. What I do with my life, what I do to my neighbours, comes under the claim of something I cannot but hold sacred, their humanity, my integrity. But leave me out of the picture; even if I am free to damn myself, I am not free to betray or outrage them.

So far, surely, we have been drawing out practical convictions which we actually entertain. Do we, then, desert the path of moral realism and begin to chase wild metaphysical geese, when we take a step further and ask, what it is in any man, that demands this practical reverence? It is not just what he happens to think or to desire, that is sacred to me. I am not to respect the villainy of villains, nor to forward the selfdehumanisation of the perverse. I may say that I respect what they have it in them to be, their proper destiny. But this may not be anything that they want, even in the depth of their hearts; and simply to say that it is what I want for them, that my volition about them commands my limitless regard, does not satisfy me; by which I mean, that I cannot believe it. Can you?

Well, what am I to do about it? What alternative is there? It is too late, surely, to hanker after Aristotelism, or hope to reinstate the timeless essence of man, the identical shaping everywhere at work in different qualities of clay, the one way of growing right, as against twenty-thousand ways of growing wrong. It is too late to reinstate the changeless rule of essence, for reasons we have named already: individualism in ethics, in sociology historicism, and in biology evolution. No, if we are to believe an objective rule of human good, it must be a flexible rule; and they are surely right who say, there is nothing for us to put our confidence in, which has not the inventiveness of volition. Only, whose? Whose will do I respect, as a will expressed in the facts and possibilities, the hopes and the claims represented by my neighbours' existence—or, indeed, by my own?

So, then, when it is said that theological belief is morally irrelevant, because after all, God or no God, we have to explore the facts to decide a policy of action, and in deciding, trust our aspiration, we make answer that moral policies are at the service of reverence and love, and that as soon as we consider what we reverence, what we love, the practical bearing of theology appears. For it is no trifling difference, whether we value our neighbour simply for what he is, or for the relation in which he stands to the will of God; a will establishing his creation, and intending his perfection. Those that are so minded reverence not a single, but a double object, God in their neighbour, and their neighbour in God. The divine is not far removed from them, but touches them as nearly as physical things touch them. For the physical is known to us by the way it conditions our physical motion; and the divine will, which is God himself, is known to us in limiting or evoking our dutiful action, through all the persons with whom we have to do.

Paradox of Creative and Creaturely Wills

A Gifford Lecturer exercises his office in a country against which it has been made a reproach by her neighbours, that she has too much tormented herself with nice reflection on the mystery of predestination. It may be indeed that the formulations of this problem by old Calvinist divinity do not greatly commend themselves to us. But the mystery itself, so far from being a needless mental agony, or subject of extreme curiosity, lies, surely, at the centre of practical religious thought; and if the Scottish people have retained a keener sense of divine power than their fellow-islanders, it may not be unconnected with a habitual dwelling on this mystery by the ministers of the word. It is true that the Calvinist paradoxes belong to revealed theology, and concern the last end of man. But this sublime issue merely draws out and emphasises a paradox already implicit in the natural theology of common moral belief. For we have seen that what commands the theist's moral response is the divine will expressed in his neighbour's being. Our neighbour is a piece of the divine handiwork, still in the making; it is the process of creation still continuing, which demands our instrumental cooperation. God (it is the theist's belief) is making our neighbour. And yet our neighbour is, in some measure at least, making himself. The same thing is true, we suppose, of ourselves; a providence shapes us, and it is this very work of God upon us, which commands our obedience in the ordering of our lives. But how, in the creating of a single life, can we accommodate two wills, one all-knowing and divine, the other fallible and human? Not, perhaps we should say, two wills side by side, for that would be a blasphemous equalisation; but rather, as it were, ranged in depth, the one behind the other, the one acting through and in the other.

To consider how best to handle such a paradox, and how philosophers or theologians have tried to handle it, would involve us in an entire theodicy, and require another book at least as long as this. All we have in mind to say here is that the mystery of the two wills is not the peculiar property of revealed theology, but arises as soon as we acknowledge in the objects of moral reverence not human volitions simply, but divine. How it arises, we may see by recurring to the comparison between Aristotle's world, and ours. The Philosopher needed to distinguish, just as we must, between the proper direction of human endeavour, and the uncertain self-direction of actual men. He managed the distinction by enlarging and extending the analogy offered by organic growth, as seen in any single generation of a species. If puppies grow to be dogs, not chimeras, it is because the formative principles of the canine species control their growth. But not all puppies come to be perfect dogs. We attribute such deviations as we find to the awkwardness of circumstance, and the intractability of material. The whole world of creatures, anyhow beneath the moon, is to Aristotelian eyes a multitude of vital forms, renewing themselves by propagation, and going right, but only in the main. What the form is, as it were, trying to do in moulding its matter constitutes the good; what comes to pass is the actual approximation. In the business of his physical growth, man is like any animal; he undergoes, and cannot directly influence, the struggle between form and matter, which makes him what he is. But in the shaping of his conduct he plays a conscious part; his thought and choice become as it were the living voice, the sensitive hand of Nature, imposing human order on what would else be the chaos of his acts. Thus the principle of our lives is perfection (for it is the human form, and form is perfect); but the performance is no more perfect than it is; the humanity in us being side-tracked and frustrated by a thousand complications of adverse circumstance.

We observe that, for Aristotle, the distinction between the standard good and the varying approximations is not a distinction between two wills, or two creative activities, both bearing upon the same material. It is the distinction between principle or form on the one side, and activity or will on the other.

Form is of its nature perfect, and functioning all more or less defective, anyhow beneath the moon; for nature is a principle which achieves its end (says Aristotle) only in the main.

Now we have found the Aristotelian picture false to science, and false to sentiment; our empirical discoveries have destroyed the doctrine of timeless, inviolable species, our moral perception sees more in the person than an accidental embodiment of the kind. The shape of that perfection after which individuals aspire is, for us, only less variable than their several aspirings after it. It is a flexible rule which, if it is to be accorded any objective being, must find it in the unsleeping creativity of a faultless mind. And so the paradox of two wills in one existence, the perfect and the imperfect, is forced upon us. And not merely as an intellectual puzzle; it is experienced by the theist as the way in which the personal world environs him.

Let us be clear what we are doing. We are presenting the relation between theism and morals; and we are bringing out its distinctive character by touching on the contrasting shape of rival systems, atheistic existentialism, philosophic humanism, or antique naturalism. We are not claiming an easy triumph, in absence, over opponents whose counter-arguments we have not so much as heard. To show that nothing but a doctrine of divine volitions will do justice to the moral sense, would be a task indeed. Should we not have to examine every philosophic alternative that has ever been propounded? If we believe our theology, it is probably because we accept a divine voice as having actually spoken; and that is not a claim which a Gifford Lecturer has any business to investigate.

What we will do here, rather than attempt any argument or justification, is to spread the trouble over a wider field. The paradox of two agents to a single activity, one finite, the other infinite, cannot be confined within the limits of personal and moral existence. For if we recognise a creative will within and behind our own, we acknowledge it as that by which we are what we are, as though it were the wellspring out of which we draw our being. And if we are insufficient to exist without the operation of such a cause, how much more insufficient are slighter and less enriched existences, such as we reckon to be the physical elements or forces of the world. There will scarcely be a theist who recognises a divine will in his neighbour and in himself, who does not believe it to be manifested in the existence of whatever is. But what is essentially the same metaphysical paradox confronts us in inanimate nature. The physical world, as well as the vital world on all its levels, operates through an activity inherent in itself, or rather, an activity which is itself; since activity is, to our present mind, the very stuff of things, and it is of this activity that we suppose our science to study the patterns. Yet, in virtue of our theism, we must take the activity to express the prior action of its creator.

We do not, indeed, attribute to the action of physical energy the special character of will; so that we do not meet, in our contemplation of the physical scene, that duality of wills which confronts us, when we consider our own dependence upon God. In the physical scene we have duality of activities, one finite, the other infinite, of which only one, the infinite, is a will. Yet the duality of activities in nature is scarcely less mysterious than the duality of wills in personal existence. We have two stories about what works the world, and each on its own level and in its own idiom appears to be complete. Omnipotence not only can dispense with, but even seems to exclude, additional or subsidiary agencies. But then on the other side the pattern of physical forces fills all the time and all the space there is, and allows of no irruption from the divine.

Men live and act under God, natural forces energise under God. Which of these two relations is the more mysterious? Here is a question which it will be illuminating to discuss, even though we shall scarcely be so simple-minded as to hope for a decisive answer this way or that. It will turn, we may suspect, on the sense we put upon the word "mysterious."

On the one hand, the case of physical nature seems the less mysterious. Natural forces, having no will of their own, do not give rise to the supreme paradox of our own case, the opposition of a finite, and often a perverse, will to the creative omnipotence. When we think of nature acting under God, we easily satisfy ourselves with familiar analogies. We can ourselves manipulate natural forces, and make them serve our will, and notably by the construction of machines. How much more readily, then, we say, can God both make and employ the mechanism of the universe. Or again, we think of the even greater immediacy and facility with which we impress the direction of our will on the forces composing our bodies. In some such manner, we may think, the whole universe answers to the control of the divine thought in every part; and following this line of analogy, Leibniz, we recall, came to see God as the transcendent Soul of his physical creation. Neither the analogy of our mind in the direction of bodily movement, nor of our person in the employment of instruments, can supply a physical theology which bears thinking out to the last point. But we need not be so rigorous. Entertained lazily on the surface of the mind, either analogy looks well enough; what a contrast to any image we may form of the relation between created will and creative! For that looks outrageous from the moment we begin to frame it. When will is set over either instruments or organs, hierarchical order is at least respected; when will is set over will, it is ignored, even if it is not flouted. If will operates physical forces, their essential character is not violated; but if will operates will, how can the subject will retain the character of being will? Is not will, by definition, self-operative? It appears, therefore, that the dependence of physical nature on divine activity is less paradoxical, or mysterious, than is the dependence of human life on divine activity.

That is as far as we will take the statement of the first case. We will now pass over to a statement of the contrary; and our initial move will be to attack the analogies on which the first thesis relied. The dependence of nature upon God is certainly not that of machines or an engineer, or of bodily motions on an embodied will. Such figures are pitiful props to a halting imagination. They give no insight whatever into the nature of the mystery on which they pretend to comment. What is it, after all, for any created act or being to draw its existence out of the Creator's act? We can have no real notion of such a relation, save by generalisation from the case where we can (however imperfectly) experience it; and what case can this be, but our own? We say of ourselves, at least, that we embrace, cooperate with, or draw upon the divine will, in doing what is right. It may be hard indeed to set out our creaturely response as an experiencing of God-dependence; and yet such phrases as we have cited mean something to theists, whose belief has become incorporated with the stuff of their lives. The insight we have into our dependence upon God is dark, when compared with God's vision of what that dependence is. But it is brightness itself, compared with the fog we are in, over the dependence on God of any physical substance.

So much for the opposing pleas. What are we to say of them? Each is, perhaps, justified in what it advances, but that is not to say that what the two advance is of equal importance; and we have, no doubt, allowed it to appear which thesis, in our judgment, has the greater weight. All that the first can honestly claim for itself is that it shows us a relation of creature to Creator which is more easily imaginable; and the second thesis may even go so far as to deny that this is any advantage. As God himself is unimaginable, so also must be the dependence of his creatures on his power. And if the relation appears imaginable, we have reason to fear that we are viewing it unrealistically, and, as it were, from a great distance. The nearer we come to it, and the more we are involved in it, the less imaginable, the more paradoxical we shall find it to be. But what we lose in imaginative clarity is made up to us in actuality; just where we cease to conceive our dependence on God, we begin to live it.

Will, action, the creative moment in man, is the only object of consideration which opens a dimension of metaphysical depth, or promises to let through a single ray of uncreated light. Here alone we find a power of making anything to be or not to be, and it is this that raises all the questions of theistic philosophy; leading us to ask, whether there is not such a power underlying all things, not merely the things we make to be; leading us to ask, whether our own creative power is underivative, or whether it does not spring continually out of a deeper source of will, the wellspring of the world; leading us to ask, how nearly analogous that prime creative will would be, to the secondary form of volition we ourselves possess and exercise. Here are questions which to formulate shortly, as we have just formulated them, is but to clothe them in stale metaphor; questions which we have not opened in this book, and will not open now. But to evoke them is to see what an importance attaches to the preliminary work which, however inadequately, we have undertaken; the work of clearing obstacles from the serious contemplation of any will whatsoever, whether human or divine; and even, perhaps, of casting some positive light on that human will, from which alone the divine can be conjectured.

Charles B. Ketcham and James F. Day / *Freedom*

as Experienced and as Thought:

The Question of Freedom

Introduction

BY NOW THE complexity and elusiveness of the term "freedom" are surely evident. As we reflect on *this* problem we seek further insight from some among those contemporary scholars who do not themselves acknowledge the tradition of Christian Faith which inspired the preceding essays. However iconoclastic the thought may seem, it is our view that these thinkers must be listened to, their claims seriously examined, as we attempt to broaden, deepen, and clarify our own perspectives on freedom.

Contemporary thought has witnessed and reflected a widespread shifting of the kinds of primary demands placed upon the terms, the concepts, and the procedures for establishing criteria for validating judgments. The consequences of this proliferation of pressures, while widely felt and acknowledged, have been of greater and more fundamental import for philosophy and theology than for other disciplines. Simply to list some of these pressures—clarity; the logic of relations, in addition to refinements of the traditional logic of predication;

234

"descriptivism" versus "prescriptivism"; the phenomena of consciousness; the "Word of God"; faithfulness; authenticity; honesty—is both to reveal and in part to account for the wide-spread confusion and tension between and within these two disciplines. The foregoing list could be easily extended by any close student of either of these fields of study. Careful inspection of this or of other possible such lists leads us to see, however, that these various pressures or demands fall into one of two primary groupings or classifications.

One of these sets, whose formal and conscious program seems to date back to the work of Husserl, is most broadly encompassed by the term "Phenomenology." The very breadth of the connotations as well as of the variety of thinkers who appeal to this term make it unusually difficult to define with any precision. But whatever the variations of its development at the hands of different thinkers, whatever the differences in actual starting point, it will serve us here as indicating two things. First, in its affirmative posture, it specifies that the starting point for genuinely significant reflection must be with the data, the "phenomena," the raw stuff of conscious experience *as experienced*. This specifies both a starting point for any sort of productive thinking and also a methodology for organizing and interpreting the materials supplied. Its emphasis is on what many thinkers have called the "subjective."

In the second place, this procedure calls upon the thinker to look only at appearances and to give no thought to a reality "behind" them. This functions chiefly as its restrictive or limiting stance, although to be applied differs quite significantly among those thinkers who employ this phenomenological method. It is our purpose in the second part of this essay to attempt a brief exercise in the phenomenology of freedom, and then to inquire whether the perspective so achieved is in significant respects phenomenologically different from the Christian experience of freedom.

The other set, whose chief practitioners are to be found in the English-speaking nations and in Scandinavia, is most generally known today by the term "analysis." It, too, has many modes of practice, a plethora of antecedent movements, and some quite significant internal tensions between its so-called "hard-headed" and "soft-headed" wings.[1] But here again, as in the case of the phenomenological method, our own interests will be served if we note two chief points, one positive, the other restrictive or limiting. The first of these has nowhere been more concisely stated than by the late G. E. Moore when he wrote: "In all . . . philosophical studies, the difficulties and disagreements, of which its history is full, are mainly due to a very simple cause: namely to the attempt to answer questions, without first discovering precisely what question it is which you desire to answer."[2] Here the stress is upon verbal, linguistic, propositional clarity; and the practitioner of such a pursuit may rightly hope for some bright light upon the object or processes of his reflections, upon the umbra if not the penumbra of his concern. This last remark suggests immediately our second, or restrictive, point. For it is evident that analysts are much more concerned with denotation than connotation, with the study of separate or separated parts than with wholes or gestalts in anything like their functional unity. It will be our purpose in the third section of this essay to examine some analytic views of freedom, and then to inquire whether the results of such a study illuminate in any significant way the Christian's way of talking about freedom.

When the foregoing tasks have been completed, we shall then be in a position to inquire, in the fourth and final section, (1) what consequences such analyses may have for Christian claims about freedom; and (2) whether, and at what price for either or both phenomenological immediacy and linguistic clarity, there are important claims that Christians make concerning freedom, which neither of the analytic schools can, with any consistency, consider. In all of this, the intention is to supply for the person who has read the other essays in this book some helpful ways of reflecting upon them in a fashion which might not have occurred to him. For it is evident that these essays and statements about freedom in the Christian tradition exhibit various assumptions, various stipulations, and various interpretations, each offering itself as *the* Christian view of freedom. The approach here proposed, of trying to see clearly just what question is being asked and, presumably answered, by a given essay; of trying to get before one's own consciousness the richness of the particular experience, with all its vividness and immediacy, to which one essayist may be appealing as primary data; of trying to see whether still another writer is asking and trying to deal with still another sort of issue—all this, we suggest, may be of some help not only in coming to grips with the significant meaning of the essays themselves, but also in the even more important task of one's own efforts to wrestle with the issues of freedom itself. No effort is made in the present essay to dictate to either the other essayists of this volume or to its readers what is rightly said or can be found in a given essay. Such issues are an intimate matter between every serious writer and every serious reader, and we deliberately withhold here any explicit reference to the other essays in this collection.

Freedom as Experienced

I have set myself this project, to write this part of this essay. I come to my study in a quiet hour. I re-read what I have already written. I uncover my typewriter, look for some paper, and roll a sheet into proper position as I adjust myself in my chair. And now, in this very moment, now, I begin to ask myself, where is the experience of freedom in all this. It does not appear out there anywhere in the world around me, nor does it appear in any of the acts that I have to this moment performed: walking to the office, unlocking the door, taking off my topcoat, readying the typewriter, the paper, myself. "Of course," I say to myself, "I might be elsewhere at *this* moment, doing something quite different. I do recall that my wife had a quite different project in mind for me this particular evening." But I am here, addressing myself to *this* project. Is freedom the feeling, the remembrance I have, of that moment of choosing to do this rather than the other? Is it to be found only in those moments where I find myself solicited by two or more prospective courses of action, when I waver between or among them, trying, as I say to myself, to make up my mind?

Is it a matter *between* me and a number of possible courses of action? I must confess that I cannot "see" freedom "out there" in the world as an aspect, characteristic, or attribute of any thing already definite. I do see that things at hand, some at least—a hatchet, a pencil, a typewriter—are "there" as possibilities for my use in doing this or that appropriate act which may solicit me. I recall just the other day having as a project the fixing of a curtain rod to a wall and looking in vain for a screwdriver, and I remember feeling frustrated, limited in effecting my project, by my inability to lay my hands upon the proper implement. Am I, then, in my experience of freedom, ready to acknowledge that I am, after all, free only when the proper implement, object, person, is at hand as means, aid, accomplice, in my projects? No, for this thing-and-person-world about me has the power only to solicit me, as I have already acknowledged, but it is I who "consent" to this or that solicitation upon *my* time, *my* money, *my* energy; it is I who give or withhold assent to, involvement in, one proposal or another. And, further, it seems, as I think about it more carefully, that these things and persons are there for me as solicitations of or for me only as and when I propose—rather than that I am somehow "there" for them. My body is mine; my acts are mine; my freedom is mine.

This freedom as experienced seems, then, to be, like my shadow (or is it more like my substance?) with, by, and of me. Yet I do not find that I have any particular organ for it—as, for example, I have a heart to pump my blood through my veins or a stomach with which to digest my food. Nor is it something for which I can find any sense—as, for example, I have a sense of smell, of taste, etc. And if I have no organ nor any sense for it, how can I hope to acquire even any idea of it, if I agree for the moment that nothing can be in the mind that is not first in the senses? But I do have an idea of it. It is a term which many of us employ, talk about, and seem to regard as in some manner "real." Are we all deceiving ourselves and one another in such talk? That remains a distinct possibility, at least to the extent that the "ourselves" and the "one another" speak to me, or in my presence, of that which is outside my own experience. But why, on what basis, do I so often respond, nodding my head in assent, sometimes dissenting, when "another" says this or that about freedom? "They" have not, really cannot—except for certain formal definitions or certain homiletical or otherwise emotive expressions—define it for me. Nor can I really remember learning about it as I can, however indistinctly, remember learning that fire burns or that twice two is four. Yet it is, quite clearly, with, by, and of me.

Freedom as experienced is *with* me. By that I seem to mean that it goes with me wherever I go. But it does not seem to be with me in quite the same sense that my hands or feet are with me, go wherever I go. For one thing, I can imagine myself as a paraplegic, but I cannot really imagine myself without my freedom. My freedom seems to be more intimately with me than hands, feet, or unessential organs. Is it with me, then, as my heart, my blood, my breath, are with me? I should say yes to this, at least in the sense of intimacy—and also in the sense of essentiality. But, at the same time, I find that I must say that freedom is not with me *as* these essentials of heart, blood, and breath are. For one thing, these physical organs and their processes support my physical life, and I experience them physiologically, but this is not the way in which I either experience or characteristically think about freedom. Another way this can be expressed is to say that the mode of my experience of freedom as with me is different than it is in the case of heart, blood, breath. Thus, if I think of myself as merely a sensate being, capable of just functioning physiologically—as a creature, in short, without the possibility of having freedom with me, then I think that I have lost the capacity to live as I.

Freedom as experienced is *by* me. It is a function, an activity, which *I* perform, exercise, carry out. As I genuinely experience freedom, it seems to be involved in my own most characteristic activities. I do not find it when I regard myself as identified with such actions as the beating of my heart, the circulation of my blood, the functioning of my lungs, nor even with the quick and automatic withdrawal of my hand from a hot substance. I do find it involved when I set out to do such a thing as to write this essay, when I am given opportunity to declare my loyalty to other persons or to causes which promise to lift the level of our common humanity. I discover it in that almost uniquely human activity of giving and receiving promises, of binding myself to others and of seeking to bind them to me. It seems to be involved in that activity whereby I seem able to go beyond, to transcend, time, place, station, duty. And in all these most characteristic human activities, freedom is either *by* me in the sense in which I energize, set in motion, certain courses of action—it is, as I experience it, either *by* me or else it is not at all. If I do not act, then this essay, these pledges of loyalty, these promises, do not come into being at all—they are *by* me. The states of affairs suggested have come to be such as they are through my activity—perhaps never entirely solely through my activity, for there are other processes and the activities of others involved; but, at the same time, these states of affairs which have come to be through my action would not be as they are if my action had been other than it was, if I had, as I say to myself, acted otherwise. Of course I know that there are those who keep saying that there is no way of either showing or proving that I *could* have acted in any way other than I did in fact act; but I am now simply setting forth these phenomena of my experience, and they constitute, taken together, what I mean by freedom. It yet remains, in the literature of this age-old debate, for someone to make good in any final way the claim that a denial of the formal validity of any statement about freedom constitutes also a denial of the possibility of the experience of freedom.

For, finally, freedom as experienced is *of* me. If I have to talk about my having an essence, then I find it impossible to describe that essence apart from the presence in or to it of freedom. If I am forced to cease talking about my essence, then I can cheerfully accept this stricture upon my thought and talk so long as it does not endanger myself as freedom. It is not that I am always cheerful about the burden of freedom, about its bondages, about its demands and its ambiguities. "If," I sometimes think to myself, "I could only be and remain a definite this or that, if I could only finally 'arrive' and know that nothing more would ever be demanded of me—what a great day that would be!" Yet this is partly what is meant when I say that freedom is *of* me. Beyond all these experiences of it—beyond the experience of freedom as burden, demand, and bondage is the experience some report, the experience of freedom as the confrontation with nothingness with the attendant sense of lostness, of the precariousness of human existence. For those of us who cannot honestly say that their own experience of freedom includes this "dimension," such reports pose something of an embarrassment. We do not like to be adjudged thicker-skinned or less sensitive than those who make such reports out of their experience of freedom; nor, further, do we wish to render dishonest reports of our own experience of freedom in an effort to be found genuinely authentic. Nevertheless, and this is the central point in this experience of freedom, freedom seems constituitive of me in as fundamental a sense as any other aspect of my experience that I can name. Yet it does not so much constitute me, as, for example, my physical appearance, my biological inheritance, my habitual behavior—it does not constitute me as these do; rather, it is that dimension, that mode, of my existence whereby I become myself. For of nothing else in the entire spectrum of my experience do I find myself able to say, as I can and do say of my free acts, "That's me." My hair is of me in the sense that it is mine to care for, to have cut short or long, to keep in its natural color or to alter artificially—yet it is basically what and how it is as a part of my genetic inheritance. It is just there, for as long as it lasts, on top of my head; and that's that. Of course, I may, out of concern for style or conformity or self-expression, make this inheritance of mine the *occasion* for the expression of my freedom or of my surrender to that bondage of the current season that is so often confused with style. Yet even here, perhaps, in this time, especially here, I am aware that the act of choice, of decision, of self-expression, whereby I set out to alter this or that part of me or of my world is more profoundly "me" than anything which provides occasion for the act itself. Thus even while I may speak of my possibilities as, at any given time and situation, constituting a rather definite set, my experience of freedom is not so much to be found in the sheer entertaining of these possibilities as it is in the act with which I initiate, with whatever energy may be at my command, one of these rather than another. With such acts, rather than primarily with my body or even some set of ideas or values in my mind, I seem to identify myself. And the final mark of this experience of freedom is that it is for such acts that I accept responsibility—for such acts are more uniquely myself, *of* me, than anything else that I am or have. Even the experience I sometimes have of mistakenly regarding an act and its attendant consequences as mine when it was, in fact, authored and energized by another, does not so much negate as further confirm the experienced reality that I am my freedom, that it is *of* me.

The foregoing may well be experientially, phenomenologically, existentially true, but there is some question whether it represents the whole truth even about men's *experience* of freedom. Many have raised this question, some from less experience-centered perspectives, others on the basis of an experience of life which finds freedom to be among persons, between self and others. Some among this latter group are those who call themselves Christians, and these seek to include in their testimony to the reality and the centrality and the meaning of freedom, concern for and involvement with others. Their model is neither the isolated individual of a Kierkegaard nor the self-regarding egoist of the Sartrean dialectic who sees others only as rivals, road-blocks to my achievement of a godlike status in a godless world. Their model is the One who spoke parables of a Kingdom in which men live for one another not out of necessity but in love and freedom. Their model is not one who calls on men to pretend that there are no tensions between and among human egos, but they do see in Him One who was, as in the act of washing his disciples' feet, in his own life, "the man for others." With this model as their guide, the Christian seeks an experience of life where freedom is found, not so much within or for his own ego as between and among men and, ultimately, as a divine permissiveness. For finally he sees, perhaps only "in a glass darkly," that the enabling legislation for human freedom is God's power and mercy, and that therefore man always needs more to be "saved" from the consequences which flow from the exercise of his own ego than from the actions of others. For the heinous acts of even a Hitler can always be "explained" in terms of a punitive Versailles or a personal *dementia*; but the really savage struggle, as the Christian at least can testify, is between the myopic bondage of the self-regarding ego and the freedom to be with and for others offered by the "eyes of faith."

That such an experience of freedom is a steady or daily part of his life is rarely, if ever, the lot of the Christian. And the power to produce it simply or solely by his own energizing action, when and where *he* wants it, under conditions of his own choosing, is not his either. For the Christian's experience of freedom happens never to him alone but to us, and its occurrence is never occasion for boasting but rather for thankfulness. It is enhanced but not deified, empowered but not overwhelmed. It is an experience which obviously lends itself to phenomenological description; yet it involves a relational experience and grasp of freedom which seems quite alien to those reports variously labeled "phenomenological" or "existential." It is an experience which seems more accurately to be described in the passive voice of "being grasped" than of "grasping," and yet its perennial witnesses testify more often to its affirmation than to its denial of self.

We may venture, then, a brief statement of the most modest and most obvious conclusion to our all-too-brief phenomenological *excursus*. It seems evident that those of Christian persuasion and experience may offer phenomenological descriptions of their experience of freedom.[3] At the same time, if our judgment that the Christian experience of freedom is of its relational rather than its primarily egoistic character has validity, it would seem an anomaly for one to speak of "Christian Existentialism" or of "Christian Phenomenology." Or if not anomalous then at least risking distortion of the Christian claim about freedom within the minds of those very phenomenologists and existentialists who are the obvious targets of such apologetic techniques. The other side of this same coin has to do with the philosopher of religion who may be of existential or phenomenological persuasion. Such a thinker may be spending himself in vain in his attempted analyses of Christian Faith if his existential or phenomenological bank notes are not legal tender or are not subject to conversion in the realm where he seeks to invest them.

The Language of Freedom

Before us is a sentence of the most common sort: "Man has a real, although limited freedom." It is grammatically quite simple, of the type in which a single attribute, characteristic, or quality is asserted of a single class of beings. Thus we say, "Water is wet," "Birds have wings," etc. Never mind, at this stage, the seemingly double modification of the primary attribute; this may well turn out to be in the interests of clarity and should not distract us from the matter that is initially and most obviously before us, which is further clarification of the term "freedom." Two immediate possibilities are apparent: one is that this assertion may be intended to function as a definition of man as the wetness of water or the wingedness of birds sometimes are asserted to do for them; the other possibility is that an assertion is being made and that the hearer or reader is being invited to verify the assertion. In the latter case, is there any one, or any combination, of our senses by which the assertion about human freedom may be tested? If not, is there any imaginable instrumental refinement of our senses by means of which such a proposition may be either verified or falsified? None seems evident on the side of verification, at least; behaviorists and other sorts of "descriptivists" have often alleged that lack of sensory evidence yields non-sensory evidence enough to convict the utterer of such a sentence of the crime of talking nonsense. However, with the observation that such a conclusion rests in turn upon the claim that descriptive sentences are the only meaningful sentences that there are, we come to a more modest and more certain conclusion, i.e. "freedom" does not function in this sentence as an attribute or characteristic open to sensory observation. We agree, in short, that it is a non-sensical term. Whether it is also, in its every possible nuance, absolutely and finally nondescriptive is a matter to which we shall have to return a bit later. We simply note here that, even if 'freedom' in some way describes man, it does not do so in the same way that color describes a man or a building.

Does the assertion about man and 'freedom' function, then, as a definition? It may well do so, we think, *in some sense*, but not evidently, or without remainder, in quite the same conclusive and undebatable manner in which the standard definition of a plane triangle functions. At least some of the time, in the minds of at least some philosophers, theologians, and others, the claim about human freedom seems to be intended as a nonempirical, yet not merely definitional, assertion. And the sensitive, resourceful analyst has not yet, in any case, exhausted his meta-linguistic arsenal.

Some analysts, at least (one thinks immediately, for example, of R. M. Hare's *The Language of Morals*) not only allow but insist that the logic of language must follow actual usage rather than dictate the limits of meaning in an *a priori* manner. Thus if a given sentence is not obviously descriptive in the manner of plain, empirically verifiable assertions, it may still be making some sort of genuinely meaningful claim. The trick is to find its peculiar logic, not to consign it immediately upon its failure of the empirical test either to the realm of the nonsensical or to that of the merely emotive. Is our sentence about man's freedom, then, some form of imperative or "prescriptive" sentence? Apart from an imaginable tone of voice in which our sentence might be spoken, it is not evident that we are dealing here with an imperative. Even to say "Be free," would still leave the issue about the meaning of 'freedom' before us. This avenue, then, seems to reach a dead end almost as soon as we have turned onto it. The most that can be derived from the prescriptivists' help is to observe that, if man is a being to whom prescriptive or "ought" statements can be meaningfully addressed, then there is some sense in which freedom is an essential precondition of such a mode of speech.

But what is the sense of this? We have already ruled out the possibility that its sense can be empirical. It is likewise apparent that, considered simply as a physiological being, man is at one with all other spatio-temporal creatures in that he stands in a chain of causation. He has no discernible control over his knee-jerk reflex, his breathing, the beating of his heart, nor the sheer physical functioning of his brain. That his total functioning as a distinctively human self is at least body-based, if not, indeed, reducible to a closed muscular-neural-electrical circuit, seems inescapable. Furthermore, as rationalists from Spinoza to R. M. Hare have pointed out, when we come to the sheerly rational effort to find reasons for alleged choices, the very success of the rationalist quest for logical and necessary "explanation" reduces freedom to the vanishing point. We are clearly blocked at both the empirical and the rationalist flanks, and if either, or both taken together, exhaust the possibilities, "freedom" remains at best a non-sense, nonrational, emotive term, "full of sound and fury, signifying nothing."

Is there, then, no further way to explicate this precarious premise? The one remaining possibility is to recall two hints in our foregoing analysis which we have not yet followed up.

One is the possibility that "freedom" may function, as we said, *in some sense* as a definition of man. The other hint comes from our observation that the effort to make out a linguistically tenable case for the "prescriptivity" of ethical terms presupposes freedom. The question of freedom, linguistically and analytically considered, does seem, then, finally to lie in the area roughly delineated by its definitional function, on the one hand, and as an essential prerequisite to the prescriptive functioning of moral language on the other. No philosophical analyst has, to our knowledge, explored these possibilities and it is not our purpose to do so in this essay. Our point is that they offer a possibly rewarding linguistic approach to freedom. In such an approach, the thinker would attempt to answer such questions as: "In its role as claiming some sense to define man, in contrast to other animals, what sort of linguistic job does 'freedom' perform?" Or again, "To what set or sets of activities, which the linguist can meaningfully assert of human selves, does 'freedom' point?" As already indicated, it would be idle to anticipate the results of such a treatment; and it would be overly sanguine, certainly, to claim that such results would establish a clearly meaningful linguistic role for the term. What is clear is that if freedom is used merely definitionally, then it is an empty, contentless term; and in the sphere of ethics and of what remains of metaphysics, it is frustrating to the new-style rationalist who sets out to discover and state the logic of freedom. Professor Hare has stated this "antimomy" in the following way:

> Some [moral philosophers] have thought it so important to preserve our freedom in moral matters, that they have denied the rationality of morals, because they thought (wrongly) that it was a restraint upon freedom. . . . Others have thought it so important to emphasize that moral thought can be a rational activity, that they have, because freedom appeared incompatible with rationality, denied our freedom to form our own opinions.[4]

To sum up, "freedom" is a term which points to an activity thought to be possible by individual human selves under conditions which are not certainly specifiable and in accordance with a logic whose lineaments are not yet clear. We cannot claim that the term has either a solely descriptive use or a merely definitional one. Beyond this, it does not seem presently possibly to go—except to note an almost certain tendency, if the line of thought suggested above is followed. This is a tendency to think of freedom as an activity, even if only of forming one's own opinions, which takes place within an individual. With such an emphasis the Christian must, in our view, find himself at odds, even at the linguistic level, because of the egoistic focus which we have noted in our study of the phenomenologists. While we note with interest this striking agreement of analysts and phenomenologists, our thought is now directed to the impact of the analysts' views of freedom upon the Christian perspective.

Can the Christian theologican accept the analytic stricture

against employing "freedom" as a descriptive term? He clearly can do so, and with profit and clarification for his own thought, to the extent that the stricture applies to *empirical* criteria. On the matter of metaphysical or quasi-metaphysical uses of freedom to describe man or the human condition, we suggest that the linguistic analyst is less prepared to shed such clear light. It does seem plausible that his insistence upon clarity should be respected, so far as this is possible in examining the Christian thinker's usage of the term in its relational function.

Can the theologian make some relevant sense of the distinction between the descriptive and "prescriptive" use of freedom? We think that such a study might be helpful. For any student of the history of Christian thought will recognize the Christian's historic concern with general arguments or inferences from the Christian's experience of moral responsibility to the allegation of a genuine, albeit limited, freedom. Whether such a usage is to be finally regarded as solely or only partly normative for his own employment of the term "freedom" is a matter which seems to us not yet settled. Certainly the issue of clarification is more vividly before us than it has yet been.

The Question of Freedom

Our reflections to this point confirm once again the persistence and the difficulty of the question of freedom. As an element ingredient in our common lives, it is a phenomenon which imposes its own unsettling demands upon each and every effort to organize life in accordance with some all-inclusive structure or scheme. Its disruptive influence intrudes upon the thinking of the language philosopher whose passion for honesty will not finally allow him to ignore the problems posed by this term. As a phenomenon of life and a term within both ordinary and technical vocabularies, it imposes its own demands with their attendant difficulties. It is a question which involves both life and our thought about life. The paradox which is freedom presents itself to phenomenologist and analyst alike; for it is apparent that no life is humanly complete without freedom, yet its very presence introduces an element of uncertainty in every moment when we think life is complete.

The question, the problem, exists, however, not only for the professional philosopher, for there is something of the phenomenologist and of the analyst in each of us. We have known the immediacy of the phenomenon of freedom as lived experience, and we have also encountered the difficulties of disciplined effort to express such experience faithfully and clearly. As those who, with St. Paul, would testify to that freedom "wherewith Christ has set us free," we too are aware of our tendency to make our witness to this gift in language whose vividness is exceeded only by its vagueness. As those who, with St. Thomas, have been called on to explain the meaning of that faith whose name we bear, we are equally aware that too often the poverty of our explication of faith's language is exceeded only by the poverty of our faithfulness. So we stand at the crossroads to which the question of freedom has brought us all.

The Christian stands here too, with his idea, his belief, that freedom is a relational term rather than one which describes some attribute which he possesses as a private, isolated self. Does he have additional demands or insights? Each of the essayists in this anthology has brought to this question his own insights, answers, further questions. The late H. Richard Niebuhr offers a strikingly minimal set of claims for Christian freedom, and we present them here with the belief that they offer a significant challenge to other perspectives on freedom: "The question of freedom arises . . . as the question of the self's ability in its present to change its past and future and to achieve or receive a new understanding of its ultimate historical context." [5] We have become accustomed to the view that, in our relation to nature, we live in response to events which we neither initiate nor normally control. It is startling, however, to be presented with the possibility that even our existence "in time and history" is largely of the same character, i.e., our freedom is limited to responding to actions that are not our own. Such action is chiefly that of reinterpreting past and future with the hope that we may achieve that final freedom which comes about from "the central work of revising our mythology of death into a history of life." [6] Many will, no doubt, regard such an interpretation of Christian freedom as granting undue concessions to determinisms and scepticisms of quite alien kinds. Yet it seems to us that anyone who has become seriously involved in rethinking the whole matter of freedom should examine Niebuhr's position with care. The view that freedom involves reinterpretation of past and future offers, at the least, a definite starting point for any reexamination of the whole matter. It is, finally, difficult to dispute the claim that, in the end, the question of freedom is a matter of our ultimate perspective.

NOTES

1. Robert R. Ammerman, "A Short History of Analytic Philosophy," in Robert R. Ammerman, ed., *Classics of Analytic Philosophy*, (New York: McGraw-Hill, 1965), pp. 1–12.

2. Ammerman, *op. cit.*, p. 4.

3. For a recent expression of this sort, see H. R. Niebuhr, *The Responsible Self*, (New York: Harper & Row, 1963), pp. 100–106.

4. R. M. Hare, *Freedom and Reason*, New York: Oxford University Press, 1965, p. 3.

5. Niebuhr, *op. cit.*, p. 101.

6. *Ibid.*, p. 107.

Appendix / Declaration on
Religious Freedom

*On the Right of the Person and of
Communities to Social and Civil
Freedom in Matters Religious*

PAUL, BISHOP
SERVANT OF THE SERVANTS OF GOD
TOGETHER WITH THE FATHERS OF THE SACRED COUNCIL
FOR EVERLASTING MEMORY

1. A sense of the dignity of the human person has been impressing itself more and more deeply on the consciousness of contemporary man.[1] And the demand is increasingly made that men should act on their own judgment, enjoying and making use of a responsible freedom, not driven by coercion but motivated by a sense of duty. The demand is also made that constitutional limits should be set to the powers of government, in order that there may be no encroachment on the rightful freedom of the person and of associations.

This demand for freedom in human society chiefly regards

This translation is taken from THE DOCUMENTS OF VATICAN II, *published by Guild Press, America Press, Association Press, and Herder and Herder, and copyrighted 1966 by The America Press. Used by permission.*

the quest for the values proper to the human spirit. It regards in the first place, the free exercise of religion in society.[2]

This Vatican Synod takes careful note of these desires in the minds of men. It proposes to declare them to be greatly in accord with truth and justice. To this end, it searches into the sacred tradition and doctrine of the Church—the treasury out of which the Church continually brings forth new things that are in harmony with the things that are old.

First,[3] this sacred Synod professes its belief that God himself has made known to mankind the way in which men are to serve Him, and thus be saved in Christ and come to blessedness. We believe that this one true religion subsists in the catholic and apostolic Church, to which the Lord Jesus committed the duty of spreading it abroad among all men. Thus He spoke to the apostles: "Go, therefore, and make disciples of all nations, baptizing them in the name of the Father, and of the Son, and of the Holy Spirit, teaching them to observe all that I have commanded you" (Mt. 28:19-20). On their part, all men are bound to seek the truth, especially in what concerns God and His Church, and to embrace the truth they come to know, and to hold fast to it.

This sacred Synod likewise professes its belief that it is upon the human conscience that these obligations fall and exert their binding force. The truth cannot impose itself except by virtue of its own truth, as it makes its entrance into the mind at once quietly and with power. Religious freedom, in turn, which men demand as necessary to fulfill their duty to worship God, has to do with immunity from coercion in civil society. Therefore, it leaves untouched traditional Catholic doctrine on the moral duty of men and societies toward the true religion and toward the one Church of Christ.

Over and above all this, in taking up the matter of religious freedom this sacred Synod intends to develop the doctrine of recent Popes on the inviolable rights of the human person and on the constitutional order of society.[4]

[I]

GENERAL PRINCIPLE OF RELIGIOUS FREEDOM

2. This Vatican Synod declares that the human person has a

right to religious freedom.[5] This freedom means that all men are to be immune from coercion on the part of individuals or of social groups and of any human power, in such wise that in matters religious no one is to be forced to act in a manner contrary to his own beliefs. Nor is anyone to be restrained from acting in accordance with his own beliefs, whether privately or publicly, whether alone or in association with others, within due limits.

The Synod further declares that the right to religious freedom has its foundation in the very dignity of the human person, as this dignity is known through the revealed Word of God and by reason itself.[6] This right of the human person to religious freedom is to be recognized in the constitutional law whereby society is governed. Thus it is to become a civil right.

It is in accordance with their dignity as persons—that is, beings endowed with reason and free will and therefore privileged to bear personal responsibility—that all men should be at once impelled by nature and also bound by a moral obligation to seek the truth, especially religious truth. They are also bound to adhere to the truth, once it is known, and to order their whole lives in accord with the demands of truth.

However, men cannot discharge these obligations in a manner in keeping with their own nature unless they enjoy immunity from external coercion as well as psychological freedom. Therefore, the right to religious freedom has its foundation, not in the subjective disposition of the person, but in his very nature. In consequence, the right to this immunity continues to exist even in those who do not live up to their obligation of seeking the truth and adhering to it. Nor is the exercise of this right to be impeded, provided that the just requirements of public order are observed.[7]

3. Further light is shed on the subject if one considers that the highest norm of human life is the divine law—eternal, objective, and universal—whereby God orders, directs, and governs the entire universe and all the ways of the human community, by a plan conceived in wisdom and love. Man has been made by God to participate in this law, with the result that, under the gentle disposition of divine Providence, he can come to perceive ever increasingly the unchanging truth. Hence

every man has the duty, and therefore the right, to seek the truth in matters religious, in order that he may with prudence form for himself right and true judgments of conscience, with the use of all suitable means.

Truth, however, is to be sought after in a manner proper to the dignity of the human person and his social nature. The inquiry is to be free, carried on with the aid of teaching or instruction, communication, and dialogue. In the course of these, men explain to one another the truth they have discovered, or think they have discovered, in order thus to assist one another in the quest for truth. Moreover, as the truth is discovered, it is by a personal assent that men are to adhere to it.

On his part, man perceives and acknowledges the imperatives of the divine law through the mediation of conscience. In all his activity a man is bound to follow his conscience faithfully, in order that he may come to God, for whom he was created. It follows that he is not to be forced to act in a manner contrary to his conscience. Nor, on the other hand, is he to be restrained from acting in accordance with his conscience, especially in matters religious.

For, of its very nature, the exercise of religion consists before all else in those internal, voluntary, and free acts whereby man sets the course of his life directly toward God. No merely human power can either command or prohibit acts of this kind.[8]

However, the social nature of man itself requires that he should give external expression to his internal acts of religion; that he should participate with others in matters religious; that he should profess his religion in community. Injury, therefore, is done to the human person and to the very order established by God for human life, if the free exercise of religion is denied in society when the just requirements of public order do not so require.

There is a further consideration. The religious acts whereby men, in private and in public and out of a sense of personal conviction, direct their lives to God transcend by their very nature the order of terrestrial and temporal affairs. Government, therefore, ought indeed to take account of the religious life of the people and show it favor, since the function of government is to make provision for the common welfare. However, it would clearly transgress the limits set to its power were it to presume to direct or inhibit acts that are religious.

4. The freedom or immunity from coercion in matters religious which is the endowment of persons as individuals is also to be recognized as their right when they act in community. Religious bodies are a requirement of the social nature both of man and of religion itself.[9]

Provided the just requirements of public order are observed, religious bodies rightfully claim freedom in order that they may govern themselves according to their own norms, honor the Supreme Being in public worship, assist their members in the practice of the religious life, strengthen them by instruction, and promote institutions in which they may join together for the purpose of ordering their own lives in accordance with their religious principles.

Religious bodies also have the right not to be hindered, either by legal measures or by administrative action on the part of government, in the selection, training, appointment, and transferral of their own ministers, in communicating with religious authorities and communities abroad, in erecting buildings for religious purposes, and in the acquisition and use of suitable funds or properties.

Religious bodies also have the right not to be hindered in their public teaching and witness to their faith, whether by the spoken or by the written word. However, in spreading religious faith and in introducing religious practices, everyone ought at all times to refrain from any manner of action which might seem to carry a hint of coercion or of a kind of persuasion that would be dishonorable or unworthy, especially when dealing with poor or uneducated people. Such a manner of action would have to be considered an abuse of one's own right and a violation of the right of others.[10]

In addition, it comes within the meaning of religious freedom that religious bodies should not be prohibited from freely undertaking to show the special value of their doctrine in what concerns the organization of society and the inspiration of the whole of human activity.[11] Finally, the social nature of man and the very nature of religion afford the foundation of the right of men freely to hold meetings and to establish educational, cultural, charitable, and social organizations, under the impulse of their own religious sense.

5. Since the family [12] is a society in its own original right, it has the right freely to live its own domestic religious life under the guidance of parents. Parents, moreover, have the right to determine, in accordance with their own religious beliefs, the kind of religious education that their children are to receive.

Government, in consequence, must acknowledge the right of parents to make a genuinely free choice of schools and of other means of education. The use of this freedom of choice is not to be made a reason for imposing unjust burdens on parents, whether directly or indirectly. Besides, the rights of parents are violated if their children are forced to attend lessons or instruction which are not in agreement with their religious beliefs. The same is true if a single system of education, from which all religious formation is excluded, is imposed upon all.

6. The common welfare of society consists in the entirety of those conditions of social life under which men enjoy the possibility of achieving their own perfection in a certain fullness of measure and also with some relative ease. Hence this welfare consists chiefly in the protection of the rights,[13] and in the performance of the duties, of the human person. Therefore, the care of the right to religious freedom devolves upon the people as a whole, upon social groups, upon government, and upon the Church and other religious Communities, in virtue of the duty of all toward the common welfare, and in the manner proper to each.[14]

The protection and promotion of the inviolable rights of man ranks among the essential duties of government.[15] Therefore, government is to assume the safeguard of the religious freedom of all its citizens, in an effective manner, by just laws and by other appropriate means. Government is also to help create conditions favorable to the fostering of religious life, in order that the people may be truly enabled to exercise their religious rights and to fulfill their religious duties, and also in order that society itself may profit by the moral qualities of justice and peace which have their origin in men's faithfulness to God and to His holy will.[16]

If, in view of peculiar circumstances obtaining among certain peoples, special legal recognition is given in the constitutional order of society to one religious body, it is at the same time imperative that the right of all citizens and religious bodies to religious freedom should be recognized and made effective in practice.[17]

Finally, government is to see to it that the equality of citizens before the law, which is itself an element of the common welfare, is never violated for religious reasons [18] whether openly or covertly. Nor is there to be discrimination among citizens.

It follows that a wrong is done when government imposes upon its people, by force or fear or other means, the profession or repudiation of any religion, or when it hinders men from joining or leaving a religious body. All the more is it a violation of the will of God and of the sacred rights of the person and the family of nations, when force is brought to bear in any way in order to destroy or repress religion, either in the whole of mankind or in a particular country or in a specific community.[19]

7. The right to religious freedom is exercised in human society; hence its exercise is subject to certain regulatory norms.[20] In the use of all freedoms, the moral principle of personal and social responsibility is to be observed. In the exercise of their rights, individual men and social groups are bound by the moral law to have respect both for the rights of others and for their own duties toward others and for the common welfare of all. Men are to deal with their fellows in justice and civility.

Furthermore, society has the right to defend itself against possible abuses committed on pretext of freedom of religion. It is the special duty of government to provide this protection. However, government is not to act in arbitrary fashion or in an unfair spirit of partisanship. Its action is to be controlled by juridical norms which are in conformity with the objective moral order.

These norms arise out of the need for effective safeguard of the rights of all citizens and for peaceful settlement of conflicts of rights. They flow from the need for an adequate care of genuine public peace, which comes about when men live together in good order and in true justice. They come, finally, out of the need for a proper guardianship of public morality. These matters constitute the basic component of the common welfare: they are what is meant by public order.

For the rest,[21] the usages of society are to be the usages of freedom in their full range. These require that the freedom of man be respected as far as possible, and curtailed only when and in so far as necessary.

8. Many pressures are brought to bear upon men of our day, to the point where the danger arises lest they lose the possibility of acting on their own judgment. On the other hand, not a few can be found who seem inclined to use the name of freedom as the pretext for refusing to submit to authority and for making light of the duty of obedience.

Therefore, this Vatican Synod urges everyone, especially those who are charged with the task of educating others, to do their utmost to form men who will respect the moral order and be obedient to lawful authority. Let them form men too who will be lovers of true freedom—men, in other words, who will come to decisions on their own judgment and in the light of truth, govern their activities with a sense of responsibility, and strive after what is true and right, willing always to join with others in cooperative effort.[22]

Religious freedom, therefore, ought to have this further purpose and aim, namely, that men may come to act with greater responsibility in fulfilling their duties in community life.[23]

[II]

RELIGIOUS FREEDOM IN THE LIGHT OF REVELATION

9. The declaration of this Vatican Synod on the right of man to religious freedom has its foundation in the dignity of the

person. The requirements of this dignity have come to be more adequately known to human reason through centuries of experience. What is more, this doctrine of freedom has roots in divine revelation, and for this reason Christians are bound to respect it all the more conscientiously.

Revelation does not indeed affirm in so many words the right of man to immunity from external coercion in matters religious. It does, however, disclose the dignity of the human person in its full dimensions. It gives evidence of the respect which Christ showed toward the freedom with which man is to fulfill his duty of belief in the Word of God. It gives us lessons too in the spirit which disciples of such a Master ought to make their own and to follow in every situation.

Thus, further light is cast on the general principles upon which the doctrine of this Declaration on Religious Freedom is based. In particular, religious freedom in society is entirely consonant with the freedom of the act of Christian faith.[24]

10. It is one of the major tenets of Catholic doctrine that man's response to God in faith must be free. Therefore no one is to be forced to embrace the Christian faith [25] against his own will.[26] This doctrine is contained in the Word of God and it was constantly proclaimed by the Fathers of the Church.[27] The act of faith is of its very nature a free act. Man, redeemed by Christ the Savior and through Christ Jesus called to be God's adopted son,[28] cannot give his adherence to God revealing Himself unless the Father draw him [29] to offer to God the reasonable and free submission of faith.

It is therefore completely in accord with the nature of faith that in matters religious every manner of coercion on the part of men should be excluded. In consequence, the principle of religious freedom makes no small contribution to the creation of an environment in which men can without hindrance be invited to Christian faith, and embrace it of their own free will, and profess it effectively in their whole manner of life.

11. God calls men to serve Him in spirit and in truth. Hence they are bound in conscience but they stand under no compulsion.[30] God has regard for the dignity of the human person whom He Himself created; man is to be guided by his own judgment and he is to enjoy freedom.

This truth appears at its height in Christ Jesus, in whom God perfectly manifested Himself and His ways with men. Christ is our Master and our Lord.[31] He is also meek and humble of heart.[32] And in attracting and inviting His disciples He acted patiently.[33] He wrought miracles to shed light on His teaching and to establish its truth. But His intention was to rouse faith in His hearers and to confirm them in faith, not to exert coercion upon them.[34]

He did indeed denounce the unbelief of some who listened to Him; but He left vengeance to God in expectation of the day of judgment.[35] When He sent His apostles into the world, He said to them: "He who believes and is baptized shall be saved, but he who does not believe shall be condemned" (Mk. 16:16); but He Himself, noting that cockle had been sown amid the wheat, gave orders that both should be allowed to grow until the harvest time, which will come at the end of the world.[36]

He refused to be a political Messiah, ruling by force,[37] He preferred to call Himself the Son of Man, who came "to serve and to give his life as a ransom for many" (Mk. 10:45). He showed Himself the perfect Servant of God; [38] "a bruised reed he will not break, and a smoking wick he will not quench" (Mt. 12:20).

He acknowledged the power of government and its rights, when He commanded that tribute be given to Caesar. But He gave clear warning that the higher rights of God are to be kept inviolate: "Render, therefore, to Caesar the things that are Caesar's, and to God the things that are God's" (Mt. 22:21).

In the end, when He completed on the cross the work of redemption whereby He achieved salvation and true freedom for men, He also brought His revelation to completion. He bore witness to the truth,[39] but He refused to impose the truth by force on those who spoke against it. Not by force of blows does His rule assert its claims.[40] Rather, it is established by witnessing to the truth and by hearing the truth, and it extends its dominion by the love whereby Christ, lifted up on the cross, draws all men to Himself.[41]

Taught by the word and example of Christ, the apostles followed the same way. From the very origins of the Church the disciples of Christ strove to convert men to faith in Christ as the Lord—not, however, by the use of coercion or by devices unworthy of the gospel, but by the power, above all, of the Word of God.[42] Steadfastly they proclaimed to all the plan of God our Savior, "who wishes all men to be saved and to come to the knowledge of the truth" (1 Tim. 2:4). At the same time, however, they showed respect for weaker souls even though these persons were in error. Thus they made it plain that "every one of us will render an account of himself to God" (Rom. 14:12),[43] and for this reason is bound to obey his conscience.

Like Christ Himself, the apostles were unceasingly bent upon bearing witness to the truth of God. They showed special courage in speaking "the word of God with boldness" (Acts 4:31) [44] before the people and their rulers. With a firm faith they held that the gospel is indeed the power of God unto salvation for all who believe.[45] Therefore they rejected all "carnal weapons." [46] They followed the example of the gentleness and respectfulness of Christ. And they preached the Word of God in the full confidence that there was resident in this Word itself a divine power able to destroy all the forces arrayed against God [47] and to bring men to faith in Christ and to His service.[48] As the Master, so too the apostles recognized legitimate civil authority. "For there exists no authority except from God," the Apostle teaches, and therefore commands: * "Let everyone be subject to the higher authorities . . . : he who resists the authority resists the ordinance of God" (Rom. 13:1-2).[49]

At the same time, however, they did not hesitate to speak out against governing powers which set themselves in opposition to the holy will of God: "We must obey God rather than men" (Acts 5:29).[50] This is the way along which countless martyrs and other believers have walked through all ages and over all the earth.

12. The Church therefore is being faithful to the truth of the

---

*The preceding 14 words are missing from the *L'Osservatore Romano* text of Dec. 11, 1965.—Ed.

gospel, and is following the way of Christ and the apostles when she recognizes, and gives support to, the principle of religious freedom as befitting the dignity of man and as being in accord with divine revelation. Throughout the ages, the Church has kept safe and handed on the doctrine received from the Master and from the apostles. In the life of the People of God as it has made its pilgrim way through the vicissitudes of human history, there have at times appeared ways of acting which were less in accord with the spirit of the gospel and even opposed to it.[51] Nevertheless, the doctrine of the Church that no one is to be coerced into faith has always stood firm.

Thus the leaven of the gospel has long been about its quiet work in the minds of men. To it is due in great measure the fact that in the course of time men have come more widely to recognize their dignity as persons, and the conviction has grown stronger that in religious matters the person in society is to be kept free from all manner of human coercion.

13. Among the things which concern the good of the Church and indeed the welfare of society here on earth—things therefore which are always and everywhere to be kept secure and defended against all injury—this certainly is preeminent, namely, that the Church should enjoy that full measure of freedom which her care for the salvation of men requires.[52] This freedom is sacred, because the only-begotten Son endowed with it the Church which He purchased with His blood. It is so much the property of the Church that to act against it is to act against the will of God. The freedom of the Church is the fundamental principle in what concerns the relations between the Church and governments and the whole civil order.[53]

In human society and in the face of government, the Church claims freedom for herself in her character as a spiritual authority, established by Christ the Lord. Upon this authority there rests, by divine mandate, the duty of going out into the whole world and preaching the gospel to every creature.[54] The Church also claims freedom for herself in her character as a society of men who have the right to live in society in accordance with the precepts of Christian faith.[55]

In turn, where the principle of religious freedom is not only proclaimed in words or simply incorporated in law but also given sincere and practical application, there the Church succeeds in achieving a stable situation of right as well as of fact and the independence which is necessary for the fulfillment of her divine mission. This independence is precisely what the authorities of the Church claim in society.[56]

At the same time, the Christian faithful, in common with all other men, possess the civil right not to be hindered in leading their lives in accordance with their conscience. Therefore, a harmony exists between the freedom of the Church and the religious freedom which is to be recognized as the right of all men and communities and sanctioned by constitutional law.

14. In order to be faithful to the divine command, "Make disciples of all nations" (Mt. 28:19), the Catholic Church must work with all urgency and concern "that the Word of God * may run and be glorified" (2 Th. 3:1). Hence the Church earnestly begs of her children that, first of all, "supplications, prayers, intercessions, and thanksgivings be made for all men. . . . For this is good and agreeable in the sight of God our Savior, who wishes all men to be saved and to come to the knowledge of the truth" (1 Tim. 2:1-4).

In the formation of their consciences, the Christian faithful ought carefully to attend to the sacred and certain doctrine of the Church.[57, 58] The Church is, by the will of Christ, the teacher of the truth. It is her duty to give utterance to, and authoritatively to teach, that Truth which is Christ Himself, and also to declare and confirm by her authority those principles of the moral order which have their origin in human nature itself. Furthermore, let Christians walk in wisdom in the face of those outside, "in the Holy Spirit, in unaffected love, in the word of truth" (2 Cor. 6:6-7). Let them be about their task of spreading the light of life with all confidence [59] and apostolic courage, even to the shedding of their blood.

The disciple is bound by a grave obligation toward Christ his Master ever more adequately to understand the truth received from Him, faithfully to proclaim it, and vigorously to

---

*The CCD translation has "the Lord" instead of "God."—Ed.

defend it, never—be it understood—having recourse to means that are incompatible with the spirit of the gospel. At the same time, the charity of Christ urges him to act lovingly, prudently and patiently in his dealings with those who are in error or in ignorance with regard to the faith.[60] All is to be taken into account—the Christian duty to Christ, the life-giving Word which must be proclaimed, the rights of the human person, and the measure of grace granted by God through Christ to men, who are invited freely to accept and profess the faith.

15. The fact is that men of the present day want to be able freely to profess their religion in private and in public. Religious freedom has already been declared to be a civil right in most constitutions, and it is solemnly recognized in international documents.[61] The further fact is that forms of government still exist under which, even though freedom of religious worship receives constitutional recognition, the powers of government are engaged in the effort to deter citizens from the profession of religion and to make life difficult and dangerous for religious Communities.[62]

This sacred Synod greets with joy the first of these two facts, as among the signs of the times. With sorrow, however, it denounces the other fact, as only to be deplored. The Synod exhorts Catholics, and it directs a plea to all men, most carefully to consider how greatly necessary religious freedom is, especially in the present condition of the human family.

All nations are coming into even closer unity. Men of different cultures and religions are being brought together in closer relationships. There is a growing consciousness of the personal responsibility that weighs upon every man. All this is evident.

Consequently, in order that relationships of peace and harmony may be established and maintained within the whole of mankind, it is necessary that religious freedom be everywhere provided with an effective constitutional guarantee, and that respect be shown for the high duty and right of man freely to lead his religious life in society.

May the God and Father of all grant that the human family, through careful observance of the principle of religious freedom in society, may be brought by the grace of Christ and the power of the Holy Spirit to the sublime and unending "freedom of the glory of the sons of God" (Rom. 8:21).

Each and every one of the things set forth in this Declaration has won the consent of the Fathers of this most sacred Council. We too, by the apostolic authority conferred on us by Christ, join with the Venerable Fathers in approving, decreeing, and establishing these things in the Holy Spirit, and we direct that what has thus been enacted in synod be published to God's glory.

Rome, at St. Peter's, December 7, 1965

I, Paul, Bishop of the Catholic Church

There follow the signatures of the Fathers.

NOTES

1. Cf. John XXIII, encyclical "Pacem in Terris," Apr. 11, 1963: AAS 55 (1963), p. 279; ibid., p. 265; Pius XII, radio message, Dec. 24, 1944: AAS 37 (1945), p. 14.

2. Vatican II has been characterized by a sense of history, an awareness of the concrete world of fact, and a disposition to see in historical facts certain "signs of the times." Hence the Declaration begins by noting two facts. The first is the recent rise of man's personal consciousness, his sense of selfhood. This increasing awareness of the dignity of the human person marks a progress of civilization. It is the good which has come out of the great evil of totalitarianism, which brutally refuses to acknowledge the reality of man's selfhood. The second fact is the related rise of man's political consciousness, his aspiration to live as a free man under a limited government which puts no obstacles to his pursuit of truth and virtue, and, in particular, leaves him unhindered in the free exercise of religion in society. (Happily, the Declaration adopts the classical phrase which the Founding Fathers likewise adopted when framing the First Amendment in 1791.)

In thus acknowledging certain realities of contemporary life, the Declaration also establishes direct continuity with two basic doctrinal themes of John XXIII in the encyclical "Pacem in Terris": the dignity of the human person and the consequent necessity of constitutional limits to the powers of government. The language of these opening sentences is, in fact, taken from this great encyclical.

3. The issue of religious freedom arises in the political and social order—in the order of the relationship between the people and government and between man and man. This is the order of human rights, and in it the principle of freedom is paramount. However, man's life is also lived in another order of reality—in the spiritual order of man's relationship to what is objectively true and morally

good. This is the order of duty and obligation. In it a man acts freely indeed, but under moral imperatives, which bind in conscience. No man may plead "rights" in the face of the truth or claim 'freedom" from the moral law. The distinction between these two orders of reality would be admitted by all men of good sense. The underlying intention of these two paragraphs of the Declaration is to make this distinction clear, lest religious freedom be made a pretext for moral anarchy.

However, the distinction is stated in Catholic terms. For the Catholic, the "truth" is not a vague abstraction; it subsists in the Church, is taught by the Church, is believed by the Church. Moreover, this truth about God and about His will for men is not the private possession of a party or sect; it is to be taught to all men, and all nations are to be its disciples. It is not to be thrust by force upon any man; in the order of man's relationship to truth, coercion has no place whatsoever. Consequently, as the Declaration will later make clear, religious freedom is an exigence of religious truth as conceived by the Church.

On the other hand, no man may say of the religious truth which subsists in the Church: "It is no concern of mine." Once given by Christ to His true Church, the true religion remains the one way in which all men are bound to serve God and save themselves. Consequently, religious freedom is not a title to exemption from the obligation to "observe all things whatsoever I have enjoined upon you." In fine, a harmony exists between man's duty of free obedience to the truth and his right to the free exercise of religion in society. The duty does not diminish the right, nor does the right diminish the duty.

This frank profession of Catholic faith, at the outset of the Declaration on Religious Freedom, is in no sense at variance with the ecumenical spirit, any more than it is at variance with full loyalty to the principle of religious freedom. Neither the spirit of ecumenism nor the principle of religious freedom requires that the Church refrain from stating publicly what she believes herself to be. The demands of truth are no more opposed to the demands of freedom than they are opposed to the demands of love.

4. In no other conciliar document is it so explicitly stated that the intention of the Council is to "develop" Catholic doctrine. This is significant, since it is an avowal that the tradition of the Church is a tradition of progress in understanding the truth. The basic truth here is the concept of the "citizen" as stated by Pius XII—the man who "feels within himself a consciousness of his own personality, of his duties, and of his rights, joined with a respect for the freedom of others" (Christmas Discourse, 1945). This conception, as the Declaration will say, is deeply rooted both in the Christian tradition and in the tradition of reason. In recent times, it was Leo XIII (in "Rerum Novarum") who first began to move it, as it were, to the forefront of Catholic social teaching. Pius XII continued this development, drawing out the implications of the dignity of man in terms of his duties and rights. He also brought forward the correlative truth, that the primary function of government is to

acknowledge, protect, vindicate, and facilitate the exercise of the rights of man. Both of these truths were taken up by John XXIII, chiefly in "Pacem in Terris," in which they are given an almost systematic form of statement.

However, in regard to the right of man to religious freedom, even "Pacem in Terris" is unclear and even ambiguous. What precisely does religious freedom mean? Does it find place among the inalienable rights of man? These are the questions to which, for the first time, the Church gives an unmistakably clear and entirely unambiguous answer. The Council brings forth out of the treasury of truth a doctrine that is at once new and also in harmony with traditional teaching.

5. The doctrinal substance of the Declaration is stated in this paragraph, which defines what religious freedom is and affirms its status as a human—and therefore civil—right. A right is a moral claim made on others that they either give me something or do something for me or refrain from doing something. Two questions always arise. First, what is the moral claim I make on others, or in other words, what is the object or content of my right? Second, on what grounds do I make this moral claim, or in other words, what is the foundation of my right?

The Declaration first defines religious freedom in terms of its object or content. The moral claim that every man makes on others —on individuals, groups, political or social powers—is that they refrain from bringing coercion to bear on him in all matters religious. This claim is twofold. First, no man is to be forced to act in a manner contrary to his personal beliefs; second, no man is to be forcibly restrained from acting in accordance with his beliefs. The affirmation of this latter immunity is the new thing, which is in harmony with the older affirmation of the former immunity.

It is to be noted that the word "conscience," found in the Latin text, is used in its generic sense, sanctioned by usage, of "beliefs," "convictions," "persuasions." Hence the unbeliever or atheist makes with equal right this claim to immunity from coercion in religious matters. It is further to be noted that, in assigning a negative content to the right to religious freedom (that is, in making it formally a "freedom from" and not a "freedom for"), the Declaration is in harmony with the sense of the First Amendment to the American Constitution. In guaranteeing the free exercise of religion, the First Amendment guarantees to the American citizen immunity from all coercion in matters religious. Neither the Declaration nor the American Constitution affirms that a man has a right to believe what is false or to do what is wrong. This would be moral nonsense. Neither error nor evil can be the object of a right, only what is true and good. It is, however, true and good that a man should enjoy freedom from coercion in matters religious.

This brings up the second question, concerning the foundation of the right. The reason why every man may claim immunity from coercion in matters religious is precisely his inalienable dignity as a human person. Surely, in matters religious, if anywhere, the free human person is required and entitled to act on his own judgment and to assume personal responsibility for his action or omission. A man's religious decisions, or his decision against religion, are inescapably his own. No one else can make them for him, or compel him to make this decision or that, or restrain him from putting his decisions into practice, privately or publicly, alone or in company with others. In all these cases, the dignity of man would be diminished because of the denial to him of that inalienable responsibility for his own decisions and actions which is the essential counterpart of his freedom.

It is worth noting that the Declaration does not base the right to the free exercise of religion on "freedom of conscience." Nowhere does this phrase occur. And the Declaration nowhere lends its authority to the theory for which the phrase frequently stands, namely, that I have the right to do what my conscience tells me to do, simply because my conscience tells me to do it. This is a perilous theory. Its particular peril is subjectivism—the notion that, in the end, it is my conscience, and not the objective truth, which determines what is right or wrong, true or false.

6. Cf. John XXIII, encyclical "Pacem in Terris," Apr. 11, 1963: AAS 55 (1963), pp. 260–261; Pius XII, radio message, Dec. 24, 1942: AAS 35 (1943), p. 19; Pius XI, encyclical "Mit Brennender Sorge," Mar. 14, 1937: AAS 29 (1937), p. 160; Leo XIII, encyclical "Libertas Praestantissimum," June 20, 1888: Acts of Leo XIII 8 (1888), pp. 237–238.

7. It was necessary for the Council to present an argument for the principle of religious freedom, lest anyone should mistakenly think that the Church was accepting religious freedom merely on pragmatic grounds or as a concession to contemporary circumstances. However, it was not the intention of the Council to affirm that the argument, as made in the text, is final and decisive. Complete and systematic study of the arguments for religious freedom is a task left to the scholars of the Church, working in ecumenical spirit with scholars of other religious Communities, and in humanist spirit with scholars of no religious convictions who are concerned with the exigencies of human dignity. The Council merely presents certain lines or elements of argument. It will be sufficient here to indicate the structure.

First, in this paragraph, the objective foundation of the right to religious freedom is presented in terms that should be intelligible and acceptable to all men, including non-believers. The simple essence of the matter is that man, being intelligent and free, is to be a responsible agent. Inherent in his very nature, therefore, is an exigency for freedom from coercion, especially in matters religious. Therefore, in the following three paragraphs, an argument is suggested that will appeal to those who believe in God, in objective order of truth and morality, and in the obligation to seek the truth, form one's conscience, and obey its dictates. To the man who so believes, it will be evident that no one is to be forced or constrained to act against his own conscience (here conscience has its technical meaning).

Two further arguments are advanced to show that a man may not be restrained from acting according to his conscience. First, by reason of man's social nature, inner acts of religion require external expression; hence their external expression enjoys the same immunity from coercion as the inner acts themselves. Second, there is the "further consideration" that no right resides in government to command or inhibit acts of religion, which by their nature lie beyond the reach of government.

American theorists are generally disposed to relate religious freedom to a general theory of constitutional government, limited by the rights of man, and the concept of civic equality. The Declaration, however, lays less stress on this political argument than it does on the ethical foundations of the right itself. In any event, the elements of the political argument are stated in later Articles (6 and 7). And one is free to construct the argument in the form which may seem more convincing.

8. Cf. John XXIII, encyclical "Pacem in Terris," Apr. 11, 1963: AAS 55 (1963), p. 270; Paul VI, radio message, Dec. 22, 1964: AAS 57 (1965), pp. 181–182.

9. The freedoms listed here are those which the Catholic Church claims for herself. The Declaration likewise claims them for all Churches and religious Communities. Lest there be misunderstanding, however, it is necessary to recall here the distinction between the content or object of the right and its foundation. The content or object always remains freedom from coercion in what concerns religious belief, worship, practice or observance, and public testimony. Hence the content of the right is the same both for the Catholic Church and for other religious bodies. In this sense, the Church claims nothing for herself which she does not also claim for them. The matter is different, however, with regard to the foundation of the right. The Catholic Church claims freedom from coercive interference in her ministry and life on grounds of the divine mandate laid upon her by Christ Himself (cf. below, note 13). It is Catholic faith that no other Church or Community may claim to possess this mandate in all its fullness. In this sense, the freedom of the Church is unique, proper to herself alone, by reason of its foundation. In the case of other religious Communities, the foundation of the right is the dignity of the human person, which requires that men be kept free from coercion, when they act in community, gathered into Churches, as well as when they act alone.

10. It is customary to distinguish between "Christian witness" and "proselytism" and to condemn the latter. This distinction is made in the text here. Proselytism is a corruption of Christian witness by appeal to hidden forms of coercion or by a style of propaganda unworthy of the gospel. It is not the use but the abuse of the right to religious freedom.

11. Implicitly rejected here is the outmoded notion that "religion is a purely private affair" or that "the Church belongs in the sacristy." Religion is relevant to the life and action of society. Therefore

religious freedom includes the right to point out this social relevance of religious belief.

12. The internal structure of family relationships and the general style of family life vary widely throughout the world. Still greater variety is exhibited in the organization of school systems, in their relation to the family, to society, and to government, and in the religious and ideological content, or lack thereof, of their teaching. In consequence, the Declaration had to confine itself to a few principles of universal import, which would enforce its doctrinal line—freedom from coercion. To descend to further detail would be to enter the realm of policy, in which contingent circumstances play a determinant role.

13. Cf. John XXIII, encyclical "Mater et Magistra," May 15, 1961: AAS 53 (1961), p. 417; idem, encyclical "Pacem in Terris," Apr. 11, 1963: AAS 55 (1963), p. 273.

14. The development of Catholic doctrine which the Declaration promised has already shown itself in the clear definition of religious freedom as a human right and in the firm claim that all Churches and religious Communities are entitled to equal freedom from coercion in what concerns religious belief, worship, practice or observance, public testimony, and the internal autonomy of the community itself. Correlative with these developments is the doctrine stated here with regard to the functions and limitations of government in what concerns religion in society. The pivotal notion is the concept of the common welfare which Leo XIII began to put forward in "Rerum Novarum," which Pius XII strongly developed, and which John XXIII defined with greater precision. The common welfare "chiefly consists in the protection of the rights, and in the performance of the duties, of the human person," who is to be the agent of the processes of society and their beneficiary. The care of the common welfare is the common task of all elements within society—individuals, groups, religious bodies, government—each in the way proper to itself.

In a special way, the care of the common good—that is to say, the care of the rights of man—devolves upon government. Consequently, in what concerns religion in society, government has a duty that is twofold. The first duty is to acknowledge the human right to religious freedom, and effectively to protect it and vindicate it against violation. The second duty derives from the general duty of government to assist the people in the performance of their duties; in this case, it is to show a general and undiscriminating favor toward religion in society (cf. above, note 3, at the end) and to assist in the creation of conditions that will help, not hinder, the people in the exercise of their religious rights and in the performance of their religious duties. This latter duty is stated with considerable generality, because the appropriate means for its performance will vary within diverse circumstances.

The concern of the Council was, first, to make entirely clear the duty of government toward religious freedom as a human right, and secondly, to make sufficiently clear the function of government with regard to religion itself as a perfection of the human person and as a social value. This latter function is not easy to define with precision. It is chiefly a matter of avoiding extremes. On the one hand, government is forbidden to assume the care of religious truth as such, or jurisdiction over religious worship or practice, or the task of judging the truth or value of religious propaganda. Otherwise it would exceed its competence, which is confined to affairs of the temporal and terrestrial order. On the other hand, government is likewise forbidden to adopt toward religion an attitude of indifference or skepticism, much less hostility. Otherwise it would betray its duty to the human person, for whom religion is the highest good, and also to the temporal and terrestrial welfare of society, whose content is not merely material but also moral and spiritual. Here then is the principle for finding the golden mean between the extremes.

15. Cf. John XXIII, encyclical "Pacem in Terris," Apr. 11, 1963: AAS 55 (1963), pp. 273–274; Pius XII, radio message, June 1, 1941: AAS 33 (1941), p. 200.

16. Cf. Leo XIII, encyclical "Immortale Dei," Nov. 1, 1885: AAS 18 (1885), p. 161.

17. This paragraph is carefully phrased. The Council did not wish to condemn the institution of "establishment," the notion of a "religion of the state." A respectable opinion maintains that the institution is compatible with full religious freedom. On the other hand, the Council did not wish to canonize the institution. A respectable opinion holds that establishment is always a threat to religious freedom. Furthermore, the Council wished to insinuate that establishment, at least from the Catholic point of view, is a matter of historical circumstance, not of theological doctrine. For all these reasons the text deals with the issue in conditional terms.

18. This statement about equality before the law as an element of the common welfare has an accent of newness in official Catholic statements. It is important for the construction of the full argument for religious freedom.

19. This condemnation of religious persecution is couched in temperate terms and without naming the guilty. However, the reference to totalitarian regimes of Communist inspiration is unmistakable.

20. It is a matter of common sense that the exercise of all freedoms in society must be subject to certain regulatory norms. The Declaration states first the moral norm—the principle of personal and social responsibility. Its restraints, of course, are self-imposed. More difficult is the question of the juridical norm which should control the action of government in limiting or inhibiting the exercise of the right to religious freedom. (Note that the right itself is always inalienable, never to be denied; only the exercise of the right is subject to control in particular instances.) The norm cannot be the common welfare, since the common welfare requires that

human rights should be protected, not limited, in their exercise. Hence the Declaration adopts the concept of public order. The concept has good warrant in constitutional law. However, it is more frequently used than defined. The Declaration undertakes to define it. In doing so, it makes a contribution to the science of law and jurisprudence.

First, the requirements of public order are not subject to arbitrary definition—at the hands, say, of tyrannical governments, which might abuse the concept for their own ends. The public order of society is a part of the universal moral order; its requirements must be rooted in moral law. Second, public order exhibits a threefold content. First, the order of society is essentially an order of justice, in which the rights of all citizens are effectively safeguarded, and provision is made for peaceful settlement of conflicts of rights. Second, the order of society is a political order, an order of peace ("domestic tranquility" is the American constitutional phrase). Public peace, however, is not the result of repressive action by the police. It is, in the classic concept, the work of justice; it comes about, of itself, when the demands of justice are met, and when orderly processes exist for airing and settling grievances. Third, the order of society is a moral order, at least in the sense that certain minimal standards of public morality are enforced at all.

Public order therefore is constituted by these three values—juridical, political, moral. They are the basic elements in the common welfare, which is a wider concept than public order. And so necessary are these three values that the coercive force of government may be enlisted to protect and vindicate them. Together they furnish a reasonable juridical criterion for coercive restriction of freedom. The free exercise of religion may not be inhibited unless proof is given that it entails some violation of the rights of others, or of the public peace, or of public morality. In these cases, in other words, a public action ceases to be a religious exercise and becomes a penal offense.

21. Secular experts may well consider this to be the most significant sentence in the Declaration. It is a statement of the basic principle of the "free society." The principle has important origins in the medieval tradition of kingship, law, and jurisprudence. But its statement by the Church has an accent of blessed newness—the newness of a renewal of the tradition. The renewal, already hesitantly begun by Pius XII, was strongly furthered by John XXIII. Catholic thought had consistently held that society is to be based upon truth (the truth of the human person), directed toward justice, and animated by charity. In "Pacem in Terris," John XXIII added the missing fourth term, freedom. Freedom is an end or purpose of society, which looks to the liberation of the human person. Freedom is the political method par excellence, whereby the other goals of society are reached. Freedom, finally, is the prevailing social usage, which sets the style of society. This progress in doctrine is sanctioned and made secure by "Dignitatis Humanae Personae."

22. The Council calls attention to the paradox of the moment. Freedom today is threatened; freedom today is itself a threat. Hence the Council calls for education both in the uses of freedom and in the ways of obedience. When freedom is truly responsible, it implies a rightful response to legitimate authority.

23. Religious freedom is not an end in itself, but a means for the fulfillment of the higher purposes of man. Its religious purpose is clear. But here the Council notes its social purpose. Respect for religious freedom rises out of a consciousness of human dignity; but this consciousness itself confronts man with the responsibilities that his freedom entails. And these responsibilities pervade the whole of community life.

24. The Declaration is the only conciliar document formally addressed to the whole world—Christian and non-Christian, religious and atheist. Therefore it first considers religious freedom in the light of reason. Moreover, in so doing it follows the structure of the problem itself, both theoretical and historical. Both as a principle and as a legal institution, religious freedom is less than two hundred years old. The First Amendment may claim the honor of having first clearly formulated the principle and established the institution. Only through centuries of experience, as the Declaration says, have the exigencies of the human dignity disclosed themselves to reason. Nevertheless, the question remains, in what sense may religious freedom be called a "Christian" principle? The Council answers by saying that the principle has its "roots in divine revelation." These roots are explored in the second part of the Declaration. This section is of high ecumenical significance. It will furnish a major theme of ecumenical dialogue.

25. Cf. CIC, c. 1351; Pius XII, allocution to prelate auditors and other officials and administrators of the tribune of the Holy Roman Rota, Oct. 6, 1946: AAS 38 (1946), p. 394; idem, encyclical "Mystici Corporis," June 29, 1943: AAS (1943), p. 243.

26. The unwavering Christian dogma that the act of Christian faith must be a free response to the Word and grace of God reveals the divine respect for human freedom and for man's inalienable responsibility toward the direction of his own life. The constitutional principle of religious freedom is not a conclusion from this Christian dogma. The connection is rather more historical. That is to say, given the Christian doctrine of the freedom of faith, men would gradually come—as over the centuries they have come—to realize that man's religious life is an affair of responsible freedom, from which all coercion is to be excluded. Given this Christian appreciation of the value of freedom (and given also the growing secular experience of freedom as a social value and a political end), men could not fail to become increasingly conscious that religious freedom is an exigency of the dignity of the person, as this dignity is disclosed by the revelation that man is made in the image of God. Moreover, experience would also make it clear that, where religious freedom prevails, a climate of freedom is created in society which

itself favors the free preaching of the gospel and the free living of the Christian life.

27. Cf. Lactantius "Divinarum Institutionum," Book V, 19: CSEL 19, pp. 463–464, 465: PL 6, 614 and 616 (ch. 20); St. Ambrose, "Epistola ad Valentianum Imp.," Letter 21: PL 16, 1005; St. Augustine, "Contra Litteras Petiliani," Book II, ch. 83: CSEL 52, p. 112: PL 43, 315; cf. C. 23, q. 5, c. 33 (ed. Friedberg, col. 939); idem, Letter 23: PL 33, 98; idem, Letter 34: PL 33, 132; idem, Letter 35: PL 33, 135; St. Gregory the Great, "Epistola ad Virgilium et Theodorum Episcopos Massiliae Galliarum," Register of Letters I, 45: MGH Ep. 1, p. 72; PL 77, 510–511 (Book I, ep. 47); idem, "Epistola ad Johannem Episcopum Constantinopolitanum," Register of Letters, III, 52: MGH Letter I, p. 210: PL 77, 649 (Book III, Letter 53); cf. D. 45, c. 1 (ed. Friedberg, col. 160); Council of Toledo IV, c. 57: Mansi 10, 633; cf. D. 45, c. 5 (ed. Friedberg, col. 161–162); Clement III: X., V. 6, 9: ed. Friedberg, col. 774; Innocent III, "Epistola ad Arelatensem Archiepiscopum," X., III, 42, 3: ed. Friedberg, col. 646.

28. Cf. Eph. 1:5.

29. Cf. Jn. 6:44.

30. The major purpose here is to show, from the example and teaching of Christ Himself, that coercion in matters religious is alien to the spirit of the gospel. The ways of God with men are not coercive. They are the ways of faithful love. And their supreme illustration is the cross. Rather than impose the truth upon men by force, Christ willingly accepted death at their hands, and He made His death itself the means of redemption, as the revelation of a love than which there is no greater. The way of Christ became the way of His first apostles, whose reliance was on the power of the Word of God, never on earthly forces.

31. Cf. Jn. 13:13.

32. Cf. Mt. 11:29.

33. Cf. Mt. 11:28–30; Jn. 6:67–68.

34. Cf. Mt. 9:28–29; Mk. 9:23–24; 6, 5–6; Paul VI, encyclical "Ecclesiam Suam," Aug. 6, 1964: AAS 56 (1964), pp. 642–643.

35. Cf. Mt. 11:20–24; Rom. 12:19–20; 2 Th. 1:8.

36. Cf. Mt. 13:30 and 40–42.

37. Cf. Mt. 4:8–10; Jn. 6:15.

38. Cf. Is. 42:1–4.

39. Cf. Jn. 18:37.

40. Cf. Mt. 26:51–53; Jn. 18:36.

41. Cf. Jn. 12:32.

42. Cf. 1 Cor. 2:3–5; 1 Th. 2:3–5.

43. Cf. Rom. 14:1–23; 1 Cor. 8:9–13; 10:23–33.

44. Cf. Eph. 6:19–20.

45. Cf. Rom. 1:16.

46. Cf. 2 Cor. 10:4; 1 Th. 5:8–9.

47. Cf. Eph. 6:11–17.

48. Cf. 2 Cor. 10:3–5.

49. Cf. 1 Pet. 2:13–17.

50. Cf. Acts 4:19–20.

51. The historical consciousness of the Council required that it be loyal to the truth of history. Hence the Declaration makes the humble avowal that the People of God have not always walked in the way of Christ and the apostles. At times they have followed ways that were at variance with the spirit of the gospel and even contrary to it. The avowal is made briefly and without details. But the intention was to confess, in a penitent spirit, not only that Christian churchmen and princes have appealed to the coercive instruments of power in the supposed interests of the faith, but also that the Church herself has countenanced institutions which made a similar appeal. Whatever may be the nice historical judgment on these institutions in their own context of history, they are not to be justified, much less are they ever or in any way to be reinstated. The Declaration is a final renunciation and repudiation by the Church of all means and measures of coercion in matters religious.

52. Cf. Leo XIII, letter "Officio Sanctissimo," Dec. 22, 1887: AAS 20 (1887), p. 269; idem, letter "Ex Litteris," Apr. 7, 1887: AAS 19 (1886), p. 465.

53. This statement, together with the declaration of religious freedom as a human right and the enunciation of the principle of the free society, must rank as one of the central doctrinal utterances of the Declaration. Its importance is emphasized by the fact that Paul VI quoted it in his address on Dec. 9 to political rulers: "And what is it that this Church asks of you, after nearly two thousand years of all sorts of vicissitudes in her relations with you, the powers of earth? What does the Church ask of you today? In one of the major texts of the Council she has told you: she asks of you nothing but freedom—the freedom to believe and to preach her faith, the freedom to love God and to serve Him, the freedom to live and to bring to men her message of life." This doctrine is traditional; it is also new. Implicit in it is the renunciation by the Church of a condition of legal privilege in society. The Church does not make, as a matter of right or of divine law, the claim that she should be established as the "religion of the state." Her claim is freedom, nothing more.

54. Cf. Mk. 16:15; Mt. 28:18–20; Pius XII, encyclical "Summi Pontificatus," Oct. 20, 1939: AAS 31 (1939), pp. 445–446.

55. Cf. Pius XI, letter "Firmissimam Constantiam," Mar. 28, 1937: AAS 29 (1937), p. 196.

56. Cf. Pius XII, allocution "Ci Riesce," Dec. 6, 1953: AAS 45 (1953), p. 802.

57. Cf. Pius XII, radio message, Mar. 23, 1952: AAS 44 (1952), pp. 270–278.

58. The Council directs a word of pastoral exhortation to the Christian faithful. They are urged, in particular, to form their consciences under the guidance of the authority of the Church. It might be noted here that the Council intended to make a clear distinction between religious freedom as a principle in the civil order and the Christian freedom which obtains even inside the Church. These two freedoms are distinct in kind; and it would be perilous to confuse them. Nowhere does the Declaration touch the issue of freedom within the Church. Undoubtedly, however, it will be a stimulus for the articulation of a full theology of Christian freedom in its relation to the doctrinal and disciplinary authority of the Church.

59. Cf. Acts 4:29.

60. Cf. John XXIII, encyclical "Pacem in Terris," Apr. 11, 1963: AAS 55 (1963), pp. 299–300.

61. Cf. John XXIII, encyclical "Pacem in Terris," Apr. 11, 1963: AAS 55 (1963), pp. 295–296.

62. At the end, the Council turns once more to the world at large. Two facts claim its attention. First, the principle of religious freedom is widely recognized; this fact takes its place among the signs of the times. Second, the principle of religious freedom is also widely violated; this fact can only be deplored. Then the Declaration, which has stated its argument in terms of principle, turns to the pragmatic aspect of the issue—the practical value and necessity of religious freedom in the world today. It is a world of diversity which is striving toward some measure of unity; it is a world of conflict which is yearning for peace; it is, above all, a world in which a new consciousness of human dignity struggles to find expression in social institutions that will guarantee to men the freedom which is due to them in justice. Most necessary of all is freedom of religion. Where it is safe, the way is open for the "glorious freedom of the sons of God" to come to men as God's gift through Christ in the Holy Spirit.

Selected Readings

Baillie, Donald M., *The Theology of the Sacraments*. New York: C. Scribner's Sons, 1957, Ch. 3.

Barth, Karl, *Church Dogmatics*, Vol II, Part 2, *The Doctrine of God*, trans. G. W. Bromiley *et. al.* Edinburgh: T. & T. Clark, 1957, pp. 598ff.

Bea, Augustine Cardinal, *Unity of Freedom*. New York: Harper & Row, 1964.

Berdyaev, Nicholas, *Freedom and the Spirit*. New York: C. Scribner's Sons, 1935.

———, *Slavery and Freedom*. New York: C. Scribner's Sons, 1944.

Bertocci, Peter, *Free Will, Responsibility, and Grace*. New York: Abingdon Press, 1957.

Brunner, Emil, *Man in Revolt*, trans. Olive Wyon. Philadelphia: Westminster Press, 1947, Ch. XI.

Bryson, Lyman, ed., *Freedom and Authority in our Time* (Twelfth Symposium). New York: Conference on Science, Philosophy & Religion, 1953.

Buber, Martin, "Prophecy, Apocalyptic, and the Historical Hour," *Union Seminary Quarterly Review*, Vol. 12 (March, 1957).

Bultmann, Rudolf, *Essays Philosophical and Theological*. New York: Macmillan, 1955, Essays III, IV, IX, XVI.

———, *Theology of the New Testament*, Vol. I, trans. K. Gobel. New York: C. Scribner's Sons, 1951, pp. 330–352.

Campbell, Charles Arthur, *On Selfhood and Godhood*. New York: Macmillan, 1957.

Cobb, John B. Jr., *A Christian Natural Theology*, Vol. III. Philadelphia: Westminster Press, 1965, pp. 92ff.

Cogley, John, ed., *Religion in America*. New York: Meridian Books, 1958.

Cole, J. P., "Function of Choice in Human Existence," *Journal of Religion*, Vol. 45 (July, 1965), 196–210.

D'Arcy, M. C., and Vincent Turner, "Freedom of Choice," *Month*, Vol. 5 (February 1951).

Duhamel, J. A., "Moral and Psychological Aspects of Freedom," *Thought*, Vol. 35 (Summer 1960).

Dupre, L., "The Constitution of the Self in Kierkegaard's Philosophy," *International Philosophical Quarterly*, Vol. 3 (1963).

———, "Philosophical Stages of Self-Discovery," *Thought*, Vol. 39 (Fall, 1964).

Fackenheim, E. L., "Human Freedom and Divine Power," *Judaism*, Vol. 12 (Summer, 1963).

Farrer, Austin, *The Freedom of the Will*. New York: C. Scribner's Sons, 1960.

Frank, Erich, *Philosophical Understanding and Religious Truth*. New York: Oxford University Press, 1945, Chapters V, VI.

"Freedom and Existence: A Symposium," *Review of Metaphysics*, Vol. 9 (September, 1955), 27–56.

Grindel, Carl W., ed., *Concept of Freedom*. Chicago: H. Regnery Co., 1955.

Gutbrod, W. and Herman Kleinknecht, *Law* from *Bible Key Words*, trans. and ed. J. R. Coates. New York: Harper & Row, 1951.

Halverson, Wm. H., "Freedom and the Self," *Journal of Religion*, Vol. 43 (April, 1963).

Hare, R. M., *Freedom and Reason*. New York: Oxford University Press, 1965.

Haroutounian, Joseph, "Grace and Freedom Reconsidered," *Journal of Religion*, Vol. 40 (April, 1960), 59–79.

Harrelson, W., "Biblical Concept of Free Man," *Review and Expositor*, Vol. 57 (July, 1960).

Hartt, J. N., and J. A. C. F. Auer, *Humanism Versus Theism*. Yellow Springs, Ohio: Antioch Press, 1951, pp. 96–106.

Hartt, J. N., "Human Freedom and Divine Transcendence," *Journal of Religion*, Vol. 31 (January, 1951), 38–51.

Herbert, A. G., "Authority and Freedom," *Anglican Theological Review*, Vol. 31 (October, 1949).

Knight, I. S., "Negation and Freedom," *Review of Metaphysics*, Vol. 13 (March, 1960), 407–411.

Kung, Hans, *Freedom Today*. New York: Sheed & Ward, 1965.

Laird, John, *On Human Freedom*, London: G. Allen & Unwin, 1947.

Love, Thomas, I., "Current Catholic Thought on Religious Liberty," *Journal of the American Academy of Religion*, Vol. XXXC, i (March, 1967), 58–64.

Lynch, W. F., "The Problem of Freedom," *Cross Currents*, Vol. 10 (Spring, 1960).

MacKay, Brian S., *Freedom of the Christian*. New York: Abingdon Press, 1965.

McKenzie, John L., *Authority in the Church*. New York: Sheed & Ward, 1966, pp. 162–174.

Maritain, Jacques, *Freedom in the Modern World*, trans. Richard O'Sullivan. New York: C. Scribner's Sons, 1936.

Melchert, N., "Freedom and Its Meanings," *Lutheran Quarterly*, Vol. 12 (November, 1960).

Morgenbesser, Sidney, and J. Walsh, *Free Will*, Englewood, N.J.: Prentice-Hall, 1962.

Murray, J. C., S. J. ed., *Freedom and Man*. New York: P. J. Kenedy, 1965.

———, *Religious Liberty: An End and A Beginning*. New York: The Macmillan Co., 1966.

Nagley, W. E., "Kierkegaard on Liberation," *Ethics*, Vol. 70 (October, 1959).

Niebuhr, H. Richard, *The Responsible Self*. New York: Harper, 1963, pp. 100–106.

Niebuhr, Reinhold, *Man's Nature and His Communities*. New York: C. Scribner's Sons, 1965, pp. 30–83.

Oden, Thomas C., *Radical Obedience: The Ethics of Rudolf Bultmann*. Philadelphia: Westminster Press, 1964.

Osborn, Robert T., "Bultmann on Freedom," *Journal of Religion*, Vol. 42 (January, 1962), 22–33.

———, *Freedom in Modern Theology*. Philadelphia: Westminster Press, 1967.

Thielicke, Helmut, *The Freedom of the Christian Man*. New York: Harper & Row, 1963.

———, *Theological Ethics*, Vol. I, *Foundations*, ed. W. H. Lazareth. Philadelphia: Fortress Press, 1966, pp. 455ff.

Torrence, T. F., "Universalism or Election," *Scottish Journal of Theology*, Vol. 2, no. 3, (1949).

Rahner, Karl, *Theological Investigations*, Vol. 2, *Man in the Church*, trans. Karl H. Kruger. Baltimore: Helicon Press, 1963, pp. 89–108.

———, *Theology for Renewal: Bishops, Priests, Laity*, trans. Cecily Hastings and Richard Strachan, New York: Sheed & Ward, 1964, pp. 95–118.

Ramsey, Ian, *Freedom and Immortality*. London: SCM Press, 1960.

"Religious Freedom in America," *Cross Currents*, Vol. XVI, i (Winter, 1963).

Rubenstein, R. L., "God and Human Freedom in Rabbinic Theology," *Cross Currents*, Vol. 11 (Spring, 1961).

Scott, E. F., *Man and Society in the New Testament*. New York: C. Scribner's Sons, 1946, Ch. IX.

Silberman, L. H., "Paradoxes of Freedom and Authority," *Hibbert Journal*, Vol. 60 (July, 1962).

Simpson, C. A., "The Biblical Idea of Freedom," *Bulletin of General Theological Seminary*, Vol. 42, n. 3 (May, 1956).

Stockhammer, M., "Responsibility and Freedom," *Judaism*, Vol. 14 (1965).

Thibon, Gustave, *Christianity and Freedom, A Symposium*. London: Hollis and Carter, 1955.

Walz, H. H., "Man's Freedom in Existence and in Christianity," *Cross Currents* (Fall, 1961).

Wild, John, *Existence and the World of Freedom*. Englewood Cliffs, N.J.: Prentice-Hall, 1967.

Williams, Daniel D., *God's Grace and Man's Hope*. New York: Harper & Row, 1949, Ch. V.

Index

INDEX

Action, freedom of, 204

Adler, Mortimer, 27

Aeschylus, 160

American way of life, and humanity, 218–219

"Amsterdam Assembly Series," 54

Analysis, 235–236; and Christian view of freedom, 247–248; and the language of freedom, 244–248

Analysts, 236; and paradox of freedom, 248–249; and phenomenologists, 247

Anarchy, 99

Anglicanism, position on the Bible, 47–48

Anglicans, 54

Antinomianism, 51, 55, 99

Anxiety, 107–108, 110–111

Aquinas, Thomas, 99, 155–156, 249; and categorial objectivity, 199; and St. Augustine, 180; and spirit as transcendence, 198; view of evil, 168–169; view of God's permission of sin, 180; view of God's will as antecedent to the good free will act, 174–178; view of God's will and the free act, 182–183

Arbitrary confinement, 157

Aristotelianism, 112, 226; and ideal humanity, 220

Aristotle, 29, 99; and definition of freedom, 108; and definition of good, 222; and the good, 222, 224, 228; and nature, 228–229; and sensation, 125; and truth of human nature, 222–223; world of, 228–229

Aspiration, 222–223, 224, 226, 229; and human nature, 222–223

Atheistic existentialism, 101, 106, 112

Augustine, St., 110, 112; and

Augustine, St. (*continued*)
affirmation of freedom-in-bondage, 44; and Aquinas, 180; and bondage of the will, 109; and concept of the heart, 206; and grace of God, 110; and Pelagianism, 32; and spiritual anxiety, 111; and voluntarism, 8
Augustinian tradition, 100
Authority, mediate, 46–48
Autonomy, 42, 45, 99

Balzac, Honoré de, 107, 109
Banez, Domingo, 166, 178; and God's predestination, 166; view of divine will and free will, 170–172; view of God's permission of sin, 180–181
Baptists, 49
Barclay, Robert, 50
Barth, Karl, 3, 14, 27, 110
Behaviorists, 244
Being: freedom of, 205; as pure source, 205; transcendental, 210
Being and Nothingness (Sartre), 116, 119, 133
Belief, moral, paradox implicit in, 227
Bennett, John, 54
Berdyaev, Nikolai, 101
Bergson, Henri, 101, 102
Bible, the, 46–47, 93; Anglican position on, 47–48, 52; and Aquinas, 180; authority of, 55; and concept of the heart, 206; and the Declaration on Religious Freedom, 59–68; and evangelical ethics, 83, 85; and exegetical findings, 88; and free theologians, 88–89, 90, 91; and freedom, 203; and historical-critical research, 88; interpretations

of, 3–8; and our neighbor, 200; Presbyterian Puritan position on, 47, 48–49, 52; re-examination by modern Protestants, 52–55; sectarian position on, 47, 49–52; and tradition, 165, 184–185
Biblical base of freedom, 65
Biblical criticism, 52–53
Biblical ethics, 54
Biblical morality, 54
Biblical teaching, and subjectivity, 209
Biblical theology, perspectives of, 3–8, 59–93
Biology, evolutionism in, 221, 226
Blondel, Maurice, and concept of action, 206
Bodily life: and arbitrary confinement, 157; and freedom, 154–157; and rape, 155; right to preservation of, 154–155; and sense of shame, 155; and slavery, 155–156; and torture, 156–157; violations of, 155–157
Bondage of the will, 109
Brunner, Emil, 27, 54
Buber, Martin, 101, 106
Byron, Lord, 107, 110

Calvin, John, 48, 49, 91, 107–108
Calvinism, 52
Calvinist divinity, 227
Calvinist paradoxes, 227
Camus, Albert, 101, 112
Candide (Voltaire), 33
Categorial experience, 205
Categorial indeterminism, 199
Categorial objectivity, 199–200
Catholic Church, the, 36–39
Catholic doctrine of faith, and salvation, 208

Catholic teaching, and subjectivity, 209
Catholic theology, and freedom, 28–39
Causality, of God, 166–171, 181
Chillingworth, William, 47
Choice, free, 41
Christian community, 74, 91
Christian ethics, 111
Christian freedomists, 99
Christian Hellenists, and nature, 224
Church constitution, Roman Catholic, and Declaration on Religious Freedom, 66–68
Church Dogmatics (Barth), 3, 82
Church tradition, Protestant, 54, 55
Cocteau, Jean, 101
Concupiscence, doctrine of, 211
Congregationalists, 49
Consciousness, and the self, Sartre's thought on, 116–123
Cosmic contingency, 105
Creative will, and creaturely will, paradox of, 227–233
Creativity, and libertarianism, 216, 218
Creaturely will, and creative will, paradox of, 227–233
Creed, Nicene, 21
Culture, Romano-Germanic, 102

Damnation, absolute, 203, 204, 206
De Beauvoir, Simone, 101, 107
"Declaration of Human Rights, The," 44
Declaration on Religious Freedom, 59–68; (*text*), 251–265
Demant, V. A., 54
Deputyship: and Jesus Christ,

158–159; and responsibility, 157–158
Descartes, René, 99, 103, 136
Descriptivists, 244
Determinism, 43, 160, 215, 218; rational, 99, 113
Determinists, 214–215
Dewey, John, 101
Dignity of the human person, 60–61, 64
Dilthey, William, 105
Divine grace, *see* Grace of God
Doctrine of concupiscence, 211
Doctrine of divine volitions, 229
Doctrine of necessity, 216
Doctrine of original sin, 211
Dogmatics, in theology, 89
Donne, John, 105
Dostoievsky, Feodor, 101, 103, 107, 111
Dynamics, and existentialist thought, 141

Einstein, Albert, 14
Eliot, T. S., 110
English Protestantism, in the 17th century, 47–52
Enlightenment, the, 43
Epictetus, 29
Epistles (Paul), 64
Epistles to the Corinthians (Paul), 67
Erasmus, Desiderius, 99
Ethics: biblical, 54; Christian, 111; evangelical, 82–86; humanistic, 45; individualism in, 220, 226; and new-style rationalists, 247; Protestant, 40–56; secular, 42; social, 53–54; special, 86; systematic, 151–152; of theology, 86–93
Ethos, of free theologian, 86–93

Evangelical ethics, foundations of, 82–86

Evil: Aquinas on, 168–169; problem of, 27, 191–192

Evolutionism, in biology, 221, 226

Exegesis, in theology, 89

Existential freedom, and Christian faith, 97–113

Existentialism: atheistic, 101, 106, 112; and dynamics, 141; perspectives of, 8–14, 97–113, 115–143; predicament of, 221–222; on the self and freedom, 115–143; theistic, 101, 106; theological, 101; and theology, 108–113; view of freedom, 104–108; and "we think" philosophies, 214–222

Existentialist antitheses, 116

Existentialists, 20–21, 26, 217

Experience, categorial, 205

Faith, natural, and the good, 224; and positivism, 222–227

Forsyth, P. T., 40

Free act, 200, 206, 207, 208; as mystery, 212

Free choice, 41, 98

Free theologian: and the Bible, 88–89, 90, 91; ethos of, 86–93

Free will: and God's sovereignty, 165–192; harmony between free will and God, 166–167; and the will of God, 167–173, 181–184

Freedom: of action, 204; of being, 205; of choice, 203–204; context of, 1–21; as freedom before God, 202; as mystery, 207, 210, 212; of will, 41, 42, 43, 214

Freedom-as-achievement, 140–141

Freud, Sigmund, 101, 102

Fromm, Erich, 45, 46

Fundamental freedom, 138–140

Fundamentalism, 52

German philosophy, 98

"Gesellschaft für evangelische Theologie" (Society for Evangelical Theology), 86

God: causality of, 166–171, 181; grace of, *see* Grace of God; image of, 108; mystery of, 212, 213; sovereignty of, 165–192; will of, *see* Will of God

God's own freedom, 69–76

Good, the: and Aristotle, 222, 224, 228; and natural faith, 224; and positivist reduction, 224

Gorgias (Plato), 98

Gospel, the, 64, 65, 73, 112

Grace, order of, 184–187

Grace of God, 110–111, 210–211, 212–213; and the Law, 203

Greek philosophy, 98, 99, 220–221, 225

Greeks, and nature, 224

Grene, Marjorie, 12

Guilt, 109–110, 211, 212

Hare, R. M., 245, 246, 247

Harmony, between God and free will, 166–167

Heidegger, Martin, 3, 101, 106, 110, 112, 126

Heilsgeschichte, 74, 77

Heim, Karl, 102

Heteronomy, 42, 45

Historicism, in sociology, 221, 226

History of revelation, 212–213
History of salvation, 212, 213
Holy Spirit, 49, 50, 51, 52, 55
Hooker, Richard, 47
Hudson, H. H., 54
Human nature: and Aristotle, 222; and aspiration, 222, 223
Human person, dignity of, 60–61
Human reason, 98, 99
Human sickness, 107–108
Humanistic ethics, 45
Humanity, 218–221; and American way of life, 218–219; and Greek philosophy, 220–221; ideal, 220; word as equivocation, 219, 220
Husserl, Edmund, 235

Idea of Freedom, The (Adler), 27
Ideal humanity, 220
Image of God, 108
Inanimate nature, and metaphysical paradox, 230
Indeterminism, 26, 160; categorial, 199; voluntaristic, 99, 113
Individualism, in ethics, 220, 226
Inner Light, 51
Inner Spirit, 50
Inner Word, 50
Institutes (Calvin), 107
Intuitionism, 51

James, St., 62
Jansenists, 100
Jaspers, Karl, 101, 104, 106, 107
Jesuits, 99
Jesus Christ, as deputy, 158–159

John, St., and Jews' rejection of Christ, 190
Judaism, law of, 64
Justice and the Social Order (Brunner), 54
Justification, doctrine of, 208

Kairos, 83, 84, 90
Kant, Immanuel, 41, 98–100, 101, 102, 103
Kantian ethic, 163
Kantian philosophy, 109
Kerygma, 74
Kierkegaard, Sören, 14, 101, 103, 104, 106, 107; and concept of subjectivity, 206; and the individual, 242
Kingdom of Heaven, 35
Kuhn, Helmut, 98

"Lack" (Sartre), 105–106, 123–124, 133
Language of Morals, The (Hare), 245
Law, Natural, 48, 49, 52
Law of Judaism, 64
Law of liberty, 111
Law of love, in Christian community, 55
"Law of love," in New Testament, 54
Law of Reason, 48, 49, 52
Legalism, 55
Leibniz, Gottfried Wilhelm von, 33, 217; and transcendent soul, 231
Liberal humanitarianism, 51
Liberalism, secular, 43, 44
Libertarianism, 215–216; and creativity, 216, 218; and liberty, 218; and responsibility, 216, 218
Libertarians, 214–215, 216, 217
Liberty, law of, 111

Love: and moral policies, 226; as therapy, 110
Luther, Martin, 46, 47, 59, 91, 109, 110, 111, 163
Lutheran doctrine of justification, 208

Man's act, and God's will in the order of grace, 184–187
Man's free will, and the will of God, 167–173, 181–184
Man's freedom, 111; and God's sovereignty, 165–192
Man's God-given freedom, 70–83
Marcel, Gabriel, 101, 106, 116; and freedom-as-achievement, 140–141; and fundamental freedom, 138; and Sartre, 126–128, 132–135; on the self and freedom, 125–133
Marcus Aurelius, 29
Maritain, Jacques, 101
Marx, Karl, 14, 101
Mediate authority, 46–48, 52
Metaphysical belief, 224, 225
Metaphysical paradox, and inanimate nature, 230
Metaphysics: and Aristotle, 222, 223, 224; and new-style rationalists, 247; and self-as-subjectivity, 137
Molina, Luis, 166, 178; and God's predestination, 166; view of divine will and free will, 170–172; view of God's permission of sin, 180–181
Molinists, 166
Moore, G. E., 236
Moral belief, paradox implicit in, 227
Moral policies: and love, 226; and reverence, 226

Moral responsibility, 102–104
Moralists, non-Christian, 41
Morals: rationality of, 247; and theism, 229
Mystery of freedom, 207, 210, 212
Mystery of God, 212, 213
Mystery of predestination, 227

Natural faith: and the good, 224; and positivism, 222–227
Natural forces: and creative will, 230–231; and human will, 231
Natural Law, 48, 49, 52, 54
Naturalists, 31–32, 33
Nature: and Aristotle, 228–229; and Christian Hellenists, 224; and the Greeks, 224; inanimate, and metaphysical paradox, 230
Nausea (Sartre), 105
Necessity: doctrine of, 216; patterns of, 216
Neo-Calvinists, 15
Neo-Lutherans, 15
Neo-Protestantism, 53
Neo-Thomists, 15
Neo-traditional thought, perspectives of, 14–18, 151–192
New Testament, 60–61, 62, 63, 65, 91, 184; and freedom, 203; "law of love," 54; thought, 53
Nicene Creed, 21
Niebuhr, H. Richard, 249–250
Niebuhr, Reinhold, 27
Nietzsche, Friedrich, 14, 101, 102, 107, 112
Non-Christian moralists, 41
Non-Christian thought, and Christian views of freedom, 234–250
Notes from the Underground (Dostoievsky), 103

Obedience, and responsibility, 161–164

Objectifications of freedom, 212

Objectivity, categorial, 199–200; and Aquinas, 199

Old Testament, 61, 184

Ontology, phenomenological, of Sartre, 115–125

Option fondamentale, 206, 207

Order of grace, God's will and man's act in the, 184–187

Original Sin, 31–32, 34, 35, 36, 39, 109–110, 211

Outer Word, 50

Parain, 97

Pascal, Blaise, 105

Paul, St., 249; and Christian freedom, 61; Epistles of, 64; Epistles to the Corinthians, 67–68; and eschatological world view, 53; and the expectation of the creature, 159; and Jews' rejection of Christ, 190; and one's neighbor, 64; and predestination, 166; and problem of freedom, 109

Pelagianism, 32

Pelagius, 99

Permission of sin, 178-181, 188–190

Personality, sickness of, 102

Phenomenologists: and analysts, 247; and paradox of freedom, 248–249

Phenomenology, 235; and Christian view of freedom, 242–244; and freedom, 237–244; and the subjective, 235

Phenomenological ontology, of Sartre, 115–125

Philo, 108

Philosophy, pressures on, 234–235

Physics, 222–223

Plato, 29, 98, 99, 101

Political liberty, and Catholic theology, 36

Pope, Alexander, 217

Positivism: and the good, 224; and natural faith, 222–227

Pragmatism, 159

Predestination, 166–167; mystery of, 227

Presbyterian Puritanism, position of on the Bible, 47, 48–49

Prescription against Heretics (Tertullian), 103

Prescriptivists, 245

Principle of Authority, The (Forsyth), 40

Problem of evil, 191–192

Protagoras (Plato), 98

Protestant doctrine of justification, 208

Protestant ethics: authority of Christ in, 55; freedom and authority in, 40–56

Protestantism, 16, 112; English, in 17th century, 47–52

Providence, 217

Puritans, 52

Quakers, 49, 50–51

Rahner, Karl, 3

Rape, 155

Rational determinism, 98, 99, 113

Rational theology, 18–21, 197–233

Rationalists, 246; new-style, 247

Rationality of morals, 247

Reason, 54, 55, 101–103; human, 98, 99

Reason, Law of, 48, 49, 52

Reckitt, M. B., 54

Reformation, the, 46

Reformers, the, 100

Religious freedom, and Roman Catholic Church: general principle of, 252–258; in the light of revelation, 258–264

Religious Freedom, Declaration on, 59–68; (*text*), 251–265

Reprieve, The (Sartre), 105

Responsibility, 205, 208–209, 217, 218, 221, 225; as deputyship, 157–158; and freedom, 151–164; and libertarianism, 216, 218; moral, 102–104; and obedience, 161–164; structure of, 157

Revelation, 197–198, 203, 208; history of, 197–198, 212–213; and religious freedom in Roman Catholic Church, 258–264

Reverence, and moral policies, 226

Roman Catholic Church: authority of, 46; and Declaration on Religious Freedom, 59–69

Roman Catholic theism, 112

Romano-Germanic culture, 102

Russell, Bertrand, 14

Salvation: absolute, 203, 204, 206; and Catholic doctrine of faith, 208; history of, 197–198, 212–213

Sartre, Jean-Paul, 100, 101, 104, 105, 106, 109, 111, 112; and the egoist, 242; and freedom-as-achievement, 140–141; "lacks," 123–124,

133; and Marcel, 126–128, 132–135; phenomenological ontology of, 115–125; and self-creation, 217; on self and consciousness, 116–123; on self and freedom, 123–125

Schiller, F. C. S., 159

Scholasticism, 113

Scripture, *see* Bible

Sectarianism, position on the Bible, 47, 49–52

Secular ethics, 42

Secular liberalism, 43, 44

Secularists, 32, 33

Self, the: and consciousness, Sartre's thought on, 116–123; and freedom, existentialist views of, 115–143; and freedom, Marcel's thought on, 125–133; and freedom, new perspectives of, 133–143; and freedom, Sartre's thought on, 123–125

Self-affirmation, and Catholic theology, 30–32

Self-as-subjectivity: and metaphysics, 137; and the social sciences, 137

Self-creation, and existentialism, 217

Self-judgment, 209–210

Self-realization, 205–206, 210, 220

Self-understanding, 210, 213

Semipelagianism, 32

Seneca, 29

Shame, 155

Sickness: human, 107–108; of freedom, 110; of the personality, 102

Simplicity and wisdom, 152–153

Sin, God's permission of, 178–181, 188–190

Slavery, 29

Smyth, John, 50

Social ethics, 53–54

Social order, fault in, 161–162

Social sciences, and self-as-subjectivity, 137

Society for Evangelical Theology ("Gesellschaft für evangelische Theologie"), 86

Socrates, 218–219

Sovereignty of God, and man's freedom, 165–192

Special ethics, 86

Spengler, Oswald, 12

Spinoza, Baruch *or* Benedict, 246

Spirit: as transcendence, 198–199; transcendentality of, 210

Stalin, Joseph, 221, 222

Stoic freedom, 61

Stoic principle, 33

Stoics, 29, 99

Subjective, the, and phenomenology, 235

Subjectivism, 51

Subjectivity: and Biblical teaching, 209; and Catholic teaching, 209; of freedom, 208–209

Systematic ethics, 151–152

Temple, William, 54

Tertullian, 103

Theism, 111–112, 232–237; and morals, 229; Roman Catholic, 112

Theistic existentialism, 101, 106

Theists, and will of God, 227, 230

Theological belief, 226

Theological existentialism, 101

Theology: biblical, 3–8, 59–93; Catholic, 28–39; ethics of, 86–93; and freedom, 25–39; of freedom, 197–213; and liberty, 214–233; pressures on, 234–235; rational, 18–21, 197–233

Theonomy, 42–43, 45

Thomistic tradition, 48

Thomists, 166

Tillich, Paul, 27, 42, 46

Timaeus (Plato), 98

Torture, 156–157

Transcendence, 198–203, 204, 210; spirit as, 198–199

"Transcendence of the Ego, The" (Sartre), 133, 135; discussion of, 116–119

Transcendent soul, and Leibniz, 231

Transcendental being, 210

Transcendental experience, 200, 207

Transcendentality of freedom, 210

Unitarianism, 51

Van Gogh, Vincent, 101

Varet, Gilbert, 134

Violations of bodily life, 155–157

Volitions, 224, 226; doctrine of divine, 229; human and divine, 228; and Stalin, 221, 222; and "we think" philosophy, 221–222

Voltaire, 33

Voluntarism, and St. Augustine, 8

Voluntaristic indeterminism, 99, 113

Voluntarists, 100

Way of life, American, 218–219

"We think" philosophies: and existential philosophies, 214–222; and volitions, 221–222

Westminster Confession, The, 48–49, 112

Whitehead, A. N., 101

Will, the, 98, 99, 103; bondage of, 109; creative, and natural forces, 230–231; freedom of, 41, 42, 43, 214; human, and natural forces, 231

Will of God, 201; as antecedent to the good free will act, 173–178; and creaturely will, paradox of, 227–233; and Jews' rejection of Christ, 189–190; and man's act in the order of grace, 184–187; and man's free will, 167–173, 181–184; and our neighbor, 226–227; and permission of sin, 178–181, 188–190; and theists, 227, 230

Wills, creative and creaturely, paradox of, 227–233

Wisdom and simplicity, 152–153

Wordsworth, William, 105